Chay. Curwother.

South boro'

To Charles D. Doyle
Ilford. 7 January
1950.

KEATS

KEATS, ON HIS DEATH BED

KEATS

by

BETTY ASKWITH

COLLINS
48 PALL MALL LONDON

THIS BOOK IS SET IN FONTANA, A NEW TYPE FACE DESIGNED
FOR THE EXCLUSIVE USE OF THE HOUSE OF COLLINS, AND
PRINTED BY THEM IN GREAT BRITAIN

COLLINS CLEAR-TYPE PRESS : LONDON AND GLASGOW

NOTE

I HAVE endeavoured throughout to preserve Keats's often characteristic spelling and punctuation. In occasional places however, where a letter has been dropped or a word misplaced through obvious carelessness and the reader would need a foot-note, I have amended it, and in one instance (the scrap of imaginary dialogue between Hunt, Ollier, Hazlitt, etc.), I have re-punctuated entirely, for clarity's sake. Anyone therefore who wishes to copy the actual letters should go to Mr. Buxton Forman's last edition of *The Letters of John Keats*. A work which for accuracy and for arrangement is quite beyond praise.

I wish to express my gratitude to The Hampstead Public Library and Keats House Committee for the permission to use their documents and to work at the Keats Museum. In particular I should like to express my warmest and most sincere thanks to Mr. Fred Edgcumbe, the Curator of the Keats Museum, for his extreme kindness and for the help that he is always so ready to give.

CONTENTS

CONTENTS

CONTENTS

CHAPTER I

Childhood—Death of Keats's father—Of his mother—Life with
his grandmother at Edmonton—Mr. Clarke's school at Enfield—
Friendship with Charles Cowden Clarke—Keats's guardian,
Mr. Abbey—Keats becomes a surgeon's apprentice.

A LITTLE boy, a very little boy, for he was unusually
small for his age, lay awake listening to music.

The memory of those childish wakeful hours when we
have been put to bed, while the world of human beings
still continues its normal daily life outside our shut
door, making us feel curiously strange and remote
almost as a ghost might, is very vivid. Sounds penetrated
to us in our imprisonment, a dog barking in the street,
voices from the garden or the notes of a piano played in
the room underneath. To the little boy lying awake in
the school dormitory came the clear precise notes of
Haydn or Mozart, and then a door shut down below and
the music abruptly ceased.

Years afterwards Keats was reading the manuscript
of *St. Agnes' Eve* to Charles Cowden Clarke, the son of his
old headmaster.

> "The boisterous, midnight, festive clarion,
> The kettle-drum, and far-heard clarionet,
> Affray his ears, though but in dying tone:
> The hall door shuts again, and all the noise is gone."

He paused on the last line, and said: "That line came
into my head when I remembered how I used to listen
in bed to your music in school."

John Keats was eight when he was sent to Mr.
Clarke's school at Enfield, and his brother George was

only six. They must have made rather a pathetic little
pair in their childish frilled suits, John being even then
the smaller of the two. But it was a good school and a
friendly one. Its very red brick front was pleasant and re-
assuring, with its moulding and acanthus leaves, its bas-
reliefs of garlands of nuts and fruit, and its cherubs'
heads

> "With hair blown back and wings put crosswise on
> their breasts"

surmounting rounded, empty niches. There was a
garden, too, where the boys could have little plots of
their own, there were strawberry beds which the more
"assiduous" scholars were allowed to water, a drying-
yard in which grew a baking-pear tree and a paddock
containing two cows. Probably those long childish
summers when the air smelt of mown grass, when
bricks and flower-pots were hot to the touch and the
strawberries tasted of the sun, were very happy ones.

John and George had not been very long at school
when they lost their father, who died from a fractured
skull after a fall from horseback in the City Road on
April 18, 1804. We do not know very much about the
Keats's parents. John was said to be like his father in
stature, so that Thomas Keats was presumably a small
man. He had come from the West Country and found a
job as an ostler at the Swan and Hoop Livery Stables on
Finsbury Pavement. He married the daughter of his
employer, Frances Jennings, at St. George's, Hanover
Square, on October 9th, 1794, and on October 31st, 1795,
at the livery stables, their eldest son, John, was born,
and baptized at St. Botolph's, Bishopsgate, on December
18th. He was followed by George on February 28th,
1797; Thomas, on November 18th, 1799; Edward, who
died in infancy, on April 28th, 1801; and finally the

family was completed by one little girl, Frances Mary or Fanny, who was born on June 3rd, 1803.

Thomas Keats was said to have been distinguished for his energy, uprightness, and common sense. He would probably have made a good father to his boys. Mrs. Keats, on the other hand, is described by an old acquaintance as a woman of unbridled temperament, who later fell into loose ways and was no credit to her family. We have no proof of this. All that is known for certain is that very shortly after her first husband's death Mrs. Keats married again, a certain William Rawlings, who was head-man at the livery stable. This marriage seems to have been an unhappy one for within a year they were parted. After that the evidence is uncertain. The gentleman who described Keats's mother as being of " unbridled temperament " was a Mr. Richard Abbey, a tea and coffee merchant, who later became guardian to the Keats children and with whom they, John in particular, never saw eye to eye. He wrote a memorandum for the information of Keats's publisher, and in this he states that Mrs. Keats, or Mrs. Rawlings, as she then was, lived for a while at Enfield with a Jew named Abraham, as his wife. Whether this statement be true or not, it is at least certain that Mrs. Rawlings resided for a considerable time, until her death in 1810, with her mother, Mrs. Jennings, now also a widow. They lived in Church Street, Edmonton, and the four children lived with them. Whatever her faults may have been, their mother was devoted to them, and they to her. Between her and her eldest son this love was particularly strong.

"My mother I distinctly remember," wrote George Keats in 1835, "she resembled John very much in the Face, was extremely fond of him and humoured him in every whim of which he had not a few." When he was a little boy and she was ill, John had mounted guard over her door, armed with an old sword. In her last illness he watched beside her for whole nights in a great chair, insisted on pouring out her medicine, and even cooking her food himself, and read novels aloud to her in her intervals of ease. When she died his grief was exceedingly bitter. There is a pathetic picture of his being found under the master's great desk, unable to control himself, sobbing his heart out. Schools have never been good places in which to indulge in the privacy of grief.

But except for this great sorrow John's childhood and schooldays probably passed pleasantly enough. Edmonton is a suburb of London now, but a hundred and thirty years ago it must have been a very pretty country village. Even in these days Church Street retains a countrified look with its grey square-towered church and its high creeper-covered, eighteenth century houses standing back from the street. Charles Lamb's cottage is still there, a charming unpretentious little house, cream-painted, with a small flagged path leading up to the front door. Nearly opposite it there is a sort of mission hall, where stands in a niche a little blue lady, her full skirts flowing demurely down to her feet, her hands holding an open book, and her head surrounded by a charming sort of blue turban. Underneath her is the inscription: "A structure of Hope, founded in Faith on the Basis of Charity, 1784," and her unseeing eyes must frequently have gazed after Keats as he walked or ran down the wide sunny street.

Pymme's Brook, too, still runs unfettered through the wilderness of high-road, suburban houses and allotments. One can climb down to it and then it seems almost like a country stream overhung with willow and alder, with elderberry and willow-herb blossoming on its banks. The current runs swiftly, and it would be easy for a small bare-legged boy to "make him ships, Of moulted feather, touchwood, alder chips, With leaves stuck in them," and to send them bobbing down the brook. It was either in this brook or in Salmon's Brook, or possibly both, that he caught little fishes, Miller's thumbs, tittlebat and minnows, which he brought home and kept in washing tubs, somewhat to the annoyance of his granny and of the maid. Yes, it must have been a pleasant home in Edmonton, with the three brothers devoted to one another, and all rivals for the sovereign affection of their one baby sister.

School, too, was very well in its way. John Keats was popular. He was so small and yet so big-hearted, generous and courageous. He would fight anybody or anything, frequently including his brother George who, being bigger and stronger, used to have to hold him down, kicking and struggling. When the youngest Keats brother came to school he was the object of a fierce protective affection on the part of his seniors, and on one occasion John squared up to an usher who had boxed Tom's ears and struck him, although the usher could, in Cowden Clarke's phrase, "have put him into his pocket." His temper was at times almost ungovernable, but it was a warm, generous temper. "He had no fears of self through intemperance in the quarrels of others, he would at all hazards, without calculating his power to defend or his reward for the deed, defend the oppressed or distressed with heart and soul, with hand and purse." So wrote his brother. Another schoolfellow wrote: "This violence and vehemence—this pugnacity and generosity of disposition—in passions of tears or outrageous fits of laughter—always in extremes—will help to paint Keats in his boyhood. Associated as they were with an extraordinary beauty of person and expression, these qualities captivated the boys and no-one was more

popular." Besides all this vitality there was the reverse
side of the picture, the black bitter fits of melancholy,
hypochondria and suspicion. He did his best to conquer
them, fighting them as manfully as he fought more ·
tangible enemies. He only confided them to his brothers,
who seem to have been inexhaustibly patient and good-
humoured. He would ask their forgiveness for bother-
ing them, but venting and discussing his miseries was a
relief. It is remarkable indeed what a degree of self-
control and of manliness this passionate, vehement,
gusty being attained in his short life. He battled all his
life with his tendencies to melancholy and the bitter hell
of neuroticism. In the end for a while ill-health and
unhappy love conquered him—but how gallantly he
fought.

The early part of Keats's schooldays seems to have
been passed more in fighting and in active exercise than
in scholastic or literary pursuits. However, in his last
two years at school he suddenly discovered literature,
and flung himself upon it with the same passionate
intensity which he devoted to everything else. He read
all day and could scarcely be detached from his books
to take exercise. There is a pleasant little picture of him
sitting at supper, tilted backwards on the form, eating
from beyond the covers of the book. Mr. Clarke's school
must have been an unusually enjoyable one, few schools
can have allowed meals to be taken in this way. He read
his way through the school library, which contained
voyages, travels, and Mavor's *Universal History*, Robert-
son's *Histories of Scotland*, *America*, and *Charles I.*, and
all Miss Edgeworth's productions. (The idea of John
Keats reading *Rosamund and the Purple Jar* has its
charms!) But it also contained, and this was what
chiefly fascinated him, Tooke's *Pantheon*, Lemprière's
Classical Dictionary, and Spence's *Polymetis*. It was un-

fortunate that his Greek classical learning came to him at second-hand. One wonders what would have been the effect if he had been brought up on the real Homer and Æschylus. Still, we need not be contemptuous of his scholastic achievements; he translated a large portion of the *Æneid* into writing, for his own pleasure, and at this time (he was almost fourteen), complained that, though he so much revelled in it, there was a feebleness in its structure.

When he had run through the school library he was still voraciously "asking for more." And it is here he met with one of the great strokes of luck in his life. Charles Cowden Clarke, the son of the headmaster, was at this time acting as assistant master to the school. He must have been one of the most delightful people who ever lived on the lower slopes of Parnassus. He was never a great artist, but he knew most of the artists of his time, and had the happiest relations with them. He was intelligent, sensitive and unselfish, and it is pleasant to record that he seems to have lived a singularly happy and unclouded life. He was a very good friend to the young Keats. He was about seven or eight years the senior of the two, just of an age when the influence of a slightly maturer intelligence and a trained taste will do wonders for a young enthusiastic boy. It was Cowden Clarke who lent Keats his *Spenser*, through which he says Keats went "as a young horse would through a spring meadow—ramping!" He also describes Keats as "hoisting himself up," and looking "burly and dominant," as he quoted: "What an image that is—sea-shouldering whales!"

Keats probably left school in 1810. After his mother's death his grandmother, Mrs. Jennings, executed a deed, putting her four grandchildren under the care of two guardians, and making over most of her property to

B

them to be held in trust. Mr. Jennings, who had died in 1805, had left a fortune of £13,000, of which he bequeathed a capital yielding £200 a year to his widow, a capital yielding £50 a year to his daughter, with reversion to the Keats children, and the remainder of the estate, about £1000, was put into Chancery, to be divided among the said children on the coming of age of the youngest. The guardians appointed were Mr. Rowland Sandell, who did not act, and Mr. Richard Abbey, who has been previously mentioned. On Mr. Abbey's authority, John Keats was taken away from school, and apprenticed to a surgeon, Mr. Thomas Hammond of Edmonton. This was not surprising, since Mr. Abbey, who seems to have been narrow-minded and John Bullish to a degree that almost amounts to caricature, probably disapproved of the school heartily. Keats once told Clarke, smiling, "that one of his guardians on being informed what books Clarke had lent him to read" (this particularly referred to Leigh Hunt's *Examiner*), "declared that if he had fifty children he would not send them to that school!"

There does not, however, seem to have been any opposition on Keats's part to the new scheme, and indeed it cannot have been too bad. Mr. Hammond lived in a pleasant creeper-covered house in Church Street, pulled down in 1926, and Keats slept in a little cottage in the garden, presumably going to the house for meals. He was not far from his grandmother's and, more important still, he was only two miles from Enfield, where he frequently walked over to see his friend Clarke. They would sit in an arbour at the bottom of the garden, reading, and "tiring the sun with talking," as young men do. Keats's expressive face, when reading aloud, has often been noted, and Clarke relates how his eyes filled and his voice faltered over the departure of Posthumus when Imogen

". . . followed him till he had melted from the smallness of a gnat to air."

Few other facts are known about this period of Keats's life. He wrote once, "this is not the hand, which seven years ago clenched itself at Hammond," and in view of his youth and exceedingly fiery temperament it was likely enough that this would occur at least once. There is another picture of Keats holding the reins of the gig, outside his old school, which Hammond was visiting professionally, and being sunk in a brown study, so that a mischievous schoolboy, remembering Keats's school reputation for pugnacity, threw a snowball at him, something in the spirit which prompts the young to thrust a stick down a wasps' nest, and made off as fast as legs could carry him.

The days of the apprenticeship on the whole probably passed happily and peacefully enough. Keats spent his plentiful leisure time in reading and translating. He finished the *Æneid*. He began himself to write a little poetry. Clarke writes that "it was the most placid period of his painful life," though in later days Keats, who hardly ever mentioned his Hammond days, once expressed his regret that he had ever undergone "a one of them." The only other piece of evidence about them we have, is a regret which comes not from the poet but from the schoolboy. Leigh Hunt, speaking of the articles that he contributed to the *Indicator*, wrote: "The paper that was most liked by Keats . . . was the one on a hot summer's day, entitled '*A Now*.' He was with me when I was writing and reading it to him, and contributed one or two of the passages." The description of the boys getting their shoes wet around the village pump, "following fish into their cool corners" in the streams and exclaiming "My eye" at the tittlebats, and that of the "green lane, thick-set with hedge-row elms," and the noise of a brook "rumbling in pebble-stones," are probably by Keats—but what must certainly be from his hand is the pathetic picture of the "apothecary's apprentice," thinking on this very hot day "with a bitterness beyond aloes . . . of the pond he used to bathe in at school."

CHAPTER II

Life at Guy's Hospital—Keats's early acquaintances—His brothers, George and Tom—George Felton Mathew—Leigh Hunt—Cowden Clarke shows Keats's poems to Leigh Hunt—Sonnet on Chapman's "Homer."

IT MUST have been a great change for Keats to move from the peaceful countrified surroundings of Edmonton to London, where he entered at Guy's Hospital as a student, in October 1810. The Borough, as he himself wrote, was "a beastly place in dirt, turnings and windings," and life at the hospital for one who was not a born doctor cannot have been too gay.

Four weeks after his appointment Keats was made dresser to Mr. William Lucas, who does not sound a very inspiring personality since he is described as "a tall ungainly awkward man, with stooping shoulders and shuffling gait, as deaf as a post, not overburdened with brains of any kind, but very good-natured and easy, and liked by everyone. His surgical acquirements were very small, his operations generally very badly performed and accompanied by much bungling if not worse. He was a poor anatomist and not a very good diagnoser which led him into ugly scrapes."

The dresser's duties consisted in accompanying his surgeon round the wards carrying a tin box with the bandages, lint, etc. After the first examination and bandaging, the work was frequently left in the dresser's hands, and since this was before the days of asceptic surgery, "each wound was or quickly became a foul-smelling festering sore, the dressing of which had to be frequently changed, often more than once a day. The responsibility for this rested with the dresser; in the actual changing of the dressings he was helped by untrained handywomen the forerunners of the present nurses."

Besides all this, the dressers had to take in rotation a week's duty at the hospital during which they lived in, the responsibility for admittances to the hospital resting upon their shoulders, though they could if necessary send for their surgeons. They also attended the crowds in the out-patient department, dressing wounds, doing minor operations, bleeding and taking out teeth.

The big excitement at the hospital was the attending of operations, which, at a time when there were no anæsthetics, must have been really horrible performances. John Flint South, who was a pupil about this time, describes them as follows: "The pupils packed like herrings in a barrel, but not so quiet, as those behind were continually pressing on those before, often so severely that several could not bear the pressure, and were continually struggling to relieve themselves of it and had not infrequently to be got out exhausted. There was also a continual calling out of "Heads, heads" to those about the table whose heads interfered with the sightseers, with various appellatives, in a small way resembling the calls in the Sheldonian Theatre during Commemoration . . . I have often known even the floor so crowded that the surgeon could not operate till it had been partially cleared. . . . So long as the patient did not make much noise I got on very well, but if the cries were great, and especially if they came from a child, I was quickly upset, had to leave the theatre, and not infrequently fainted . . . the atmosphere almost stifling."

One can pity Keats living in such an uncongenial atmosphere, one is also inclined to pity his patients. "My last operation," he told a friend, "was the opening of a man's temporal artery. I did it with the utmost nicety, but reflecting on what passed through my mind at the time, my dexterity seemed a miracle, and I never took up the lancet again." His heart was never really in his work. He would sit abstracted at lectures, writing doggerel rhymes on some other student's syllabus.

> "Give me women, wine and snuff
> Until I cry out, 'hold enough,'
> You may do so, sans objection
> Till the day of resurrection;
> For bless my beard they aye shall be
> My beloved Trinity——"

was scribbled on the paper cover of someone else's chemical lectures, and one of the margins of his own anatomical note-book is crowded with little pen and ink drawings of flowers. Or a long shaft of light would come through the windows of the dusty lecture-room, "a whole troop of creatures floating in the ray," and he would be "off with them to Oberon and fairyland."

On the other hand Keats was a conscientious and not untalented student. In after years he showed a certain knowledge and authority when he talked about medicine. He even thought occasionally of going back to it as a profession, though never, perhaps, very seriously. He later wrote to his sister, ". . . if I cannot lead that life of competence and society I should wish, I have enough knowledge of my gallipots to ensure me an employment and maintenance."

"He once talked to me," writes Cowden Clarke, "upon my complaining of stomachic derangement, with a remarkable decision of opinion, describing the functions and actions of the organ with the clearness and, as I presume, technical precision of an adult practitioner."

Keats characteristically adorned his lecture with one of his vivid concrete images, "the stomach," he said, "was like a brood of callow nestlings gaping for nourishment." And he opened and shut his own wide mouth to illustrate his point.

To return to his capacities as a medical student. His notes are well taken, showing an ability to record the important fundamental points of a lecture. (There is a humorous flavour about one statement that: "In disease Medical Men guess, if they cannot ascertain a disease they call it nervous.") He passed his Apothecaries Examination in 1816 with ease, though it must be admitted that his fellow students put it down more to his knowledge of Latin than his knowledge of medicine, and he in some way attracted the notice of Astley Cooper, the greatest surgeon then at Guy's. Astley Cooper was the most popular lecturer and the most brilliant doctor of his day, and it was his lectures on anatomy and physiology that Keats followed. A great many sentences in the note-book begin "Mr. C. says." Though again it must be admitted that another fellow student called Denny relates—"Even in the lecture-room of St. Thomas' I have seen Keats in a deep poetic dream; his mind was on Parnassus with the Muses and here is a quaint fragment which he one evening scribbled while the precepts of Sir Astley Cooper fell unheeded on his ear." The fragment is a bit of would-be archaic prose, telling how Alexander the Great saw and loved a beautiful lady in his march through India. Why Astley Cooper noticed Keats among the three hundred students or so who crowded his lectures we do not know, but that he did is proved by the fact that he placed him in the charge of his own dresser, George Cooper, with whom, in consequence, Keats went to live. They shared lodgings at a tallow-chandler's in St. Thomas' Street with two other medical students, George Wilson Mackerett and Henry Stephens.

This last has undoubtedly earned a small niche in English literature. It was he who, when Keats suggested "A thing of beauty is a constant joy," as a possible opening line for a poem, declared that it would not quite do, there was something lacking, whereupon the poet cried, "I have it!" and produced the celebrated "joy for ever," which he was to use later as the first line in *Endymion*.

Keats may well have been a little trying to fellow-students at this moment. This same Stephens wrote:

"Poetry was to his mind the zenith of all his aspirations: the only thing worthy the attention of superior minds: so he thought: all other pursuits were mean and tame. He had no idea of fame or greatness but as it was connected with the pursuits of poetry, or the attainment of poetical excellence. The greatest men in the world were the poets and to rank among them was the chief object of his ambition. It may readily be imagined that this feeling was accompanied with a good deal of pride and some conceit, and that amongst mere medical students he would walk and talk as one of the Gods might be supposed to do when mingling with mortals. This pride exposed him, as may be readily imagined, to occasional ridicule and some mortification."

Little he cared! He was entering into his own heritage of poetry. Whether he was sitting apart in a half dream at Astley Cooper's lectures, or following Mr. Lucas through the wards, or hunched up on the window seat in St. Thomas' Street gazing into space, he was not living in this world but, to adapt his own words:

". . . naught he sees
In water, air or earth, but poesy."

Nor was Keats's outer life, any more than his inner imagination, bounded by Guy's Hospital. For one thing in 1816, Cowden Clarke came up to live with a brother-in-law in Clerkenwell, ready to resume the long talks on books and poetry that had taken place in the arbour at Enfield. The renewing of Clarke's companionship was to be of great importance in Keats's life, leading up to the consequential friendship with Leigh Hunt.

Before the advent of Clarke, Keats had been moving, socially, in a little circle that was probably pleasant enough but not very exciting. He owed most of his early acquaintances to his brother George, who was now a clerk in the tea and coffee business belonging to their guardian, Richard Abbey. The three Keats brothers, unlike as they were in many respects, were very devoted to each other.

"He had two brothers," wrote Henry Stephens, his fellow medical student, "and they worshipped him. They seemed to think their brother John was to be exalted and to exalt the family name . . . their praise of their brother John amounted almost to idolatry."

John fully repaid this devotion. "My brother George has ever been more than a brother to me, he has been my greatest friend," he wrote. And in a passage that gives the greatest impression of intimacy, of the kinship that ought to exist between brothers brought up together in childhood, he writes to George in America: "Now the reason why I do not feel at the present moment so far from you is that I remember your Ways and Manners and actions; I know your manner of thinking, your manner of feeling: I know what shape your joy or your sorrow would take; I know the manner of your walking, standing, sauntering, sitting down, laughing, punning, and every action so truly that you seem near to me."

George Keats was considerably taller than his elder brother. Cowden Clarke says that John was like his father whereas both George and Tom resembled their mother, having long faces with big thick features. In his miniature however, George is not unlike John, though with a far less interesting face and less well-cut features. He must have gone bald at a phenomenally early age, as the picture shows a high expanse of dome-like forehead, and it must have been taken before he was twenty-two.

In character he appeared to be a downright, rather sensible, outspoken fellow, and John seems to have depended on him to a certain extent in practical matters. "My brother George always stood between me and my dealings with the world," he wrote, a year after George had gone to America. "Now I find I must buffet it."

As for Tom, the youngest of the three, his short life story is infinitely pathetic. On an October Sunday evening, a few months before Tom's death, John Keats, sitting with a heavy heart, over his folio Shakespeare, underlined the words "poore Tom" in the third act of *King Lear*. And somehow that brief phrase seems to sum up Thomas Keats's life better than any other. He was a tall, fair, narrow-chested boy, very like his sister Fanny. The only two letters we have from him are brave, rather school-boyish little productions making light of his ill-health. He had, according to John, "an exquisite love of Life," but more pathetically even than his unhappy brother, he was called away, a pale little shadow, before he could taste any of its sweets.

However, in 1816, he was probably happy enough, especially when John left the hospital, and the three brothers joined in lodgings together at 76 Cheapside. There is a pleasing touch of happiness, of peaceful well-

being in the beginning of the sonnet, which John wrote
on Tom's birthday, November 18th, 1816:

"Small, busy flames play through the fresh laid coals,
   And their faint cracklings o'er our silence creep
   Like whispers of the household gods that keep
   A gentle empire o'er fraternal souls."

Tom's sentiment for his brothers, especially for John,
whom he adored, ("no one understood John as Tom did,"
wrote George Keats,) was probably the strongest emotion
the affectionate sensitive boy knew, though it is said that
his death was hastened by the discovery of a cruel hoax
practised on him by a schoolfellow, C. J. Wells, who
wrote him fabricated love-letters from a fictitious lady
called "Amena." John's anger when he discovered this
wicked practical joke after Tom's death was terrible.
"The instigations to this diabolical scheme," he wrote to
George, "were vanity, and the love of intrigue. It was
no thoughtless hoax—but a cruel deception on a sanguine
temperament, with every show of friendship. I do not
think death too bad for the villain."

Next to his brothers, Keats's best friend at this time
was probably George Felton Mathew, to whom the poet's
first biographer, Monckton Milnes, applied for such
details as he could remember. Perhaps Mr. Mathew's
recollections throw more light on his character than on
that of his friend, nevertheless they provide an animated
picture of the young Keats of 1816. The Keats of
Severn's silhouette, with the lifted chin, the pugnacious
upper lip, the whole air of resolution and of gay
confidence.

"Keats and I though about the same age," wrote
George Felton Mathew, "and both inclined to literature,
were in many respects as different as two individuals
could be. He enjoyed good health—a fine flow of animal

spirits—was fond of company—could amuse himself admirably with the frivolities of life—and had great confidence in himself. I, on the other hand was languid and melancholy—fond of repose, thoughtful beyond my years—and diffident to the last degree. But I always delighted in administering to the happiness of others: and being one of a large family it pleased me much to see him and his brother George enjoy themselves so much at our little domestic concerts and dances." It is pleasant to think of Mathew, too languid and poetical to enjoy the frivolities of life, watching Keats being the life and soul of the party. He goes on: "He was of the sceptical and republican school. An advocate for the innovations which were making progress in his time. A fault finder with everything established. I, on the contrary, hated controversy and dispute—dreaded discord and disorder—loved the institutions of my country— believed them founded in nature and truth—best cal- culated to uphold religion and morality—harmonising on the one hand with the Theocracy of heaven, and on the other with the paternal rule at home. But I respected Keats's opinions, because they were sincere—refrained from subjects on which we differed, and only asked him to concede with me the imperfection of human know- ledge and the fallibility of human judgment: while he, on his part, would often express regret on finding that he had given pain and annoyance by opposing with ridicule or asperity the opinions of others."

In fact, Keats, at this period, according both to Henry Stephens and to Mathew, seems to have been rather a cocksure young man. But it must be remembered that he was only twenty, and also that he was consorting with those who were considerably below him in intel- lectual calibre. Not that he ever came to suffer fools gladly, but his gentleness and sweet temper in his relations with his friends was frequently remarked upon by them.

However, to return to Mr. Mathew who "delighted in administering to the happiness of others," Keats does seem to have been at one time very fond of him, possibly because he was, while Cowden Clarke remained at Enfield, the only young man in London he knew who was a "brother Poet."

There is some ground for believing that Keats's Sonnet on *Solitude*, with the lines:

> "Yet the sweet converse of an innocent mind
> Whose words are images of thoughts refin'd,
> Is my soul's pleasure and it sure must be
> Almost the highest bliss of human kind
> When to thy haunts two kindred spirits flee"

was addressed to Mathew, and that Mathew responded with an equally enthusiastic poem entitled: *To a Poetical Friend*, beginning:

> "O Thou who delightest in fanciful song
> And tellest strange tales of the earth and the fay,"

to which Keats in turn replied with the *Epistle to George Felton Mathew*, beginning:

> "Sweet are the pleasures that to verse belong,
> And doubly sweet a brotherhood in song,"

and ending with the curious fancy that Mathew was once a "flowret blooming wild," then was changed by Apollo into a "fish of gold," next becoming a "black-eyed swan," till at last he saw in the mirror of the stream "the placid features of a human face." There is a wild kind of fancy and immature poetry in these lines, though the thoughts of Mathew's metamorphoses are somewhat dizzying. Keats rather liked them himself,

for he wrote to Cowden Clarke: "I have copied out a
sheet or two of Verses which I composed some time ago,
and find so much to blame in them that the worst part
will go into the fire—those to G. Mathew I will suffer
·to meet the eye of Mr. H."

Mr. H. stood for Mr. Hunt, and we now come to one
of the great stepping-stones in Keats's early career.
George Felton Mathew fades into obscurity and the far
more interesting personality of Leigh Hunt takes his
place.

Leigh Hunt was, at this time, only thirty-two, that is
to say eleven years older than Keats, but he was already
celebrated in the world of literature. With his brother
John he started in 1808 a weekly newspaper called the
Examiner, which soon became one of the principal and
best journals of the day. He published, in 1814, his
Feast of the Poets, and in 1816, the *Story of Rimini*, which
had a success out of all proportion to its deserts, or so it
seems to modern tastes. It is written in a chatty, informal
style, the verse slipping along with ease but constantly
tipping over into bathos.

That he did have a certain amount of influence on
Keats's early work is proved by the resemblance between
their styles.

> "And when you listen you may hear a coil
>   Of bubbling springs about the grassy soil,"

might have been written by the youthful Keats. Just as

> "So I straightway began to pluck a posey
>   Of luxuries, bright, milky, soft and rosy,"

might have been by Hunt.

On the other hand in his worst lines he dropped to
extraordinary depths of bathos:

"Fain would I haste indeed to finish all
And so at once I reach the funeral,
Private 'twas fancied it would be, but some
Thought that her sire, the poor old duke, would come."

Nevertheless *Rimini* was much appreciated in its day. Byron's copy is scored with marginalia: "Very, very good." "The whole passage is very fine and original." "Superlative." "Many more beauties than there is time or place to express here." And Charles Lamb wrote to the author: "We congratulate you most sincerely on the taste of your prison fruit." (*Rimini* was written while Leigh Hunt was in the Surrey Jail.)

In spite of his somewhat chirruping personality, Leigh Hunt must have had a great deal of charm, an unusually happy disposition and a fund of genuine good-nature. Hazlitt, the crabbed, bitter Hazlitt, wrote to him:

"You are one of those people that I like, do what they will; there are others that I do not like, do what they may. I have always spoken well of you to friend or foe, viz. I have said that you were one of the pleasantest and cleverest persons I ever knew, but that you teased anyone you had to deal with out of their lives."

Since Leigh Hunt had no sense of time and still less sense of money, this last sentence must have been all too true. He was, moreover, rather heavily encumbered by domestic bonds; one becomes quite unfairly irritated by the prevalence of Mrs. Hunt and the six little Hunts. No wonder they nearly drove Byron crazy, and it is possible that Keats's often expressed dislike of domesticity may have been due to a surfeit of a poet's "amiable wife and sweet Children" in early days.

Nevertheless, there was a great deal more to Hunt than his sweet temper and chronic out-of-pocketness,

and to regard him as a Skimpolian figure is simply
absurd. He was a brilliant conversationalist, and a very
fine critic. His review, for example, of Keats's first book
of poems is unusually good and discerning, and he not
only possessed principles but was ready to suffer for
them.

The *Examiner*, which "began with being of no party;
but Reform soon gave it one," to quote its own foreword,
stood for liberalism and freedom, and was very strong
against such abuses as flogging in the army. In particular it launched a violent campaign against the Regent.
Its editors were continually being prosecuted for libel by
the powers that be—in fact, in 1811, the annual summary
recorded a "remarkable event," "the cessation of the
usual notice on the part of His Majesty's Attorney
General—the non-appearance of a legal Information for
the space of a whole twelve-month." But such immunity
was not to last. On March 22nd, 1812, an article appeared
on the Prince Regent, which stigmatized him as "a
violator of his word, a libertine over head and ears in
debt and disgrace, a despiser of domestic ties, the companion of gamblers and demireps, a man who has just
closed half a century without one single claim on the
gratitude of his country or the respect of posterity!" It
is not altogether surprising that, on December 9th,
John and Leigh Hunt found themselves being tried for
libel. They were adjudged guilty and condemned to a
year's imprisonment in separate jails. Hunt went down
with his flag flying. We find in the *Examiner* of December
13th, the following pleasant mock-recantation. "The
Regent," he writes, "has kept his word with the Irish—
he lives with his wife—he is a little advanced in years,
young, indeed, rather than otherwise; and in one word,
he is thin."

Cowden Clarke was one of Leigh Hunt's many friends

c

who came to visit him in prison, taking with him
baskets of fruit from the pleasant school-garden at
Enfield. It was on one of those occasions, in fact the last
of them, since it was the day of Hunt's release, that Keats
walking across the fields with his friend, turned back
at the last gate, and with a "conscious look," as Clarke
describes it, and a hesitating hand, had thrust on Clarke
the sonnet entitled: *Written on the Day Mr. Leigh Hunt Left
Prison*. It was the first of his poems that he had shown
to any one, even to this most intimate friend, and it is a
promising sonnet with a certain amount of vigour,
eulogizing Hunt, not for his liberalism and political
significance, but because he strayed "in Spenser's halls,"
and "flew with daring Milton," because to "regions of
his own, his genius true took flight." This was characteristic of Keats at this period, poetry was still to him "the
only thing worthy the attention of superior minds."

Now that Hunt was released, Clarke determined to see
if he could introduce him to his young admirer. The
sonnet on *Solitude*, already quoted, had been published in
the *Examiner*, on May 5th, 1816, but, according to his
own testimony, Leigh Hunt then knew nothing of the
anonymous contributor, but now Clarke walked over to
his cottage in the Vale of Health, bringing one or two of
Keats's poems with him. Leigh Hunt with a critical
intuition that was very near genius, broke into enthusiastic praises of the new young poet. Horace Smith, the
author of *Rejected Addresses*, who was also there, seconded
them, reading aloud the sonnet, *How many Bards gild
the lapses of time*, and remarking as he reached the
penultimate line of the sextet:

"That distance of recognizance bereaves,"

"What a well-condensed expression for a youth so
young!"

The sequel to this was an invitation to Cowden Clarke to bring Keats over to the Vale of Health. But before the first visit took place, an incident occurred which must have established Clarke's belief in Keats's genius more than all the praise of all the critics in the world.

A Mr. Alsager, who unpoetically enough conducted the money market department for the *Times*, lent Cowden Clarke his folio edition of Chapman's *Homer*. So that, one evening, Clarke and Keats sat up till dawn, reading and re-reading, and turning up all the famous passages they had known so scrappily in Pope's translation, Keats sometimes literally shouting with enthusiasm. Clarke read aloud the description of the shipwreck of Ulysses:

"Then forth he came, his both knees falt'ring, both
His strong hands hanging down, and all with froth
His cheeks and nostrils flowing, voice and breath
Spent to all use, and down he sank to death.
The sea had soaked his heart through; all his veins
His toils had wracked t'a labouring woman's pains.
Dead weary was he,"

and "had the reward," as he says of one of Keats's "delighted stares." Those earnest stares and the thrusting out of the upper lip remained very vividly in Clarke's memory.

As day was breaking Keats walked back to his solitary lodgings at 8 Dean Street,[1] or perhaps he did not go home at all but wandered about, loitering around the river and on the bridges. Certain it is he did not sleep, for at ten o'clock the next morning, Clarke found on his breakfast table the famous sonnet, *On First looking into Chapman's Homer*. Clarke may very well have felt that a "new planet" had swum into *his* ken.

[1] *See* Appendix I.

CHAPTER III

"AND I shall ever bless my destiny,
 That in a time, when under pleasant trees
  Pan is no longer sought, I feel a free
 A leafy luxury, seeing I could please
  With these poor offerings, a man like thee"—

wrote Keats, in the dedicatory sonnet to Leigh Hunt which prefaced his first volume of poems, published in March 1817.

In later days Keats rightly resented the assumption made by the curiously blind critics of the day that he was a pupil and disciple of Hunt's. Even in this very early book, which contains the loveliness of *I stood tiptoe upon a little hill*, and the rushing youthful vigour of *Sleep and Poetry*, he had far outstripped the older man. When Hunt does influence his style, as in *Calidore*, it is nearly always unfortunately; none the less, he deserved the enthusiastic dedication, for he did a very great deal for Keats. It was partly owing to his influence that Keats made the great decision of his life and communicated it to his guardian, Mr. Abbey, who records it, writing of himself in the third person, not without a certain dry humour. "It was Mr. Abbey's advice," he wrote, "that John commence business at Tottenham as a Surgeon. He communicated his plans to his Ward, but his surprise was not moderate to hear in reply that he did not intend

to be a surgeon. Not intend to be a Surgeon! Why
what do you mean to be? I mean to rely on my ability
as a Poet—John you are either Mad or a Fool to talk in
so absurd a Manner. My Mind is made up said the
youngster very quietly. I know that I possess abilities
greater than most men, and therefore I am determined
to gain my living by exercising them. Seeing nothing
could be done Abbey called him a Silly Boy, and pro-
phesied a speedy Termination to his inconsiderate
enterprise."

A very natural reaction on the part of a guardian.

The change from the uncongenial profession, and the
not very intellectual middle-class social circle which was
all he knew, must at first have been delightful to that
young eager mind. Hunt not only introduced him to the
best literary society of the time, but made him a constant
companion and an unquestioned intimate of the little
cottage in the Vale of Health. Apart from his genius,
he found, as indeed did all who came in contact with
him, something intensely lovable about the young man.

"I found the young poet's heart as warm as his
imagination," he writes. "We read and walked together,
and used to write verses of an evening on a given subject.
No imaginative pleasure was left unnoticed by us, or
unenjoyed, from the recollections of the bards and
patriots of old to the luxury of a summer's rain at our
windows or the clicking of the coal in winter time."

One of the pleasantest sensations in the whole world
is to become an intimate of a house which is not one's
own home. Home, however beloved, must always be a
little dull, a little over-familiar, there is a romantic glow
about this substitute, an awareness of its charm that is
infinitely satisfying. This is especially so when it provides, perhaps for the first time, a congenial atmosphere,
rich satisfying talk, a friendly freedom.

Keats found all these in Leigh Hunt's Cottage in the Vale of Health. That he really was at home there, and one of the family, is proved by the following extract from a letter from Hunt to Vincent Novello: "We set off at eleven to-morrow morning, and are in all the chaos of packed trunks, lumber, litter, dust, dirty dry fingers &c. . . . The ladies join with me in these devoirs and so does Mr. Keats, as in poetry bound." Mr. Keats must then have been in the midst of the lumber and litter and may have helped in packing the trunks. He could stay with the Hunts whenever he wished; a bed was made up for him on the sofa in the small parlour, and there he lay awake watching in the flickering firelight the prints and the busts with which the small room was adorned, happy to be so familiar with them. They were a mixed collection. There was Alfred the Great in one corner; in another Kosciusko, of whom Keats had noted down, not so long ago, from one of Astley Cooper's lectures, "that the patriot K . . . had the sciatic nerve divided by a pike-wound;" and in yet a third there was Sappho, who should have looked down at her young descendant with especial pity, since he was to know, too intimately, the torments of which she wrote.

The whole atmosphere of Leigh Hunt's untidy, welcoming, intellectual house must have been very agreeable. Keats shows how delightful it was to him in the sonnet beginning: "*Keen fitful gusts are whispering here and there,*" which tells of his walk returning from Hampstead on a winter's evening, with his mind "brimfull of the friendliness that in a little cottage I have found," and of the eager literary talk in which the evening had been passed; while Cowden Clarke has left us one charming sketch of an evening, when, as was a frequent custom, Keats and Leigh Hunt set themselves to write verses on a given subject. On this occasion the subject proposed was *The Grasshopper and the Cricket*, and the two protagonists were soon scribbling, with Cowden Clarke tucked away with a book, on the end of the sofa. He afterwards wrote: ". . . the effect of the after scrutiny was one of many such occurrences which have riveted the memory of Leigh Hunt in my affectionate regard and admiration for unaffected generosity and perfectly unpretentious encouragement. His sincere look of pleasure at the first line

" The poetry of earth is never dead."

"Such a prosperous opening!" he said; and when he came to the tenth and eleventh lines:

"On a lone winter evening, when the frost
    Has wrought a silence——"

"Ah! that's perfect! Bravo Keats!"

Here is Hunt's sonnet:

"Green little vaulter in the sunny grass
        Catching your heart up at the feel of June,
        Sole voice that's heard amidst the lazy noon,
When ev'n the bees lag at the summoning brass;
And you, warm little housekeeper, who class
        With those who think the candles come too soon.
        Loving the fire, and all your tricksome tune
Nick the glad silent moments as they pass:
Oh sweet and tiny cousins, that belong
        One to the fields, the other to the hearth,
Both have your sunshine, both though small are strong
        At your clear hearts; and both were sent on earth
To sing in thoughtful ears this natural song,—
        In doors and out, Summer and Winter. Mirth."

And here is Keats's:

"The poetry of earth is never dead:
When all the birds are faint with the hot sun,
And hide in cooling trees, a voice will run
From hedge to hedge about the new-mown mead;
That is the Grasshopper's—he takes the lead
In summer luxury,—he has never done
With his delights; for when tired out with fun
He rests at ease beneath some pleasant weed.
The poetry of earth is ceasing never:
On a lone winter evening, when the frost
Has wrought a silence, from the stove there shrills
The Cricket's song, in warmth increasing ever,
And seems to one in drowsiness half lost,
The Grasshopper's among some grassy hills."

Keats, on the walk home, confided to Cowden Clarke that he preferred Leigh Hunt's sonnet but one cannot agree with him. Even the fearful bathos of "when tired out with fun, He rests at ease beneath some pleasant weed," presenting a happy picture of the grasshopper as a sort of romping old Caspar, doesn't equal Leigh Hunt's archness, "the warm little housekeeper," and "the tricksome tune." It may be noted, too, that Hunt, ever a better critic than poet, had seized on the only good line in the two sonnets:

> "... when the frost
> Has wrought a silence ..."

Another little scene which has provided posterity with four not very remarkable sonnets, took place on an occasion, when the two poets saw fit to crown each other with wreaths of laurel and ivy and to write verses celebrating the occasion. Some ladies were announced while they were thus employed and Keats enthusiastically refused to take off his wreath.

Later he became rather ashamed of the silliness of the intercoronation episode, and expressed it in a few lines of what he called "ranting" verse:

" God of the golden bow,
    And of the golden lyre
And of the golden hair
    And of the golden fire,
      Charioteer
      Of the patient year,
Where—where slept thine ire,
When like a blank idiot I put on thy wreath,
    Thy laurel, thy glory
    The light of thy story,
Or was I a worm—too low ' crawling for death,'
    Delphic Apollo!"

In fact, Keats began very soon to grow out of the Hunt atmosphere. It was not Hunt's fault. He was genuinely extremely fond of Keats, who perhaps evoked from him deeper feelings than any, except Shelley, were able to arouse in that genial, sunshiny, easy-going nature. But Hunt's whole atmosphere was that of a small literary coterie. Keats probably hit it off well enough in a little sketch he made of the Hunt circle for his sister-in-law, in 1818.

"(Scene, a little Parlour. Enter Hunt, Gattie, Hazlitt, Mrs. Novello, Ollier.)

GATTIE: Ha! Hunt! Got into your new house? Ha! Mrs. Novello seen *Altham and his Wife*?[1]

MRS. NOVELLO: Yes (*with a grin*). It's Mr. Hunt's, isn't it?

GATTIE: Mr. Hunt's? No, Ha! Mr. Ollier I congratulate you on the highest compliment I ever heard paid to the book. Mr. Hazlitt I hope you are well?

---

[1] *Altham and his Wife* was a "domestic tale" newly written by Charles Ollier.

HAZLITT: Yes sir, no sir.

HUNT (*at the Music*): ' La Biondina etc.'—Hazlitt did you ever hear this?—' La Biondina etc.'

HAZLITT: O no Sir—I never.

OLLIER: Do Hunt, give it us over again—divino.

GATTIE: Divino—Hunt when does your Pocket-Book come out?

HUNT: ' What is this absorbs me quite?' O we are spinning on a little, we shall floridize soon I hope—Such a thing was very much wanting—people think of nothing but money-getting—now for me I am rather inclined to the liberal side of things—I am reckoned lax in christian principles etc. etc. etc."

The "divino" and the "floridize" give the tone of the little scene. Keats apparently got pretty sick of the mutual admiration and the set enthusiasms of the Hunt coterie. He wrote to George and Georgiana Keats in March, 1818: "It is a great Pity that People should be associating themselves with the finest things, spoil them. Hunt has damned Hampstead and Masks and Sonnets and italian tales . . ." And eight months later: "The night we went to Novello's" (Vincent Novello was a well-known musician, a friend of Hunt and of Lamb, and father-in-law to Charles Cowden Clarke) "there was a complete set-to of Mozart and punning—I was so completely tired of it that if I were to follow my own inclinations I should never meet any one of that set again, not even Hunt—who is certainly a pleasant fellow in the main when you are with him—but in reallity he is vain, egotistical, and disgusting in matters of taste and in morals. He understands many a beautiful thing; but then, instead of giving other minds credit for the same degree of perception as he himself possesses—he begins an explanation in such a curious manner that our taste and self-love is offended continually. Hunt does one harm by making fine things petty and beautiful things hateful—Through him I am indifferent to Mozart, I care not for white Busts— and many a glorious thing when associated with him becomes a nothing—This distorts one's mind— makes one's thoughts bizarre—perplexes one in the standard of Beauty."

Had he been older and maturer, he might have got more from the Hunt circle, since, after all, it included Lamb and Hazlitt. (He had a tremendous admiration for Hazlitt but never seems to have become intimate with him.) But Keats was too great a poet and too sincere a person to relish the rôle of infant genius which Hunt, in all goodness of heart, wished to thrust upon him. He certainly was not fitted, as he wrote later, to be "a versifying pet-lamb." Another reason why Keats diverged from Hunt and never became intimate with Hazlitt and Lamb, with Horace and James Smith, and with the other wits and men of letters of this day was a division of centuries. They were all of them, Hunt included, children of the eighteenth century. Their minds were at the same time romantic and robust, sentimental and cynical. They never bothered about contradictions in their natures. They could wear laurel crowns and shed tears without feeling foolish, just as they could demolish their own accepted standards in a coolly witty phrase, without feeling daring. To us, nostalgic for the eighteenth century, they appear extraordinarily charming. But Keats had nothing of the eighteenth century in his mental make-up. He was too unsophisticated, too sincere, and above all too well integrated, to get on with them. On his last voyage, it is recorded that he threw Byron's *Don Juan* on to the floor of the cabin in a transport of indignation, exclaiming: "Oh this is a paltry originality which consists in making solemn things gay and gay things solemn."

Yet this is not to say that Keats was a prig. He held no theories, defended no moral codes, only he had the high seriousness of youth and he was so sincerely unaffected that he never attempted to try to show himself as other than he was. Nevertheless, he preserved a fund of sturdy common sense, an excellent sense of proportion, and a complete lack of vanity, which saved him from becoming either priggish or preposterous. Contrast him for example with another enthusiastic character with an unflinching belief in his own genius, a member of Hunt's circle, the painter, Benjamin Robert Haydon.

Haydon must have been one of the queerest and in some ways one of the most trying personalities of that queer and trying galère. Packed with vitality, obstinate as a mule, convinced about everything in heaven and earth, particularly about his own rightness and his own genius, he was a stimulating but aggravating companion.

His story is a tragic one and should be read thoughtfully by the youthful aspirant to genius. It is a far greater deterrent than the story of Keats. For, however Keats suffered, however little reward his genius brought him, yet it was there. When he said so quietly and firmly to Mr. Abbey, "I know I possess abilities greater than most men," he was unquestionably right. But Benjamin Haydon possessed just this same firm unshakeable opinion about his own powers, this fiery single-minded devotion to his own genius, and he was wrong. In his autobiography he relates how very early one morning, his mother slipped into his room and, sitting down beside him, implored him very movingly not to leave his parents. "My dear Benjamin you are my only support," she said, "and in the delicate state of your poor father's health God only knows how soon I may be left alone and unaided. It will break my heart, if, after all my care and anxiety for your infancy, you leave me just as you are becoming able to comfort and console me."

"I was deeply affected," Haydon continues, "but checking my tears I told her, in a voice struggling to be calm, that it was of no use attempting to dissuade me. I felt impelled by something I could not resist. 'Do not,' said I, ' my dear mother, think me cruel; I can never forget your love and affection; but yet I cannot help it —I must be a painter.'"

It is the classic reply. And Haydon's life followed the classic course, poverty, lack of appreciation, near starvation, and finally a bullet through the brain. The whole sordid story only redeemed by his devotion to Art, his steady unwavering belief in his own genius. Only there was no genius. The pendant half of the story is not there. Posterity has found even less to admire than his own generation did in Haydon's enormous historical pictures, for which he sacrificed so much.

But, in 1816, the end was still far off, and when Keats met Haydon, he was immensely attracted by his vivid personality, his sincerity, and his passionate devotion to art. Their friendship started off at a high level:

"My dear Sir—" wrote Keats, on November 20th, 1816, "Last evening wrought me up, and I cannot forbear sending you the following—Yours unfeignedly, John Keats." And he encloses a sonnet beginning *Great spirits now on Earth are sojourning*, which includes Haydon with Wordsworth and Hunt.

The acquaintance ripened rapidly. They met frequently, at Haydon's studio in Great Marlborough Street, at 76 Cheapside, where Keats lodged with his brothers, and whenever they met they plunged into a vortex of talk. It may have been with Haydon that Keats became so thoroughly soaked in Shakespeare as his correspondence proves him to have been. There are scarcely ever twenty consecutive lines in his letters which do not contain some Shakespearean quotation, never dragged in, but springing naturally and appropriately from a mind which seems to have known the plays backwards, forwards and inside out. Certainly, Haydon wrote in his journal: "I have enjoyed Shakespeare with John Keats more than with any other human being," and Keats, in his first long letter to Haydon, starts off with a quotation from *Love's Labour Lost*:

"Let Fame, which all hunt after in their Lives
Live register'd upon our brazen tombs, etc."

continues with three references to *King Lear*, and ends with a disquisition on *Antony and Cleopatra*. He also writes in the course of the letter: "I remember your saying that you had notions of a good Genius presiding over you. I have of late had the same thought . . . Is it too daring to Fancy Shakespeare this Presidor?" And a little later: "I never quite despair and I read Shakespeare—indeed I shall I think never read any other Book much," and he concludes: "So now in the name of Shakespeare, Raphael and all our Saints I commend you."

Haydon's real burning enthusiasm for art, his love of classic sculpture (it was he who forced the British Museum to purchase the Parthenon frieze from Lord Elgin), his sense of the high calling of an artist, influenced and were very useful to Keats's development; though his really monstrous egoism made it impossible for any one to keep him as a permanent friend. Yet at the beginning their intimacy was very close and the picture that he draws of Keats in his autobiography shows an excellent observation and perception of character. "In fireside conversation he was weak and inconsistent, but he was in his glory in the fields. The humming of a bee, the sight of a flower, the glitter of the sun, seemed to make his nature tremble; then his eye flashed, his cheek glowed, his mouth quivered. He was the most unselfish of human creatures: unadapted to this world, he cared not for himself, and put himself to any inconvenience for the sake of his friends. He was haughty and had a fierce hatred of rank; but he had a kind gentle heart and would have shared his fortune with any man who wanted it."

Unfortunately, in matters of fact, Haydon, with his sense of the dramatic and vivid imagination, is a most unreliable witness. It is he who tells an oddly distorted version of the story given in Chapter I, of Keats watching by his mother's bedroom door during her illness. Haydon has it that Keats being a child of ungovernable temper, terrorized the household, and kept his mother imprisoned by flourishing an old sword. Haydon is also responsible for the legend that Keats peppered his tongue with cayenne pepper in order better to enjoy the coolness and freshness of claret, and also reports him in later years as having "flown to dissipation," and adds, for "six weeks he was scarcely sober." About the claret and cayenne there is, of course, no proof, though it is a highly unlikely story, scouted as impossible by Cowden Clarke, but the six weeks drunkenness is sheer nonsense, disproved by Keats's letters at the time and the testimony of all his friends.

There are occasions however, when Haydon's prose style, and his unaffected pleasure and interest in himself and his own affairs, do combine to give a wonderfully vivid picture. Such is the account of the "immortal dinner" (it is typically Haydon so to describe his own hospitality), which he gave at the end of 1817.

"On December 28th the immortal dinner came off in my painting-room, with Jerusalem towering up behind us as a background." (This was Haydon's enormous picture of " *The entry of Christ into Jerusalem*." The heads of the disciples and of the crowd were those of famous writers and philosophers. Wordsworth was drawn from life, as was Keats, and Haydon was mightily perplexed about this time as to whether Voltaire was worthy of the honour of being included.) "Wordsworth was in fine cue, and we had a glorious set-to,—on Homer, Shakespeare, Milton and Virgil. Lamb got exceedingly merry and exquisitely witty; and his fun in the midst of Wordsworth's solemn intonations of oratory was like the sarcasm and wit of the fool in the intervals of Lear's passion. He made a speech and voted me absent and made them drink my health. 'Now,' said Lamb, 'you old lake poet, you rascally poet, why do you call Voltaire dull?' We all defended Wordsworth, and affirmed there was a state of mind when Voltaire would be dull. 'Well,' said Lamb, 'here's to Voltaire—the Messiah of the French nation, and a very proper one, too.'

"He then, in a strain of humour beyond description, abused me for putting Newton's head into my picture,— 'a fellow,' said he, 'who believed nothing unless it was as clear as the three sides of a triangle.' And then he and Keats agreed he had destroyed all the poetry of the rainbow by reducing it to prismatic colours. It was impossible to resist him, and we all drank, 'Newton's health, and confusion to mathematics.' It was delightful to see the good-humour of Wordsworth in giving in to all our frolics without affectation and laughing as heartily as the best of us. . . .

"In the morning of this delightful day, a gentleman, a perfect stranger, had called on me. He said he knew my friends, had an enthusiasm for Wordsworth, and begged I would procure him the happiness of an introduction. He told me he was a Comptroller of Stamps, and often had correspondence with the poet. I thought it a liberty; but still, as he seemed a gentleman, I told him he might come.

"When we retired to tea we found the comptroller. In introducing him to Wordsworth I forgot to say who he was. After a little time the comptroller looked down, looked up and said to Wordsworth, ' Don't you think, sir, Milton was a great genius?' Keats looked at me, Wordsworth looked at the comptroller. Lamb who was dozing by the fire turned round and said, ' Pray, sir, did you say Milton was a great genius?' ' No, sir; I asked Mr. Wordsworth if he were not.' ' Oh,' said Lamb, ' then you are a silly fellow.' ' Charles! my dear Charles!' said Wordsworth; but Lamb, perfectly innocent of the confusion he had created, was off again by the fire.

"After an awful pause the Comptroller said, ' Don't you think Newton a great genius?' I could not stand it any longer; Keats put his head into my books. Ritchie squeezed in a laugh. Wordsworth seemed asking himself, ' Who is this?' Lamb got up and, taking a candle, said, ' Sir, will you allow me to look at your phrenological development?' He then turned his back on the poor man, and at every question of the comptroller he chaunted—

Diddle diddle dumpling, my son John
Went to bed with his breeches on.

The man in office, finding Wordsworth did not know who he was, said in a spasmodic and half-chuckling anticipation of assured victory, ' I have had the honour of some correspondance with you, Mr. Wordsworth.'

D

'With me, sir?' said Wordsworth, 'not that I remember.' 'Don't you sir? I am a comptroller of stamps.'

"There was dead silence;—the comptroller evidently thinking that was enough. While we were waiting for Wordsworth's reply, Lamb sung out

> Hey diddle diddle,
> The cat and the fiddle.

'My dear Charles!' said Wordsworth,—

"'Diddle diddle dumpling, my son John,' chaunted Lamb, and then rising, exclaimed, 'Do let me have another look at that gentleman's organs.' Keats and I hurried Lamb into the painting-room, shut the door, and gave way to inextinguishable laughter. Monkhouse followed and tried to get Lamb away. We went back but the comptroller was irreconcilable. We soothed and smiled and asked him to supper. He stayed, though his dignity was sorely affected. However, being a good-natured man, we parted all in good humour, and no ill effects followed.

"All the while, until Monkhouse succeeded, we could hear Lamb struggling in the painting-room and calling at intervals, 'Who is that fellow? Allow me to see his organs once more.'

"It was indeed an immortal evening. Wordsworth's fine intonation as he quoted Milton and Virgil, Keats's eager inspired look, Lamb's quaint sparkle of lambent humour, so speeded the stream of conversation, that in my life I never passed a more delightful time. All our fun was within bounds. Not a word passed that an apostle might not have listened to. It was a night worthy of the Elizabethan age, and my solemn Jerusalem flashing up by the flame of the fire, with Christ hanging over us like a vision, all made up a picture which will long glow upon—

                        that inward eye
which is the bliss of solitude.

"Keats made Ritchie (a young explorer just going to Africa) promise he would carry his *Endymion* to the great desert of Sahara and fling it in the midst."

The evening does not seem to have made nearly such an impression on Keats, who mentions it, very passingly, in a letter to his brothers; but Haydon does provide for us an enchanting picture of the " man in office " "making" literary conversation with such startling effects, and of Wordsworth's half-amused, half-shocked efforts to repress the irrepressible Lamb. Surely only Lamb could obtain so much toleration from the rugged domineering Wordsworth!

CHAPTER IV

Keats's relationship with other poets—Wordsworth—Coleridge—Shelley—Byron.

WILLIAM WORDSWORTH was, of course, the third member of the "great spirits now on Earth," eulogized in Keats's sonnet, and the "immortal dinner" was the first time that he and Keats met. Keats had a great admiration for Wordsworth and when Haydon proposed sending him the sonnet, Keats wrote: "The idea of your sending it to Wordsworth puts me out of breath—you know with what Reverence I would send my Well wishes to him."

Alas, the actual meetings with the poet seem to have proved a little disappointing, though there was one occasion on which Wordsworth invited him to supper, which so pleased him that he had to burst into a friend's rooms late at night to tell him all about it. But Wordsworth was both dictatorial and pompous, he had notoriously no sense of humour and he must have been in a very light-hearted mood when he asked Haydon, who had spent ten years over the painting of his picture "Jerusalem," what Dutch painter he most resembled. The answer being Teniers (ten years).

Leigh Hunt describes him thus: "He had a dignified manner, with a deep and roughish but not unpleasing voice, and an exalted mode of speaking. He had a habit of keeping his left hand in the bosom of his waistcoat; and in this attitude . . . he sat dealing forth his eloquent but hardly catholic judgments."

His judgments were indeed hardly catholic. He disliked all modern poetry except his own and expressed his opinions with the finality of a Church Council. Keats, one evening at Haydon's, was induced to recite the "Hymn to Pan," from *Endymion*. All waited in silence for Wordsworth's approbation, but after a long pause all that Wordsworth, who "looked red, though grave," could find to say was: "A pretty piece of paganism." After which the party broke up. On another occasion when someone mentioned that Scott was about to publish his novel, *Rob Roy*, Wordsworth went to the bookcase and taking down his own ballad of that name read it aloud, remarking at the end: "I do not know what more Mr. Scott can have to say on this subject." It is hardly to be wondered at that Keats wrote to his brothers, in February, 1818, that: "I am sorry that Wordsworth has left a bad impression wherever he visited in town by his egotism, Vanity and bigotry."

One small circumstance probably slightly ruffled Keats. Any one who reads Wordsworth's life must discover that, in spite of all the plain living and high thinking, he was not insensible to the distinctions of society and of the world. In fact, he was something of a snob. He liked titles and he liked great folk. It is a harmless foible, but Keats was so entirely untouched by it that he may have found it hard to comprehend. The first time he called on Wordsworth shortly after the immortal dinner, he found the elder poet in full fig, silk stockings, knee-breeches, etc., on his way to dine with Kingston, the Commissioner of Stamps, the very man who had made such a fool of himself at Haydon's. Keats, who had a high idea of the calling of a poet, must have found it jarring to see one of the greatest of living poets hastening to accept the hospitality of a man who, whatever his merits, cut such a very poor figure in literary society.

Wordsworth's just appreciation of his own talents presents a contrast to the attitude of Coleridge who, Leigh Hunt records, "speaks very modestly of his Poetry —not affectedly so, but out of a high notion in the art of his predecessors. He delighted the late Mr. Keats in the course of conversation, with adding, after he had alluded to it,—' if there is anything I have written which may be *called* poetry.'"

This is an interesting sidelight on the relations of two poets whom Rudyard Kipling coupled together when he wrote: "Remember that in all the millions permitted there are no more than five—five little lines— of which one can say: ' These are the pure Magic. These are the clear Vision. The rest is only poetry.' " And even more interesting is the famous description of Keats's meeting with Coleridge on an April day in 1819. The account of the conversation chimes in curiously with those "five little lines," since they talked of nightingales and poetry, and perhaps, as has been suggested, the echoes of Coleridge's beautifully-modulated voice were still in Keats's ears as he lay out in the garden under the plum tree a month or so later, writing the *Ode to the Nightingale*. And they talked of "different genera and species of dreams," perhaps referring, modestly without doubt on Coleridge's part, since he published it "rather as a psychological curiosity than on the grounds of any supposed *poetic* merits," to that famous dream which was interrupted by "a person on business from Porlock." But let us have the account of it in Keats's own words.

"Last Sunday," writes Keats, "I took a walk towards Highgate, and in the lane that winds by the side of Lord Mansfield's park I met Mr. Green our Demonstrator at Guy's in conversation with Coleridge—I joined them, after enquiring by a look whether it would be agreeable—I walked with him at his alderman-after-dinner pace for nearly two miles I suppose. In those two Miles he broached a thousand things—let me see if I can give you a list—Nightingales, Poetry—on Poetical Sensation Metaphysics—Different genera and species of Dreams—Nightmare—a dream accompanied by a sense of touch—single and double touch—A dream related—First and second consciousness—the difference explained between will and Volition—so many meta-physicians from a want of smoking the second conscious-ness—Monsters—the Kraken—Mermaids—Southey be-lieves in them—Southey's belief too much diluted—A Ghost story—Good morning—I heard his voice as he came towards me—I heard it as he came away—I had heard it all the interval—if it may be called so."

The vanity of human evidence is well exemplified in Coleridge's account of this same interview. It is true that he wrote it thirteen years later and that accuracy was not one of the qualities for which he was dis-tinguished, but it certainly shows what imagination will do.

"A loose, slack not well-dressed youth met Mr. Green and myself in a lane near Highgate." The com-ment on Keats's dress may well have been just, since two years previously his publisher's brother, Henry Taylor, had written: "Your interesting description of Mr. Keats gave me great pleasure, he must be a bold young man to affect such a singular style of dress. Cowley's dress was agreeable to the costume of the day but Mr. Keats violates all decorum and can only excite ridicule and pity." While Mr. Reynell, the printer to the firm, retained an impression that Keats used to wear "some sort of sailor costume." But Keats was certainly neither "slack" nor "loose," since he was but five feet high, with broad shoulders, compact and well knit. Coleridge's narrative continues: "Green knew him, and spoke. It was Keats. He was introduced to me, and stayed a minute or so." (The whole two hours walk and conversation have slipped Coleridge's memory.) "After he had left us a little way, he came back, and said, ' Let me carry away the memory, Coleridge, of having pressed your hand! ' ' There is death in that hand,' I said to Green when Keats was gone; yet this was, I believe, before the consumption showed itself."

The remark about "death in that hand," seems to have been rather a favourite one of Coleridge's, since he made it, according to himself, not once or twice, but several times, on his friend, Adam Steinmetz.

If ghosts ever do walk what would one not give to meet those three in a shady lane by the side of Ken Wood? Mr. Green would be unknown to us but I think we should at once recognize the other figures, the one excessively corpulent, with broad, high forehead, with "gross, voluptuous, open, eloquent" mouth, and purple tinged complexion; the other barely five feet high, but broad-shouldered and well-knit, with the curling reddish-brown hair as "soft as the plumage of a bird," with the projecting upper lip and beautiful, lambent, expressive hazel eyes. I think we should recognize that celebratedly melodious voice, rising and falling but never stopping as it passed from one to another of the magic subjects, nightingales, poetry, metaphysics, monsters, and Southey's belief in mermaids, as they strolled along, so very slowly, beneath the budding April branches.

There is one other figure with whom Keats is linked imperishably and for ever, that other youthful poet, three years his senior, who also perished untimely, with a volume of Keats's poetry in his coat-pocket, surviving just long enough to leave for his contemporary one of the most nobly beautiful elegies in English literature. Yet if Keats could have seen into the future, nothing would have surprised him more than this posthumous alliance, for their relationship, though friendly, was cool and distant.

They first met at Hunt's in 1817. Leigh Hunt writes: "Keats did not take to Shelley as kindly as Shelley did to him. Shelley's only thoughts of his new acquaintance were such as regarded his bad health, with which he sympathized, and his poetry, of which he has left such a monument of his admiration in *Adonais*. Keats, being a little too sensitive on the score of his origin, felt inclined to see in every man of birth a natural enemy."

This may have been true. It is quite a usual occurrence, having been observed a thousand times before, and will probably be observed as many times again, and Leigh Hunt was a shrewd observer of such foibles, as when he wrote of Byron: ". . . Lord Byron, besides being a lord, was a man of letters, and he was extremely desirous of the approbation of men of letters. He loved to enjoy the privileges of his rank, and at the same time to be thought above them. It is true, if he thought you were not above them yourself, he was the better pleased."

On the other hand attractive as Shelley may sound to us, to a young man, his contemporary, he may have seemed rather preposterous. Leigh Hunt describes him as "a youth not come to his full growth; very gentlemanly, earnestly gazing at every object that interested him, and quoting the Greek dramatists." Hazlitt says: "he has a fire in his eye, a fever in his blood, a maggot in his brain, a hectic flutter in his speech . . . He is sanguine complexioned and shrill-voiced . . . His bending, flexible form appears to take no strong hold of things, does not grapple with the world about him, but flows from it like a river." While Lamb simply states that: "his voice was the most obnoxious squeak I ever was tormented with." We know, in addition, that Shelley held opinions on humanity, morality and the Universe as decided as Wordsworth's and Haydon's, though he advanced them with a great deal more courtesy. Keats, on the other hand, once wrote: "You know my ideas about Religion. I do not think myself more in the right than other people, and that nothing in the world is proveable."

Leigh Hunt goes on to say that "Keats, notwithstanding his unbounded sympathies with ordinary flesh and blood, and even the transcendental cosmopolitics of Hyperion, was so far inferior in universality to his great acquaintance, that he could not accompany him in his dædal rounds with nature, and his Archimedean endeavours to move the globe with his own hands." That is one way of putting it. In more ordinary language, Keats probably thought Shelley rather an ass.

There are not many, perhaps one or two, references to Shelley in Keats's letters. One, which shows a complete misunderstanding of Shelley's nature, runs as follows: "The fact is he (Leigh Hunt) and Shelley are hurt, and perhaps rightly, at my not having showed them the affair (*Endymion*) officiously—and from several hints I have had"—these hints came from Haydon and John Hamilton Reynolds, both of whom had quarrelled with Hunt and to whom, obviously, the misunderstanding is due—"they appear much disposed to dissect and anatomize, any trip or slip I may have made—But who's afraid?"

The fact was that long before the newspaper attacks on the Cockney school Keats was anxious to escape from the reputation of having been influenced by Hunt. "You see," he wrote, "how independant my writing has been—Hunt's dissuasion was of no avail—I refused to visit Shelley that I might have my own unfetter'd Scope —and after all, I shall have the reputation of being

Hunt's elevé. His corrections and amputations will, by
the knowing ones be traced in the Poem. This to be sure
is the vexation of a day—nor would I say so many
Words about it to any but those whom I know to have
my wellfare and Reputation at heart."

In another letter to his brothers he writes: "Shelley's
poem is out and there are words about its being objected
to as much as ' Queen Mab ' was. Poor Shelley I think
he has his Quota of good qualities, in sooth la!!"; which
sounds like a private joke of some kind, possibly an echo
of someone's way of speaking.

But the most striking reference is the first one which
occurs, in a letter to Hunt in May, 1817. It is a joking
enquiry as to whether "Shelley goes on telling sad stories
of the deaths of Kings?" This was a quotation of which
Shelley was very fond and which came out at the most
unexpected moments. "Going with me to town once in
the Hampstead stage," Hunt records, "in which our only
companion was an old lady, who sat silent and stiff
after the English fashion, he startled her into a look of
the most ludicrous astonishment by saying abruptly:
' Hunt, for God's sake let us sit upon the ground and tell
sad stories of the deaths of kings.' The old lady looked
on the coach floor, as if she expected us to take our seats
there accordingly." Keats had probably heard this
story and was making an allusion to it but the next
sentence in the letter gives one a curious shock. "Tell
him," writes Keats, and he is writing at the very opening
of his career, "there are strange Stories of the death of
Poets—some have died before they were conceived."
The jesting sentences run on. "Does Mrs. S. (Mrs.
Shelley) cut Bread and Butter as neatly as ever? Tell her
to procure some fatal Scissors and cut the thread of life
of all to be disappointed Poets. Does Mrs. Hunt tear
linen in half as straight as ever? Tell her to tear from the

book of Life all blank leaves." "Strange stories of the death of Poets!" If the theory about Time be true, that it is continuous running both backward and forward, and that the already mapped-out future can be apprehended by the dreaming or unconscious mind, it would seem as if Rome and Pisa and that "slope of green access" were already lurking in the shadows.

Shelley and Keats never corresponded till towards the end of the latter's life. The following letter speaks for itself.

"Pisa, July 27th, 1820.

"MY DEAR KEATS,—I hear with great pain the dangerous accident that you have undergone, & Mr Gisborne who gives me the account of it, adds that you continue to wear a consumptive appearance. This consumption is a disease particularly fond of people who write such good verses as you have done, and with the assistance of an English winter it can often indulge its selection;—I do not think that young and amiable poets are at all bound to gratify its taste; they have entered into no bond with the Muses to that effect. But seriously (for I am joking on what I am very anxious about) I think you would do well to pass the winter after so tremendous an accident in Italy, and (if you think it necessary as I do) so long as you could find Pisa or its neighbourhood agreeable to you, Mrs. Shelley unites with myself in urging the request, that you would take up your residence with us.—You might come by sea to Leghorn, (France is not worth seeing, and the sea air is particularly good for weak lungs) which is within a few miles of us. You ought at all events to see Italy, and your health which I suggest as a motive, might be an excuse to you.—I spare declamation about the statues and the paintings and the ruins—and what is a greater piece of forbearance—about the mountains the streams and the fields, the colours of the sky, and the sky itself—

I have lately read your *Endymion* again and ever with a new sense of the treasures of poetry it contains, though treasures poured forth with indistinct profusion. This, people in general will not endure, and that is the cause of the comparatively few copies which have been sold.—I feel persuaded that you are capable of the greatest things so you but will.

I always tell Ollier to send you copies of my books.— *Prometheus Unbound* I imagine you will receive nearly at the same time with this letter. *The Cenci* I hope you have already received—it was studiously composed in a different style ' Below the *good* how far! but far above the *great*.' In poetry *I* have sought to avoid system and mannerism; I wish those who excel me in genius, would pursue the same plan—

Whether you remain in England, or journey to Italy,—believe that you carry with you my anxious wishes for your health happiness and success, wherever you are or whatever you undertake—and that I am

Yours sincerely
P. B. SHELLEY."

Keats replied to this letter in August, 1820, as follows:

"MY DEAR SHELLEY,—I am very much gratified that you, in a foreign country, and with a mind almost over-occupied, should write to me in the strain of the letter beside me. If I do not take advantage of your invitation, it will be prevented by a circumstance I have very much at heart to prophesy. There is no doubt that an English winter would put an end to me, and do so in a lingering, hateful manner. Therefore, I must either voyage or journey to Italy, as a soldier marches up to a battery. My nerves at present are the worst part of me, yet they feel soothed that, come what extreme may, I shall not be destined to remain in one spot long enough to take a hatred of any four particular bedposts. I am glad you take any pleasure in my poor poem, which I would willingly take the trouble to unwrite, if possible, did I care so much as I have done about reputation. I received a copy of the *Cenci*, as from yourself, from Hunt. There is only one part of it I am judge of—the poetry and dramatic effect, which by many spirits now-a-days is considered the Mammon. A modern work, it is said, must have a purpose, which may be the God."

(It is interesting to note how the old discussion of "With what purpose?" or "Art for Art's sake," swings backwards and forwards. In 1820 already artists are bordering on to Victorian days when art must have a mission. This was all upset again at the end of the century and now we seem to be coming back to it, with the sole difference that the "purpose" or "God," instead of being ethical or religious is now political.) Keats continues:

"An artist must serve Mammon; he must have self-concentration—selfishness, perhaps. You, I am sure, will forgive me for sincerely remarking that you might curb your magnanimity, and be more of an artist, and load every rift of your subject with ore. The thought of such discipline must fall like cold chains upon you, who perhaps never sat with your wings furled for six months together. And is not this extraordinary talk for the writer of *Endymion*, whose mind was like a pack of scattered cards? I am picked up and sorted to a pip. My imagination is a monastery, and I am its monk. I am in expectation of *Prometheus* every day. Could I have my own wish effected, you would have it still in manuscript, or be but now putting an end to the second act. I remember you advising me not to publish my first blights, on Hampstead Heath. I am returning advice upon your hands. Most of the poems in the volume I send you," (the 1820 volume containing *Lamia, Isabella, The Eve of St. Agnes, Hyperion* and the *Odes*) "have been written above two years, and would never have been published but for hope of gain; so you see I am inclined enough to take your advice now. I must express once more my deep sense of your kindness, adding my sincere thanks and respects for Mrs Shelley. In the hope of soon seeing you,

I remain most sincerely yours,

JOHN KEATS."

These two long letters are rather moving in their simplicity and dignity. Shelley's is perhaps the more generous as it is certainly the warmer of the two, but that is natural since he was a born giver, and Keats was too young and too proud to be altogether an easy taker. Nevertheless, in both letters there is a note of spacious equality, of acknowledged greatness, in spite of the mutual criticism, which is on both sides extremely just. To the imagination they seem like two great ships of the line, dipping their flags in salutation before they pass on their diverse ways.

Shelley wrote once more to Keats at Naples, with anxious enquiries, and a pressing invitation to come to Pisa, and on November 11th, 1820, he wrote to Hunt:

"Where is Keats now? I am anxiously expecting him in Italy, when I shall take care to bestow every possible attention on him. I consider his a most valuable life, and I am deeply interested in his safety. I intend to be the physician both of his body and his soul, to keep the one warm, and to teach the other Greek and Spanish. I am aware, indeed, in part, that I am nourishing a rival who will far surpass me; and this is an additional motive and will be an added pleasure."

Few writers could have written the last sentence quite sincerely but Shelley was one of the few.

Shelley's attitude is very much in contrast to that of the most popular romantic poet of the day. Byron's famous stanza in *Don Juan*:

> "John Keats, who was killed off by one critique
>   Just as he really promised something great
> If not intelligible, without Greek,
>   Contrived to talk about the gods of late,
> Much as they might have been supposed to speak.
>   Poor fellow! his was an untoward fate;
> 'Tis strange the mind, that very fiery particle,
> Should let itself be snuffed out by an article,"

has given rise to the impression that in his flippant, half-patronizing way Byron was, like Shelley, an admirer of poetic genius, and that he was moved by something of the same generous impulse to protect the weak against the strong. His correspondence, however, disproves this.

He never knew Keats personally but Murray sent him the 1820 volume while he was at Ravenna, which he acknowledges as follows:

> "I'm thankful for your books dear Murray;
> But why not send Scott's *Monastery*? the only book in four volumes I would give a baioces to see, abating the rest by the same author. Instead of this here are Johnny Keats's p-ss a bed of poetry and three novels by God knows whom. . . . Pray send me no more poetry but what is rare and decidedly good. There is such a trash of Keats' and the like upon my tables I am ashamed to look at them. . . . No more Keats I intreat:—flay him alive, if

some of you don't I must skin him myself. There is no bearing the drivelling idiocy of the Mankin."

Byron's wrath was further aroused about three months later (this was in 1820) by a belated article in the *Edinburgh*, praising not only the 1820 book but the *Endymion*, which had provoked such savage attacks from the other critical journals.

Exactly what Keats had foretold was now taking place. A year earlier he had written: "They (the *Edinburgh*) do not know what to make of it (*Endymion*), and they will not praise it for fear. They are as shy of it as I should be of wearing a Quaker's hat. The fact is they have no real taste. They dare not compromise their judgment on so puzzling a question. If on my next publication they should praise me, and so lug in *Endymion* I will address them in a manner they will not at all relish. The cowardliness of the *Edinburgh* is more than the abuse of the *Quarterly*."

Keats was extremely prescient, but by the time the review came out he was in Rome, waiting only for death and long past caring for men's praise or blame. Byron, on the other hand, was worked up into a fury of excitement, and expressed himself to Murray in terms which do little credit either to his critical insight or to his good breeding.

"The *Edinburgh* praises Jack Keats or Ketch, or whatever his names are:" he writes on November 4th, 1820, "why his is the Onanism of poetry—something like the pleasure an Italian fiddler extracted from being suspended daily by a Street Walker in Drury Lane."

And again, on November 9th: "Mr Keats whose poetry you enquire after appears to me what I have already said. Such writing is a sort of mental masturbation, he is always" (unprintable) "his Imagination. I don't mean that he is indecent, but viciously soliciting his own ideas into a state which is neither poetry nor anything else but a Bedlam vision produced by raw pork and opium."

On November 18th he is still pursuing the subject: Of the praises of that dirty blackguard Keats in the *Edinburgh*, I shall observe as Johnson did when Sheridan the actor got a pension: ' What, has he got a pension? Then it is time I should give up mine.' Nobody could be prouder of the praises of the *Edinburgh* than I was, or more alive to their censure. At present all the men they have ever praised are degraded by that insane article."

In pursuance of his expressed policy of flaying the Mankin alive, Byron wrote a letter abusing "Mr. John Ketch" for a controversy he was having with William Lisle Bowles on the subject of Pope. (Keats's depreciation of Pope in *Sleep and Poetry* was the original cause of Byron's abusive bitterness.) But Keats died and the letter was held over. A little later the already quoted stanza in *Don Juan* appeared, and Byron, "having been at first thus savagely bent on hunting with the hounds, turned and chose to run part of the way, as far as suited him, with the hare."

Leigh Hunt records that Byron showed him the *Don Juan* passage in manuscript, adding: "I told him the real state of the case, proving to him that the supposition," (that Keats's death was attributable to the *Quarterly Review*) "was a mistake, and therefore, if printed, would be a misrepresentation. But a stroke of wit was not to be given up."

CHAPTER V

Keats's more intimate friends—John Hamilton Reynolds—His early promise as a poet—His parody of Wordsworth—His relationship with, and influence on, Keats—A little circle of talented young men—James Rice—Benjamin Bailey.

So much for Keats's celebrated acquaintances. His more intimate friends, and they were many, are hardly known to posterity, except through the light that his letters cast on them, and remain, perhaps for that reason, curiously shadowy personages. Nevertheless, they played an important part in Keats's life. "I could not live without the love of my friends," he wrote to John Hamilton Reynolds, in 1818.

Reynolds, at one time, might have seemed to his contemporaries to qualify for a place among the celebrated names. He was considered a rising star of considerable promise. In his article on "Young Poets" published in the *Examiner*, December 1st, 1816, Leigh Hunt places him between Shelley and Keats, and quotes twenty-seven lines from his poem, *The Naiad*.

Yet Reynolds's poetic career dropped and died. For one thing, he was sternly discouraged by Miss Eliza Powell Drewe, a dark-eyed young lady from Exeter, with whom he fell in love, and whom he afterwards married. Miss Drewe thought literature an unsafe pursuit for a good steady husband, and persuaded him to forgo his literary career and to enter a solicitor's office. Reynolds, who was very much in love, agreed to this, not without a good many backward glances.

In the charming rhymed dedication to the *Garden of*

67

Florence, his last book of serious Verse, he addressed Miss Drewe as follows:

"Thou has intreated me ' to write no more,'
  To turn aside from the consuming art;
And can I shun the voice that I adore,
The voice that hath an echo in my heart?
Perchance a gentleman of twenty-four,
  And *upwards*, should abandon verse in part,
And keep a house, and plunge in tax vexations,
And die, and leave a will for his relations."

It is true that Keats wrote to Reynolds: "I must see you marry your lovely wife—My sensations are sometimes deadened for weeks together—but believe me I have more than once yearne'd for the time of your happiness to come, as much as I could for myself after the lips of Juliet.—From the tenor of my occasional rhodomontade in chit-chat, you might have been deceived concerning me in these points—upon my soul, I have been getting more and more close to you, ever since I knew you, and now one of the first pleasures I look to is your happy Marriage——" but it is probable that Reynolds's example must have accentuated what he felt instinctively as the gulf between poetry and domesticity. To one whose whole aim and life was poetry, "to keep a house and plunge in tax-vexations," must have seemed a very dreadful alternative. And it was partly this feeling led him to struggle against love when his own time came, or rather, since struggle was unavailing, seeing that "heart and soul and senses, world without end were drowned," to resent love.

Reynolds was not, of course, a poet of anything like the calibre of his friend. He knew this and not only knew it but accepted it with a readiness and a generous good grace that are very heart warming. It cannot have been altogether easy for him, a year older than Keats, already an accepted poet when the latter began to publish, with a brilliant start in his poetical career; but he never showed a sign of the least jealousy or envy. While he was on the staff of the *Champion*, a correspondent wrote to the newspaper: "I have seen some lines in your paper, occasionally, signed J.H.R. which have pleased me much. I think that the writer (whoever he is) can furnish something much better than your favourite Mr Keats, whom my perverseness of taste forbids me to admire."

When the *Champion* printed Keats's *Sonnet on the Sea*, two weeks later, the editor added the comment that it was "quite sufficient . . . to justify all the praise we have given (the author)—and to prove to our correspondent . . . his superiority over any poetical writer in the *Champion*.—J.H.R. would be the first to acknowledge this himself."

This probably came from the pen of Reynolds, at any rate, he must have given his approval and consent. At all times, his attitude was, as he once wrote to Keats: "I set my heart on having you high as you ought to be. Do *you* get Fame, and I shall have it in being your affectionate and steady friend." It is good that a man has such friends, it is a proof of Keats's extraordinary nature that he had so many. Commonplace, ordinary men enough, quarrelling bitterly among themselves, often jealous and petty, they were united in this. They not only loved Keats but to him they showed themselves, always, generous, constant, delicate-minded and noblehearted.

Reynolds's recognition of his own limitations as a poet must, of course, have made it easier for him to abandon the slopes of Parnassus. But one cannot help feeling that there is a certain poetical justice in the fact that he did not make much of a success in his legal career; even from a purely worldly point of view he might have done better to stick to literature.

His real talent seems to have lain in the direction of light verse, as is shown in the *Fancy*, which contains the best verses on the "noble art" in the English language. This humorous talent was again very pleasantly employed when, in April, 1819, he read in the papers that Wordsworth intended publishing a new long poem entitled *Peter Bell*. Reynolds was strongly of the opinion of the modern poet who, writing of Wordsworth, held that:

> "Two voices had he, one was of the deep,
> The other of an old half-witted sheep."

Besides, Wordsworth had once advised him to cut fifty-four lines from his poem, *The Naiad*! He sat down and, in five hours produced a parody, which was rushed through the press by Taylor & Hessey with almost equal speed, and on April 16th, *The Times* announced the forthcoming publication of "*Peter Bell*: A Lyrical Ballad. 'I do affirm that I am the REAL SIMON PURE.'" (This was a quotation from a seventeenth century play.)

This premature parody had a great success. On April 26th, Lamb told Wordsworth that it was "in every bookseller's window in London," and a second edition was published within two weeks of the first.

Keats wrote to his brother and sister-in-law: "when Reynolds was here on Monday—he asked me to give Hunt a hint to take notice of his *Peter Bell* in the *Examiner* —the best thing I can do is to write a little notice of it myself which I will do here and copy it out if it should suit my Purpose—*Peter Bell*. There have been lately advertized two Books both *Peter Bell* by name; what stuff the one was made of might be seen by the motto 'I am the real Simon Pure.' This false florimel," (a word taken from Spenser's *Færy Queen*) "has hurried from the press and obtruded herself into public notice while for aught we know the real one may be still wandering about the woods and mountains. Let us hope she may soon appear and make good her right to the magic girdle. The Pamphleteering Archimage we can perceive has rather a splenetic love than a downright hatred to real florimels—if indeed they have been so christened . . . but he has a fixed aversion to those three rhyming Graces Alice Fell, Susan Gale and Betty Foy; and now at length especially to Peter Bell . . . It may be seen from one or two passages in this little skit, that the writer of it has felt the finer parts of Mr. Wordsworth, and perhaps expatiated with his more remote and sublimer muse; this as far as it relates to *Peter Bell* is unlucky. The more he may love the sad embroidery of the *Excursion*; the more he will hate the worse Samplers of Betty Foy and Alice Fell; and as they come from the same hand, the better will be able to imitate that which can be imitated—to wit *Peter Bell*—as far as can be imagined from the obstinate Name. We repeat, it is very unlucky—this real Simon Pure is in parts the very Man, there is a pernicious likeness in the scenery, a 'pestilent humour' in the rhymes and an inveterate cadence in some of the Stanzas that must be lamented. If we are one part amused at this we are three parts sorry that an appreciator of Wordsworth should show so much temper at this really provoking name of Peter Bell!'

"This will do well enough—I have coppied it and enclosed it to Hunt. You will call it a little politic—seeing I keep clear of all parties. I say something for and against both parties—and suit it to the tune of the *Examiner*—I mean to say I do not unsuit it—and I believe

I think what I say nay I am sure I do—I and my conscience are in luck to-day—which is an excellent thing."

The review is indeed quite well and deftly done,
steering a neat course between admiration of Reynolds
and courtesy towards Wordsworth.

Wordsworth is an easy mark for the parodist but
Keats is right when he admits that "this real Simon
Pure is in parts the very man." The skit is far too long
to reproduce in full but I will quote the beginning of the
preface which beautifully hits off Wordsworth's solemn
style and his well-known foible of admiring no poetry
but his own.

PREFACE

"It is now a period of one-and-twenty years since I wrote
some of the most perfect Compositions (except certain
pieces I have written in my later days) that ever dropped
from poetical pen. My heart hath been right and power-
ful all its years. I never thought an evil or weak thought
in my life. It has been my aim and my achievement to
deduce moral thunder from butter-cups, daisies,[1] cel-
andines, and (as a poet, scarcely inferior to myself hath
it) 'such small deer.' Out of sparrows' eggs I have
hatched great truths, and with sextons' barrows have I
wheeled into human hearts, piles of the weightiest philosophy . . . The sneers and scoffings of impious Scotch-
men, and the neglect of my poor uninspired countrymen,
fall as dew upon the thorn, (on which plant I have written
an immortal stanza or two) and are as fleeting as the
spray of the waterfall, (concerning which waterfall I
have composed some great lines which the world will
not let die. . . .)

"Of PETER BELL I have only thus much to say: it

[1] A favourite flower of mine. It was a favourite with Chaucer, but he did not
understand its moral mystery as I do. "Little Cyclops, with one eye."
                                                            Poems by ME.

completes the simple system of natural narrative, which
I began so early as 1798. It is written in that pure un-
laboured style, which can only be met with among
labourers;—and I can safely say, that while its imagina-
tions spring beyond the reach of the most imaginative,
its occasional meaning falls far below the meanest
capacity . . . I commit my Ballad to posterity. I love
to read my own poetry: it does my heart good.

W.W."

It is difficult to select from the poem the best stanzas
to quote, (there are forty-two in all) but the following
three do illustrate rather well the Wordsworthian note
of simple narrative mingled with nature's uplift and also
the Wordsworthian habit of footnotes.

> "The hand of Peter Bell is busy,
> Under the pent-house of his hairs;
> His eye is like a solemn sermon;
> The little flea severely fares,
> 'Tis a sad day for the vermin.
>
> . . . .
>
> "At home his foster child is cradled—
> Four brown bugs are feeding there;[1]
> Catch as many, sister Ann,
> Catch as many as you can[2]
> And yet the little insects spare.
>
> "Why should blessed insects die?
> The flea doth skip o'er Betty Foy,
> Like a little living thing:
> Though it hath not fin or wing,
> Hath it not a moral joy?"

[1] I have a similar idea in my Poem on finding a Bird's Nest:
"Look five blue eggs are gleaming there."
But the numbers are different, so I trust no one will differ with the numbers.
[2] I have given these lines before, but in thus printing them again, I neither tarnish
their value, nor injure their novelty.

It is interesting to compare Reynolds's irreverent parody with a letter written to him by Keats nearly a year previously. He was probably not thinking of it when he sat down to his five hours' task, but Keats's words may have been lying dormant in his mind.

"I will have no more Wordsworth or Hunt in particular," writes Keats. "Why should we be of the tribe of Manasseh when we can wander with Esau? Why should we kick against the Pricks, when we can walk on Roses? Why should we be owls, when we can be Eagles? Why be teased with 'nice Eyed wagtails'" (a quotation from Hunt's poem, *The Nymphs*), "when we have in sight, 'the Cherub Contemplation'?" (*Il Penseroso*.) "Why with Wordsworth's 'Matthew with a bough of wilding in his hand' when we can have Jacques' 'under an oak etc.'? The secret of the Bough of Wilding will run through your head faster than I can write it—Old Matthew spoke to him some years on some nothing, and because he happens in an Evening Walk to imagine the figure of the Old Man—he must stamp it down in black and white, and it is henceforth sacred—I don't mean to deny Wordsworth's grandeur and Hunt's merit, but I mean to say we need not be teazed with grandeur and merit when we can have the uncontaminated and Unobtrusive."

Reading the whole of the letter in which this paragraph occurs, it will be seen at once what great benefit this friendship was to Keats. Reynolds was of great practical help in many ways; his journalistic pen was always at Keats's service and he fought the critics of the *Quarterly* and of *Blackwood's* with as weighty weapons as he could command; but Reynolds was of most use to Keats not for what he did, but for what he was—a young man, and a poet, like himself. We have seen how Keats, after the very first, was anxious to escape from Hunt's influence, but Reynolds was not an elder and a mentor, he was a contemporary, to be talked to and argued with, someone with whom Keats could "talk shop."

Keats's letters to his brothers are mostly impressions, very vivid ones; news; and gossip. His letters, later, to Bailey, are metaphysical and speculative, and those to Rice are generally in a joking vein. But although he often expounded to Reynolds his theories of life or was led into them by his subject, and although his letters are nearly always touched with fun and gaiety, here we have the only correspondent of whom he wrote as a conscious artist, with whom he was able to discuss the technicalities of his craft.

As an instance let us take the letter already quoted. It starts by thanking Reynolds for two sonnets on *Robin Hood*, which he had sent Keats by the twopenny post. Keats makes his comments on the sonnets, the first is the best, he considers, because of certain lines, "moreover (and this is the only word or two I find fault with, the more because I have had so much reason to shun it as a quicksand) the last has ' tender and true.'" (Any one who has ever written verse, and known the irritating persistence with which rhyming cliches will come into the head, will sympathize with Keats and Reynolds. It is rather a shock, incidentally, to find that Reynolds replaced it with "young as the dew," or presumably "doo," on revision.)

After these practical remarks Keats goes on to a general discussion of poetry, which with its rightness, its calm certainty, its piercing in a few sentences to the very heart of the matter, stamps him as one of the masters of writing on his art. Many a critic has written volume after volume on the appreciation of poetry, wandering around and outside the subject in a fog of cotton-wool, and never getting a tenth part as near as Keats in these few luminous sentences.

"It may be said that we ought to read our Contemporaries," he begins, "that Wordsworth &c. should have their due from us. But for the sake of a few fine imaginative or domestic passages, are we to be bullied into a certain Philosophy engendered in the whims of an Egotist—Every man has his speculations, but every man does not brood and peacock over them till he makes a false coinage and deceives himself. Many a man can travel to the very bourne of Heaven, and yet want confidence to put down his half-seeing. Sancho will invent a Journey heavenward as well as anybody. We hate poetry that has a palpable design upon us—and if we do not agree, seems to put its hand into its breeches pocket. Poetry should be great and unobtrusive, a thing which enters into one's soul, and does not startle nor amaze it with itself, but with its subject.—How beautiful are the retired flowers! how would they lose their beauty were they to throng into the highway crying out, admire me I am a violet!—dote upon me I am a primrose!"

Then follows a passage comparing the largeness of conception of the Elizabethan poets with the moderns who each "governs his petty state and knows how many straws are swept daily from the Causeways in all his dominions." "The antients," concludes Keats, in one of his carelessly beautiful phrases, "were Emperors of vast Provinces, they had only heard of the remote ones and scarcely cared to visit them."

He then proceeds with the criticism of Hunt and Wordsworth already quoted and finishes by returning Reynolds some lines on *Robin Hood*, and some on the *Mermaid Tavern*, signing himself "Your sincere friend and Co-scribbler, John Keats."

This is but one of the letters in which Keats discusses

poetry with Reynolds, echoes of the long talks that took place between the young poets, when they lay on Hampstead Heath with a book on the ground between them.

Shakespeare was, naturally, a great theme of theirs. "Whenever you write say a Word or two on some passage of Shakespeare that may have come rather new to you; which must be continually happening, notwithstanding that we read the same Play forty times." And in another letter Keats comes despairingly on that problem which Shakespeare has left for all subsequent writers: "One of the three Books I have with me is Shakespeare's Poems: I neer found so many beauties in the Sonnets—they seem to be full of fine things said unintentionally—in the intensity of working out conceits. Is this to be borne? Hark ye!

> ' When lofty trees I see barren of leaves
>> Which erst from heat did canopy the herd,
> And summer's green all girded up in sheaves,
>> Borne on the bier with white and bristly beard.'

He has left nothing to say about nothing or anything."

In the last years of his life the letters to Reynolds became sparser, partly owing to Keats's ill-health and absorption in his love, partly owing to the fact that Charles Brown with whom he shared a house had, in a way, taken Reynolds's place. But, in September, 1819, there is a long letter from Winchester, with the prose notes, as it were, for the *Ode to Autumn*: "How beautiful the season is now—How fine the air. A temperate sharpness about it. Really, without joking, chaste weather—Dian skies—I never lik'd stubble-fields so much as now—Aye better than the chilly green of the Spring. Somehow a stubble-plain looks warm in the way that some pictures look warm." Keats goes on to mention Chatterton as the purest writer of English since unlike Chaucer he has no

French idiom, and tells Reynolds that he has given up
Hyperion, as there were too many Miltonic inversions in
it. "English ought to be kept up. It may be interesting
to you to pick out some lines from *Hyperion* and put a
mark X to the false beauty proceeding from art, and one
// to the true voice of feeling."

Keats wrote once more to Reynolds on the 28th of
February, 1820. And this last letter again proves that
Reynolds was the friend with whom Keats could
discuss poetry, not as a high and holy mystery, but as a
craft.

Barry Cornwall or Bryan Waller Procter, had sent
Keats copies of his books. Keats was touched by his
kindness, and in writing to Charles Dilke, he says: "I
have experienced a specimen of great politeness from Mr.
Barry Cornwall. He has sent me his books. Some time
ago he had given his first publish'd book to Hunt for
me; Hunt forgot to give it and Barry Cornwall, thinking
I had received it must have thought me a very neglectful
fellow. Notwithstanding he sent me his second book and
on my explaining that I had not received his first he sent
me that also." Even to his love he only wrote: "Mr
Barry Cornwall has sent me another book, his first, with
a polite note. I must do what I can to make him sensible
of the esteem I have for his kindness." But to Reynolds,
although he acknowledges the kindness, he adds: "I
confess they" (the poems) "teare me—they are composed
of Amiability—the Seasons, the Leaves, the Moon etc.
upon which he rings (according to Hunt's expression)
triple bob majors."

This was the last letter Keats wrote to Reynolds,
but in his last letter of all, written in Rome, on November
30th, 1820, to Charles Brown, Keats says: "I have not
written to Reynolds yet, which he must think very
neglectful; being anxious to send him a good account,

I have delayed it from week to week. If I recover, I will do all in my power to correct the mistakes made during sickness; and if I should not, all my faults will be forgiven."

The letter was never written and three months later Keats's bitter agony was over, and his contemporary, his co-scribbler, was left "to grow old as we who are left grow old."

Reynolds died at Newport, in the Isle of Wight, in 1852. "He was buried in the churchyard of the town—a broken-down discontented man, whose great literary abilities had brought him no success in life. Few, probably, of the islanders, were aware that the assistant County-Court clerk, who professed himself an Unitarian and a bitter Radical, and whose drunken habits placed him beyond the pale of society, had promised to be one of the stars of English literature at the period of its poetical revival."

If, somewhere, there are Elysian fields where time and eternity mingle and stand still, perhaps there is a place where two young poets are still discussing poetry with "a black-letter *Chaucer* printed in 1596: aye I've got one huzza!"—lying between them on the grass.

Keats did not only quickly become intimate with Reynolds, but through him he met most of Reynolds's other great friends. The chief of these were James Rice and Benjamin Bailey. The three young men knew each other well; a pleasant picture of their intimacy is given by Rice in a letter to Thomasina Leigh of Sidmouth, where they frequently went down to spend their holidays. There were three Misses Leigh, cousins of the Miss Drewe who caused Reynolds to forsake the Muses, and judging by the playful intimate letters they received, and the amount of poetry addressed to them, the latter chiefly by Bailey, they probably slightly touched the hearts of the visitors from London. Here is Rice's letter to Thomasina:

"I'll tell you what is the only comfortable part of my present existence. It is when the Evening closes in and we ' stir the fire and wheel the sofa round and draw the curtains close' when ' we retire the world shut out.' Then it is that Bailey, Reynolds and myself in all the luxury of mental relaxation indulge our fancies our feeling and our humours, and without any of the prescriptions of form, ramble over the fields of imagination running after every butterfly subject that starts before us. . . . We have always some project on the carpet, some game ever afoot—Either Reynolds or Bailey have ever got the Muses Spur in their side that will not allow them rest or respite—and very sad things their productions *may* be for ought I know—but they give us pleasure and make us every now and then cry ' excellent ' and that serves our turn you know as well as if they were better."

This description of the three young men, all under twenty-five, sitting in the firelit room, talking and scribbling letters and verses and philosophical essays, and reading them aloud, was written in 1815, before Keats had met any of them; but he very quickly became as intimate with them as they were with each other. Reynolds was the most talented, Bailey the most serious of the three. "You have had enough of steady, grave Prose from Bailey," writes Rice in the same letter to Thomasina, "and it is for me, as indeed it most suits me to saunter along the pathway of my lines with a sort of easy slip-shod gossiping and I like to appear before my friends in the same style of dress that I used to come down in at Slade in the morning slippered and *loose at the legs*—at the *legs* only I hope."

Actually Rice was not only "loose at the legs," by which he presumably means he came down without wearing the skin-tight pantaloons of 1815, he was quite sufficiently loose in the tongue as well, and as gay about town as his health permitted him.

"I have had a great deal of pleasant time with Rice lately, and am getting initiated into a little band," wrote Keats, in the beginning of 1818, "they call drinking deep dying scarlet and when you breathe in your wartering they bid you cry hem and play it off—" (The quotation is from Pistol, *Henry IV.*, the next bit is presumably the slang actually used by Rice and his friends) "They call good Wine a pretty tipple, and call getting a Child Knocking out an apple—" (This piece of argot was perhaps in Keats's mind when he wrote *Eve's Apple*) "stopping at a Tavern they call hanging out? Where do you sup? is where do you hang out?" And again, about six months later: "Rice may begin to crow for he got a little so-so, (i.e., tipsy) at a Party of his the other night and was none the worse for it the next morning—". There is another account of a party given by an old gentleman called Mr. Redhall, who rather touchingly, having no idea of the quantity of wine needed, put eight dozen bottles in readiness on the stairs. Possibly, in consequence of this liberality, it seems to have been quite a riotous evening, with Rice in fine form, cutting several dirty jokes, faithfully recorded by Keats for the benefit of George and Tom.

Rice had wretched health, he was always ill and suffering, but he never allowed it to quench his wit, his kindness, and his unconquerable gaiety of spirit. He fought it as much as possible. "There were some miserable reports of Rice's health," wrote Keats in January, 1818, "I went and lo! Master Jemmy had been to the play the night before and was out at the time—he always comes on his Legs like a Cat." "Rice continues to everyone his friendly behaviour:" he wrote nearly two years

later, "his illness and his wit stick by him as usual. In a note to me the other day he sent the following Pun—
Tune—The Harlot's Lament

> Between the two P-x's I've lost every
>   Lover,
> But a difference I found 'twixt the
>   great and the small:
> For by the Small Pox I gott (pitted) all over,
>   By the other I did not get (pittied) at all."

And yet, in spite of his wit, and unquenchable good-humour, the thing that seems to have struck Keats about Rice was his wisdom. "He is the most sensible and even wise man I know—he has a few John Bull prejudices but they improve him." And again: "I know three witty people all distinct in their excellence—Rice, Reynolds, and Richards. Rice is the wisest, Reynolds the play-fullest, Richards the out of the wayest." His wisdom must have been of the unpretentious, unpreaching sort that comes to a man through his own suffering. This is borne out by Keats's last letter to him. It is written in February, 1820, and Keats was very ill at the time. It is obvious from the letter that Rice was trying to cheer and counsel him not by throwing advice at his head, but by drawing on the depths of his own experience, exhibiting himself not as an example but as a fellow sufferer. Here is Keats's letter:

"I have not been well enough to make any tolerable rejoinder to your kind letter. I will as you advise be very chary of my health and spirits. I am sorry to hear of your relapse and hypochondriac symptoms attending it. Let us hope for the best as you say. I shall follow your example in looking to the future good rather than brooding upon present ill. I have not been so worn with lengthen'd illnesses as you have therefore cannot answer you on

your own ground with respect to those haunting and
deformed thoughts and feelings you speak of. When I
have been or supposed myself in health I have had my
share of them especially within this last year. I may say
that for 6 Months before I was taken ill I had not passed
a tranquil day."

Another occasion which proves the reliance Keats
placed on Rice's judgment was the "affaire" Bailey.
Benjamin Bailey, who, we have already seen, wrote
"steady grave Prose" even to young ladies, was a serious,
good-looking, rather plump, young man, who, in the
course of 1818 entered orders. Keats was very fond of
him and admired him immensely but his admiration
received a shock. Actually the matter does not seem very
grave. Bailey had for some time been paying court to
Mariane, the sister of John Hamilton Reynolds, but she
would have none of him, and no wonder, since Keats
records: "She liked him as a Brother, but not as a
Husband—especially as he used to woo her with the
Bible and Jeremy Taylor under his arm—they walked in
no grove but Jeremy Taylor's." (*Golden Grove* was a
devotional manual written by Taylor.)

Bailey, however, entreated her to take time and to
think over his proposal. Meanwhile, he himself went up
to Scotland, where "his susceptible heart was conquered by Miss Gleig," the daughter of the Bishop of
Stirling. He immediately sent back Mariane's letters
and demanded his own, writing at the same time "some
very abrupt letters" to Mrs. Reynolds. The Reynolds'
family were furious, since, although Mariane showed
reluctance to be wooed by such a paragon of Holy Living,
her mother and sisters were excessively pro-Bailey—as
Keats, who got a little tired of the feminine side of the
Reynolds family, records with glee: "Nothing would
serve but Bailey—If you mentioned the word Tea pot

some one of them came out with an apropos about Bailey—noble fellow—fine fellow! was always in their mouths."

There seems no particular harm in a young man who has been firmly refused by one young lady picking up the pieces and consoling himself with another, but it was no wonder it was a shock to Keats, since Bailey was one of those excessively ethical, idealistic men who make heavy weather of everything. Nor were these the only two young ladies in his life. "You know," writes Keats, "that Bailey was very much cut up about a little jilt in the country somewhere;" (possibly one of the Miss Leighs?) "I thought he was in a dying state about it when at Oxford with him: little supposing as I have since heard, that he was at that very time making impatient love to Marian Reynolds—and guess my astonishment at hearing after this that he had been trying at a Miss Martin." (For Bailey's credit it ought to be mentioned that Keats may have been misinformed on this, since Miss Martin subsequently married another Bailey, an upholsterer of London; nevertheless, to be passionately attached to three young ladies in so short a time is perhaps overdoing it, especially for such a solemnly romantic man as Bailey.) "His so quickly taking to Miss Gleig can have no excuse," says Keats roundly, "except that of a Ploughman's who wants a wife." And he goes on: "The thing which sways me more against him than anything else is Rice's conduct on the occasion; Rice would not make an immature resolve: he was ardent in his friendship for Bailey; he examined the whole for and against minutely; and he has abandoned Bailey entirely."

It is uncommonly pleasant to find the loose-tongued, volatile Rice, sitting in judgment on Bailey, since Bailey was a prig of the first water. He had solid undeniable merits. Keats was very fond of him and was much struck with his scholarship and with his character. In September, 1817, we find him writing, rather ironically, in view of later events, to Jane Reynolds: "To your brother John . . . and to you my dear friends Marriann and Jane I shall ever feel grateful for having made known to me so real a fellow as Bailey. He delights me in the Selfish and (please God) the disinterrested part of my disposition. If the old Poets have any pleasure in looking down at the Enjoyers of their works, their eyes must bend with double satisfaction upon him—I sit as at a feast when he is over them and pray that if after my death any of my Labours should be worth saving, they may have as 'honest a Chronicler' as Bailey. Out of this his Enthusiasm in his own pursuit" (the Church), "and for all good things is of an exalted kind—worthy a more healthful frame and an untorn Spirit. He must have happy years to come—he shall not die by God." (He did nothing of the sort, at least not for thirty-six years, but lived and prospered and became Archdeacon of Colombo.) And in January, 1818, Keats wrote again of Bailey that "he is one of the noblest men alive at the present day," and later in the same letter, that "that sort of probity and disinterestedness which such men as Bailey possess, does hold and grasp the tip-top of spiritual honours which can be paid to anything in this world." It is no wonder that Bailey's behaviour in his love-affairs was a slight disillusionment!

Bailey, in his turn, was sincerely fond of Keats, and gives us one of the best descriptions of his personal appearance that we have. "He bore," writes Bailey, "along with the strong impress of genius, much beauty of feature and countenance. The contour of his face was . . . not square and angular, but circular and oval; and this is the proper shape for a poet's head. His hair was beautiful—a fine brown, rather than auburn I think, and if you placed your hand upon his head, the silken curls felt like the rich plumage of a bird. I do not particularly remember the fullness of the upper lip, which is so generally described, and doubtless correctly; but the mouth struck me as too wide, both in itself and as out of harmony with the rest of the face, which, with this single blemish, was eminently beautiful. The eye was full and fine, and softened into tenderness, or beamed with a fiery brightness, according to the current of his thoughts and conversation. Indeed the form of his head was like that of a fine Greek statue!—and he realized to my mind the youthful Apollo, more than any head of a living man whom I have ever known."

He was also a great admirer of Keats's poetry. "Nothing but the finest poetry can now touch me," he wrote in April, 1818, "but that does touch me in the most secret springs the ' resting places calm and deep', of my soul. Keats's is of this power."

But there is all the same, an unpleasantly patronizing flavour about Bailey's comments. He writes to John Taylor, Keats's publisher, in an exceedingly lofty strain. He had been defending *Endymion*, in Scotland (in the intervals of courting Miss Gleig), and had found it a dangerous subject.

"But the quarter I *fear*, and cannot defend is the *moral* part of it. There are two great blotches in this respect. The first must offend every one of proper feelings; and indelicacy is not to be borne; and I greatly reproach myself that I did not represent this very strongly to him before it was sent to the Press, not that I apprehend it would have had any great effect, but it would have been more self-satisfaction . . . The second fault I allude to I think we have noticed—the approaching inclination it has to that abominable principle of Shelley's—that *sensual Love* is the principle of *things*. Of this I believe him to be unconscious, and can see how by a process of imagination he might arrive at so false, delusive and dangerous conclusion. . . . My taste has been called 'parasitic' in relation to him. No matter." (One is somehow reminded of Mr. Crummles, one almost expects Bailey to add, with a dark frown and a hand thrust into the bosom, "We shall see.") He concludes his letter by saying, "I think this had better not be mentioned to Keats . . ."

His later letters to Taylor are even more annoying in their high moral tone. On July 27th, 1820, he wrote of Keats: "He has not kept the best society for one of his character and condition. Many of his moral principles are consequently loose, his moral conduct not very exact; and the Phantom of Honour is substituted for the truth and substance of *Religion*."

"What you say of the progress of his mind," wrote the Reverend Bailey again, on February 12th, 1821, "affords me sincere pleasure. I confess there are traces of it in his last volume. Much, however, requires to be yet done." And a little later he writes that, "there is consolation in the dispensation of a Kind Providence— that his sanguine temper would have been rendered miserable by the excitement produced by successive disappointments. And I fear he is not possessed with philosophic nor religious Resignation enough to have borne the slow ascent up the ladder of literary Fame. Poor fellow, my heart bleeds for him; but human sorrow is very unavailing."

Poor fellow, indeed!

CHAPTER VI

Keats's publishers—Ollier's—Taylor and Hessey—Taylor and Hessey contract for " Endymion "—Keats begins to write it—He goes to the Isle of Wight—The effect poetry has on him—He stays at Oxford with Bailey—His letters to his sister Fanny— Return to London—Quarrels among his friends.

SEVERAL references have been made in the preceding chapter to Keats's publishers, the firm of Taylor and Hessey. They were not his original publishers. The 1817 book went to Ollier's. It was not a success. "Alas," wrote Cowden Clarke, "the book might have emerged in Timbuctoo with far stronger chance of fame and approbation." This was an exaggeration, since it obtained several long reviews, including, of course, Leigh Hunt's own in the *Examiner*, which still reads as a first-class piece of literary criticism. Nevertheless, the first edition of the book was never sold off.

George Keats, as authors' relatives will, put the blame on Ollier's and finally wrote to them taking them pretty roundly to task. The fact that the failure of any book is always attributed to its publishers' stinginess, mishandling or general foolishness by the interested parties, must begin to get boring for the firms in question, who, after all, presumably wish to sell their wares if only from self-interest, but, however impatient they may become, there is no excuse for a reply such as Ollier's sent back!

"SIR,—We regret that your brother ever requested us to publish this book, or that our opinion of its talents should have led us to acquiesce in undertaking it. We are, however, much obliged to you for relieving us from the unpleasant necessity of declining any further con-

88

nexion with it which we must have done, as we think the curiosity is satisfied and the sale has dropped—By far the greater number of persons who have purchased it from us have found fault with it in such plain terms, that we have in many cases offered to take the book back rather than be annoyed with the ridicule which has, time after time, been shower'd on it. In fact it was only on Saturday last that we were under the mortification of having our own opinion of it's merits" (the agitation of the firm has been communicated to its grammar), "flatly contradicted by a Gentleman who told us he considered it ' no better than a take in.'—

These are unpleasant imputations for any one in business to labour under, but we should have borne them and concealed their existence from you had not the stile of your note shewn us that such delicacy would be quite thrown away. We shall take means without delay for ascertaining the number of copies on hand, and you shall be informed accordingly.

We are,

Your most obedt. Servts.,
C & J OLLIER."

It is possible that this overflowing of bitterness may not have been due to the fact that Keats had already become a Taylor & Hessey author. In any case he was well out of Ollier's who nearly drove Shelley distracted over *Laon and Cynthia*. The book was actually printed and ready for issue when Charles Ollier, stricken with cold feet, insisted on withdrawing it and toning it down by means of numerous cancel-leaves, doing away with the blood-relationship between the hero and heroine and modifying the antitheistic passages. Keats had his own troubles with his publishers on the score of propriety, as will be seen later, but on the whole his relationship with them was extraordinarily happy and their generosity to him deserves the greatest praise.

John Taylor, the dominant character in the firm, was the son of a Northamptonshire bookseller. At the age of twenty-one he came to London and got a job in a bookshop, Messrs. Lackington & Allen in Finsbury Square. There he met a young man called James Augustus Hessey and in 1806 the two set up business together. It was a very happy partnership, Hessey attended more to the commercial side of the business, Taylor to the policy of the house. They began more as booksellers, but Taylor was determined to develop the publishing side. They started in a modest but probably extremely practical way with didactic tales, books on moral conduct, etc., many of them being by Taylor's namesakes Jane and Ann, whose works at any rate in verse, about Matilda who was so proud of making a purse of beads and the slatternly Harriet, "who cut her pin-cushion in two," have survived to a much later date. They were very popular in their own period; a copy of *Essays in Rhyme* inscribed "John Keats to His Dear Sister" was discovered on a Madrid bookstall in 1924, and in his first letter to Fanny Keats he writes: "How do you like Miss Taylor's *Essays in Rhyme*—I just look'd into the Book and it appeared to me suitable to you—especially since I remembered your liking for those pleasant little things the Original Poems—the essays are the more mature production of the same hand."

But Taylor was more ambitious, especially after he had made the acquaintance, in 1811, of Richard Woodhouse. Woodhouse was a young lawyer, then twenty-two, a member of the famous family of port importers. Taylor describes him as follows: "He is about my own size but thinner, has red hair and a florid complexion. His eyes are deep seated. . . . He is an excellent Classic, having been last of all at Eton School—has a turn for poetry by no means contemptible though he thinks meanly enough of it—is abstemious to a remarkable degree, of great industry, averse to pleasure (in the London acceptation of the word), rises early, reads much and with the strictest attention—Above all things he is extremely attentive to religious duties, has the highest veneration for the Scriptures in which he delights to read, is of a retired modest behaviour, and possesses more real humility than (I was going to say) any one I know; but certainly, I think, as much." But what was really remarkable about Woodhouse, at least in our eyes, was not his abstemiousness nor his veneration for the Scriptures, but his real knowledge and love of literature and his passionate unswerving devotion to the poetry of John Keats.

Woodhouse soon became very closely connected with the firm of Taylor & Hessey, giving them his legal advice, finding them authors, drafting their advertisements, etc. It may have been he who introduced Keats to the firm, since the young poet was already acquainted with Woodhouse's cousin, Miss Mary Frogley, who had many of his early verses copied out into her album. However that may be, Taylor's designs for a more extensive and more distinguished list were beginning to mature. Taylor & Hessey had published the first edition of Leigh Hunt's *Story of Rimini* and also *The Naiad* by John Hamilton Reynolds, it is not strange that their next venture was young Keats.

It may here be noted that Taylor's ambition to publish what was good in English literature was finely fulfilled. In 1824 the firm had published Hazlitt's *Characters of Shakespeare's Plays*, *Lectures on the English Poets*, *Lectures on the English Comic Writers* and *Sketches of the Principal Picture Galleries in England*; Landor's *Imaginary Conversations* (there was a lot of difficulty about this book!); Cary's *Dante* and *Birds of Aristophanes*; Coleridge's *Aids to Reflection*; *Elia*; De Quincey's *Confessions of an English Opium Eater*; all John Clare's poetry; and *Endymion* and the 1820 volume containing *Isabella, Eve of St. Agnes, Lamia, Hyperion* and the *Odes* by John Keats. Their profits from such a remarkable series of works were not very startling, and though they published enough devotional and instructional books to carry them over for some time, in 1825 they were forced to dissolve partnership.

But to return to Keats. On the strength of the 1817 *Poems* alone, which as we have seen was a failure, they arranged to publish his next long poem and to keep him in funds while he wrote it. Poetry was, of course, in those days more of a commercial speculation than it is now. Byron, Scott and Moore were all best sellers, Moore had been offered £3000 as an advance for *Lallah Rookh*—nevertheless it was a courageous decision and one which could only have been made by some one who really cared for poetry and for English literature.

This arrangement was come to early in April, 1817, and on the 15th Keats left London in order to begin his first long poem, *Endymion*. He writes an excellent description to his brother, of the night journey down to Southampton, so vivid that one almost feels as if one were on the coach glimpsing the passing countryside in the orange light of the lamps.

"I saw dusty Hedges sometimes Ponds—then nothing —then a little Wood with trees look you like ' Launce's Sister ' as white as a lilly and as small as a Wand"— (presumably the silver birches of Surrey, and a very good description of them too)—"then came houses which died away into a few straggling Barns then came hedge trees aforesaid again. As the Lamp light crept along the following things were discovered: ' long heath brown furze '—Hurdles here and there half a Mile—Park palings when the Windows of a House were always discovered by reflection—One Nymph of Fountain *N. B. Stone*—lopped trees—Cow ruminating—ditto Donkey—Man and woman going gingerly along—William seeing his Sisters over the Heath—John waiting with a Lanthen for his Mistress—Barbers Pole—Docter's Shop —However after having had my fill of these I popped my Head out just as it began to Dawn."

Keats crossed from Southampton to the Isle of Wight but the solitude and the intense excitement which his poetry caused him made him almost ill and he left there after barely a week and went to Margate where his brother Tom joined him. Poetry had always the most intense emotional effect on him. "I find that I cannot exist without poetry—without eternal poetry—half the day will not do—the whole of it—I began with a little but habit has made me a Leviathan—I had become all in a Tremble from not having written anything of late— the Sonnet over leaf" (that on the Sea) "did me some good. I slept the better last night for it—this Morning, however, I am nearly as bad again—Just now I opened Spencer, and the first Lines I saw were these.—

" 'The noble heart that harbors virtuous thought,
    And is with Child of glorious great intent,
    Can never rest, until it forth have brought
    Th' eternal Brood of Glory excellent——'"

So he wrote to Reynolds from the Isle of Wight and two and a half years later he wrote to the same correspondent: "I think if I had a free and healthy and lasting organization of heart, and lungs as strong as an ox's so as to be able to bear unhurt the shock of extreme thought and sensation without weariness, I could pass my life very nearly alone though it should last eighty years. But I feel my body too weak to support me to the height' I am obliged continually to check myself and strive to be nothing. It would be vain for me to endeavour after a more reasonable manner of writing to you. . . . If you should have any reason to regret this state of excitement in me, I will turn the tide of your feelings in the right Channel, by mentioning that it is the only state for the best sort of Poetry—that is all I care for, all I live for."

This was written at a time when although he did not know it Keats was already touched by the consumption that killed him, and when the "shock of extreme thought" may well have been too much for his enfeebled body, but it is clear from his earlier letters, written when he was in perfect health, how consuming the vital flame of poetry was to him.

"I went to the Isle of Wight," he says to Hunt, "thought so much about Poetry so long together that I could not get to sleep at night—and moreover, I know not how it was I could not get wholesome food—By this means in a Week or so I became not over capable in my upper Stories and set off pell mell for Margate, at least 150 Miles—because forsooth I fancied I should like my old Lodging here and could contrive to do without Trees. Another thing I was too much in Solitude, and consequently was obliged to be in continual burning of thought as an only resource."

His friend Dilke says of this passage that it was: "An exact picture of the man's mind and character," adding, "He could at any time have ' thought himself out ' mind and body. Thought was intense with him, and seemed at times to assume a reality that influenced his conduct—and I have no doubt helped to wear him out."

One difference there is between the Keats of 1817 and him of 1819. The earlier letters are preoccupied with the idea of Fame. The idea that he has been chosen as one of the great poets and that he will earn immortality haunts his letters at this date as it does his verse. Sometimes it almost frightens him with its immensity. But two years later he had nearly put that idea behind him. All he cared for and lived for was to write "the best sort of poetry."

Meanwhile in spite of this horrid "Morbidity of Temperament" as he describes it to Haydon, Keats was working hard on *Endymion*, writing every day except when he was actually travelling. From Margate he writes to Taylor & Hessey thanking them for £20, and after describing how he will use it to "destroy some of the Minor Heads of that spiny-headed Hydra the Dun" he goes on to say, "I went day by day at my Poem for a Month—at the end of which time the other day I found my Brain so overwrought that I had neither Rhyme nor reason in it." Any one who has ever written will sympathize with the further account of Keats's symptoms—"Instead of Poetry—I have a swimming in my head—And feel all the effects of a Mental Debauch —lowness of Spirits—anxiety to go on without the Power to do so."

This letter shows the excellent terms Keats was on with his publishers and so does the following written less than a month later.

"My Dear Sirs,—I must endeavour to lose my Maidenhead with respect to money Matters as soon as possible—and I will to—so here goes. A Couple of Duns that I thought would be silent till the beginning, at least, of next Month (when I am certain to be on my legs for certain sure) have opened upon me with a cry most 'untunable'; never did you hear such an un-' gallant chiding.'

Now you must know that I am not desolate but have thank God 25 good Notes in my fob—but then you know I laid them by to write with and would stand at Bay a fortnight ere they should grab me. In a Month's time I must pay but it would relieve my mind if I owed you instead of these Pelican duns.

I am affraid you will say I have 'wound about with circumstance' when I should have asked plainly. However, as I said I am a little maidenish or so—and I feel my virginity come strong upon me—the while I request the loan of a £20 and a £10—which if you would enclose to me I would acknowledge and save myself a hot forehead. I am sure you are confident in my responsibility—and in the sense of squareness that is always in me.

Your obliged friend,
"JOHN KEATS."

The money affairs were presumably satisfactorily settled and there is a gap in Keats's correspondence after this letter written on the 10th of June till September. He went on from Margate to Canterbury and after that was probably in London, where his friends were around him and did not need to be written to. But during September Keats went down to Oxford to stay with Bailey who was reading for orders at Magdalen Hall. And if one is sometimes inclined to resent Bailey's priggishness and patronising style one can at least remember that he gave Keats some of the happiest and most untroubled weeks in his short, saddened life. "He was pleased with everything that occurred in the ordinary mode of life," writes Bailey, "and a cloud never passed over his face except at the wrongs of others."

It was one of those long golden Septembers, when the lovely curving High Street is empty and deserted; when if one mounts the hill towards Elsfield in the early morning, the dome of the Radcliffe, the spire of St. Mary's and all the towers, seem to be enchanted and half real, rising from the curling white mist; when there is a faint blue bloom on all the distances and when the Cherwell slips along silently through the cut hayfields and the meadows heavy with ripe corn. The days passed smoothly and placidly. The two young men worked in the mornings, sometimes at the same table, sometimes at separate desks. Keats was writing the third book of *Endymion*, it was running easily now and he seldom failed in his allotted task of fifty lines a day. When he had finished he would read over the completed lines to Bailey and then read or write letters till the other was ready to come out. It was at this time that he wrote the first of those charming letters to his sister Fanny which make up a large part of his correspondence.

Fanny Keats was still under the guardianship of Mr. and Mrs. Abbey, who as might be expected did not much approve of her elder brothers, particularly of the self-willed John. She was not allowed to see much of him, but he was determined that the little sister who bore his mother's name should not forget him nor lose her childish affection for him, and he wrote to her continually, delightful, spontaneous, loving letters. Even when he was most ill, and his correspondence with all the world else was too much of an effort for him, he did not forget her. He wrote twice as often to her as to any one else except to that other Fanny who was his love. But those days were far ahead and though to her he nearly always wrote cheerfully in any case, it is probable that this pleasant letter was written from a genuinely contented heart.

"My dear Fanny," he wrote on September 10th, 1817, "Let us now begin a regular question and answer—a little pro and con; letting it interfere as a pleasant method

G

of my coming at your favouirte little wants and enjoyments that I may meet them in a way befitting a brother.

We have been so little together since you have been able to reflect on things that I know not whether you prefer the *History of King Pepin* to Bunyan's *Pilgrim's Progress*—or Cinderella and her glass slipper to Moor's *Almanack*. However, in a few Letters I hope I shall be able to come at that and adapt my scribblings to your Pleasure. You must tell me about all you read if it be only six Pages in a Week—and this transmitted to me every now and then will procure you full sheets of Writing from me pretty frequently—This I feel as a necessity: for we ought to become intimately acquainted, in order that I may not only, as you grow up love you as my only Sister, but confide in you as my dearest friend. When I saw you last I told you of my intention of going to Oxford and 'tis now a Week since I disembark'd from his Whipship's Coach the Defiance in this place. I am living in Magdalen Hall on a visit to a young Man with whom I have not been long acquainted, but whom I like very much—we lead very industrious lives he in general Studies and I in proceeding at a pretty good rate with a Poem which I hope you will see early next year. Perhaps you might like to know what I am writing about. I will tell you.

Many Years ago there was a young handsome Shepherd who fed his flocks on a Mountain's side called Latmus—he was a very contemplative sort of a Person and lived solitary among the trees and Plains little thinking—that such a beautiful Creature as the Moon was growing mad in Love with him—However so it was; and when he was asleep on the Grass, she used to come down from heaven and admire him excessively for a long time; and at last could not refrain from carrying him in her arms to the top of that high Moun-

tain Latmus while he was a dreaming—but I dare say
(you) have read this and all the other beautiful Tales
which have come down from the ancient times of that
beautiful Greece. If you have not let me know and I
will tell you more at large of others quite as delightful.

This Oxford I have no doubt is the finest City in
the world—it is full of old Gothic buildings—Spires—
towers—Quadrangles—Cloisters Groves &(c) and is
surrounded by more clear streams than ever I saw
together. I take a Walk by the Side of one of them every
Evening and thank God, we have not had a drop of rain
these many days."

He goes on to tell her about a letter from George
and Tom who are in Paris and who "like most English-
men . . . feel a mighty preference for every thing
English." He sends the query about Miss Taylor's *Essays*
we have already referred to and a longish dissertation,
following Hunt, on the superiority of the Italian to the
French language.

"Now Fanny you must write soon—and write all
you think about, never mind what—only let me have a
good deal of your writing—You need not do it all at
once—be two or three or four days about it, and let it
be a diary of your little Life. You will preserve all my
Letters and I will secure yours—and thus in the course
of time we shall each of us have a good Bundle—which,
hereafter, when things may have strangely altered and
god knows what happened, we may read over together
and look with pleasure on times past—that now are to
come. Give my Respects to the Ladies" (Fanny Keats,
who was now aged fourteen, was at the Misses Tuckeys'
School at Walthamstow) "—and so my dear Fanny I
am ever

You most affectionate Brother,

JOHN."

When the reading and writing were done, there were walks beside clear streams and about the quiet bell-haunted city, and boating on the Isis, or the streams around; "which are more in number than your eye-lashes," till the nose of the boat became tangled in the thick green rushes and out came the volume of poetry, often enough Wordsworth, for Bailey was an ardent Wordsworthian.

Or Keats would recite aloud in his peculiar chanting tone verses from Chatterton:

> "Come with acorn cup and thorn
> Drain my hertè's blood away;
> Life and all its good I scorn
> Dance by night and feast by day."

The first line of this haunting little poem was the one Keats loved and he probably applied to it his favourite expression of commendation for poetry, that it was "nice," the word pronounced in a low undertone.

Or they would discuss vowel sounds in poetry, about which Keats had a theory of his own that "they should be so managed as not to clash one with another so as to hear the melody,—and yet that they should be inter-changed, like differing notes of music to prevent monotony." And then they would go on to Homer and the character of Achilles and so back to Wordsworth and the long discussions on the "burthen of the mystery." Though Keats seemed to Bailey to "value this great Poet rather in particular passages than in the full length portrait, as it were, of the great imaginative and philosophic Christian poet." The lines of Wordsworth that Keats loved most were that starkly simple, almost pathetic couplet which yet conveys the deep, selfish sorrow of all men better than any more exalted lines on death:

> "But she is in her grave, and oh,
> The difference to me."

Then there was a visit to Stratford-on-Avon, a day of "unalloyed happiness." There they visited the birthplace and the church, where they were much aggravated by a commonplace guide, which must have been infuriating to one who wished to muse, as Keats surely did, on the strangeness of Alexander stopping a bunghole, on the mystery of that brain and that heart being in "a little dust quiescent."

There was also the affair of the "young man whose Name is Crips," a young artist in whom Haydon discerned promise and whom he was anxious to have as a pupil if enough money could be provided for him to live on. The trouble which Keats took over this affair bears witness to his disinterested good-nature; as the subsequent letter he sent to Bailey, to whom Haydon had in his usual impetuous bull-like way apparently written a very rude, tactless note, is proof of his good sense. "What occasions the greater part of the World's Quarrels?" he writes, "simply this, two Minds meet and do not understand each other time enough to prevent any shock or surprise at the conduct of either party."

Haydon must have been feeling in a particularly belligerent mood that winter, since he later quarrelled both with Reynolds and with Hunt. The quarrel with Reynolds arose over an invitation to meet Wordsworth for which Reynolds never turned up nor sent excuse. Haydon wrote "a very sharp high note," followed up by another whose effect seems to have been worse than the first. "Considering all things," writes Keats, "Haydon's frequent neglect of his appointments etc., his notes were bad enough to put Reynolds on the right side of the question—but then Reynolds has no powers of sufferance;

no idea of having the thing against him; so he answered Haydon in one of the most cutting letters I have ever read; exposing to himself all his own weaknesses and going on to an excess, which whether it is just or no, is what I would fain have unsaid, the fact is they are both in the right and both in the wrong.

The quarrel with Hunt I understand this far. Mrs. H. was in the habit of borrowing silver of Haydon—the last time she did so, Haydon asked her to return it at a certain time—she did not—Haydon sent for it—Hunt went to expostulate on the indelicacy &c.—they got to words and parted for ever. All I hope is at some time to bring them all together again."

The childishness and triviality of such quarrels among talented men are not, alas, unusual; what is remarkable is the real fundamental good sense and feeling shown by a young man so temperamental and mercurial as Keats. And here it may be remarked that in spite of his warm, outspoken nature, Keats never quarrelled with any of his friends. He was the least touchy of men. And though he was extremely sensitive it was not about trifles like these. He once wrote to Rice, in answer to a letter which we have not got: "Your amende honorable, I must call 'un surcroit d'amitié' for I am not sensible of any thing but that you were unfortunately engaged and I was unfortunately in a hurry. . . . I have long made up my mind to take for granted the genuine heartedness of my friends notwithstanding any temporery ambiguousness in their behaviour or their tongues."

Keats was extremely, fierily, youthfully proud, but there lived in him none of the small vanities that leave a man touchy and sore. He was great in more ways than in his genius.

CHAPTER VII

" Endymion " finished—Keats's mental development—His character—The will to live and the will to die—His vitality and joy in life.

ALMOST directly after his return from Oxford, Keats went down to the Burford Bridge Hotel near Dorking, where he finished *Endymion* on November 28th, 1817.

It is difficult in these days to judge *Endymion's* merits—the long poem which tells a story has so completely gone out of fashion. Keats himself wrote that "a long Poem is a test of Invention, which I take to be the Polar Star of Poetry." Now a young man in these days who wished to test his invention would not write a long poem; it would be a novel, or at worst a poetical play; and certainly to modern taste the four thousand lines of *Endymion* are pretty heavy going. There are lovely things in the poem, as well as the two famous extracts, the *Ode to Sorrow* and the *Hymn to Pan*, and some quite startlingly bad ones.

It is rather like the story one child will tell another. There is a wealth of imagination without much consecutive plan, improbable incidents in bright colours surge out of the undisciplined fancy; now there is a butterfly, now suddenly an old man seated on a rock; here is Adonis and here a pair of horses, and here without any previous introduction:

"Sighing, an elephant approached and bowed."

One feels, as one often does with very young poetry, that it is all rather a matter of luck. The wind bloweth where it listeth and the result may be either:

103

"How tiptoe Night holds back her dark gray hood."

Or:

"And once above the edges of our nest
    An arch face peep'd—an Oread as I guessed."

It is the first stage of creation, when, as it were, poetry seems almost to pour through the poet, effortless, inspired and undirected.

But whatever the immediate result may be, it is obvious that there can be little better training for a young poet than to sit down and deliver himself of four thousand consecutive lines. He must, and Keats obviously did, by these means gain a mastery over the sheer technical expression of his art which is beyond all price. One has only to compare the fragment of *Hyperion* with *Endymion* to see how far, in that direction only, Keats had advanced in one year.

Even in *Endymion* he was moving towards greater control of his expression and of his thought. On January 30th, 1818, he wrote to Taylor:

"These lines, as they now stand, about Happiness have rung in my ears like a ' chime a mending.' See here,

                    Behold
    Wherein lies Happiness Pœona? fold—

This appears to me the very contrary of blessed. I hope this will appear to you more elegible.

    Wherein lies Happiness? In that which becks
    Our ready minds to fellowship divine;
    A fellowship with essence, till we shine
    Full alchymized and free of space. Behold
    The clear Religion of heaven—fold &c.—

You must indulge me by putting this in for setting aside the badness of the other, such a preface is necessary to the subject. The whole thing must I think have appeared to you, who are a consequitive Man, as a thing almost of mere words—but I assure you that when I wrote it it was a regular stepping of the Imagination towards a Truth. My having written that Argument will perhaps be of the greatest Service to me of anything I ever did. It set before me at once the gradations of Happiness even like a kind of Pleasure Thermometer—and is my first Step towards the chief attempt in the Drama—the playing of different Natures with Joy and Sorrow."

This letter contains a phrase of variants which are continually cropping up in his writings about this time: "The stepping of Imagination towards a Truth." During this winter, after his stay at Oxford with Bailey, he was to a certain extent occupied with abstract thoughts and in attempting to set down coherently his philosophy of life. Yet such a description is wrong, for a philosophy is just what he refused to have. He had one of those rare minds which refuses to believe in more than it knows. It is not at all a sceptical, it is a very humble, attitude, and it is founded on complete sincerity of soul.

"Every man has his speculations," he wrote, as we have already seen, "but every man does not brood and peacock over them till he makes a false coinage and deceives himself."

Keats's openness of mind and of heart are remarkable, especially when we consider the age in which he lived. Most men of his day believed in Christianity; among his own particular circle Haydon, Bailey and Joseph Severn at least, were devout and fervent Christians. Those who could not accept the faith were generally even more devout and fervent atheists, as was Shelley. There were also the Nature worshippers who founded their beliefs on the philosophy of the *Excursion*. Only Keats said that he did not think himself more in the right than other people, and that nothing in this world is provable.

He was far from being a scoffer at Christianity. One has only to read his grave, lucid letter clarifying Scriptural points for his little sister for her Confirmation; a letter which she treasured so much that when, as an old woman, she gave up the rest to be published, this one and the last that he ever wrote to her she held back. Then again he wrote: "I have no doubt that thousands of people never heard of have had hearts completely disinterested: I can remember but two— Socrates and Jesus—their Histories evince it. What I heard a little time ago, Taylor observe with respect to Socrates, may be said of Jesus—That he was so great a man that though he transmitted no writing of his own to posterity, we have his Mind and his sayings and his greatness handed to us by others. It is to be lamented that the history of the latter was written and revised by Men interested in the pious frauds of Religion. Yet through all this I see his splendour."

And on the margin of Burton's *Anatomy of Melancholy*, against a list of names, "Moses, Elias, Daniel, CHRIST, and . . . his apostles . . ." he wrote: "I would decapitate these large letters, but really they being in such very bad company have *without sneer* a right to pre-eminence."

But he could not accept Christianity—since for him there were no half-measures, no acceptances for the sake of consolation or of future hope, although he felt certain of immortality. He had the strength of mind to know that he knew not and he was not forced by weakness to accept the conclusions of others.

He was aware of it himself, for he wrote of that

"quality . . . which Shakespeare possessed so enormously—I mean *Negative Capability*, that is, when a man is capable of being in uncertainties, mysteries, doubts, without any irritable reaching after fact and reason—Coleridge, for instance, would let go by a fine isolated verisimilitude caught from the Penetralium of mystery, from being incapable of remaining content with half-knowledge. This pursued through volumes would perhaps take us no further than this, that with a great poet the sense of Beauty overcomes every other consideration, or rather obliterates all consideration."

And there at last we come to it, the thing that Keats did believe in passionately, that was to him the heart and kernel of all things, "the sense of Beauty" obliterating all else. "I am certain of nothing," he writes to Bailey, "but of the holiness of the Heart's affections and the truth of the Imagination—What the Imagination seizes as Beauty must be truth—whether it existed before or not—for I have the same idea of all our Passions as of Love, they are all in their sublime, creative of essential Beauty."

This may seem a very vague doctrine, as indeed it is, but the essential part of it is that it is not a doctrine but a personal revelation. The Grecian Urn whispered its message to Keats alone; that was what he felt and knew for himself; he never meant it to be used as a flat common denomination for all the world. Keats was the most undidactic of men. Our attitude towards him should be that of his own towards the thrush, whom, in a lovely unrhyming sonnet he imagines saying:

"O fret not after knowledge—I have none,
And yet my song comes native with the warmth.
O fret not after knowledge—I have none,
And yet the Evening listens."

His songs indeed "come native with the warmth."

Nor is the "essential Beauty" that he talks of so refined, abstract and colourless a thing as many of his disciples have made it. For Keats beauty denoted intensity, and intensity of almost any kind. Let a thing be vital and real enough, it was in his mind beautiful. He did not, as the Pre-Raphaelites did, separate beauty into a compartment of life, seeing some things as beautiful and romantic, others as sordid and ugly. And more and more as his art developed did he draw away from the over-romantic conception of subject that he showed in his early days. One writes early days, and there is less than a year between the two quotations, but with Keats such distinctions must stand.

For instance in the lovely opening of *Endymion* he writes:

"in spite of all
Some shape of beauty moves away the pall
From our dark spirits."

And he goes on to a catalogue of obvious poetical beauties, sun, moon and trees, "daffodils with the green world they live in," clear streams, the wild roses in the forests, "the grandeur of the dooms

"We have imagined for the mighty dead;
All lovely tales that we have heard or read."

About a year and a half later we find him writing to Woodhouse in a long and penetratingly clear letter on poetical genius, as follows: "As to the poetical Character itself (I mean that sort of which, if I am anything, I am a Member; that sort distinguished from the wordsworthian or egotistical sublime; which is a thing *per se* and stands alone) it is not itself—it has no self—it is every thing and nothing—It has no character—

it enjoys light and shade; it lives in gusto, be it foul or fair, high or low, rich or poor, mean or elevated—It has as much delight in conceiving an Iago as an Imogen. What shocks the virtuous philosopher, delights the camelion Poet. It does no harm from its relish of the dark side of things any more than from its taste for the bright one; because they both end in speculation. A Poet is the most unpoetical of any thing in existence." And a little later he writes: "Though a quarrel in the Streets is a thing to be hated, the energies displayed in it are fine; the commonest Man shows a grace in his quarrel."

Like Shakespeare, like Chaucer, he could see beauty in common things. Although he was a "romantic" poet, he was yet of the racy, earthy English stock which produced the Elizabethans. He did "live in gusto." It is this, I think, which makes him differ so much from the conventional portrait of Adonais, the Muses' youngest son, dying of consumption and a broken heart. He did die of these, but it must not be forgotten that he lived, too.

He bore within himself, in full measure, as do most men of strong temperament and of genius, both the will to live and the will to die. At a later period they were to come into conflict, bringing him an agony of which it is almost unbearable to read, but in the early part of his life the will to live was very predominant. He was packed with vitality, instinct with life. He was gay, pugnacious and rowdy. He got a black eye thrashing a butcher who ill-treated a kitten. He went to a bear-baiting and came home and imitated the whole scene with enormous gusto; impersonating first the enthusiastic bear-baiting "fan" overcome with gratification by being hurled out of the ring by the comptroller, "My eyes! Bill Soames giv' me such a licken!"; then the bear itself, legs and arms bent and shortened, dabbing

at the dogs; and then the dogs gasping as they were
suddenly caught and hugged, "his own capacious
mouth," Cowden Clarke records, adding force to the
presentation. He went to prize-fights. He got a little
tipsy on claret. He and his friends used to amuse themselves by playing at concert parties, where they each
imitated one particular instrument, Keats taking the
bassoon. He made uncommonly bad puns and enjoyed
bawdy stories.

There was, of course, the other side of the picture.
He had, as all poets have, the sense of despair. Also, he
was excessively sensitive. He could not have had that
"trembling delicate and snail-horn perception of Beauty"
if he had not been; but "Lord," as he wrote to Reynolds,
"a man should have the fine point of his soul taken off
to become fit for this world," and his own never was.

At this time before his own troubles came "thick
upon him," he was oppressed with the heavy, mounting,
unintelligible tide of the world's sorrow. It is a proof
of his quick ripening maturity that he felt it so soon.
The young may generally escape it for a few years, but
for Keats, to use the imagery of his own famous simile,
the doors were being set open.

"I compare human life," he writes to Reynolds, "to
a large Mansion of Many Apartments, two of which I
can only describe, the doors of the rest being as yet shut
upon me. The first we step into we call the infant or
thoughtless Chamber in which we remain as long as
we do not think—We remain there a long while, and
notwithstanding the doors of the second Chamber
remain wide open, showing a bright appearance, we care
not to hasten to it; but are at length imperceptibly
impelled by the awakening of the thinking principle
within us—we no sooner get into the second Chamber,
which I shall call the Chamber of Maiden-Thought,

than we become intoxicated with the light and the atmosphere, we see nothing but pleasant wonders, and think of delaying these for ever in delight: However among the effects this breathing is father of is that tremendous one of sharpening one's vision into the heart and nature of Man—of convincing one's nerves that the world is full of Misery and Heartbreak, Pain, Sickness and oppression—whereby this Chamber of Maiden-Thought becomes gradually darken'd and at the same time on all sides of it many doors are set open—but all dark—all leading to dark passages—we see not the ballance of good and evil. We are in a Mist."

But this letter was written a little later in the May of 1818 when he was down at Teignmouth with Tom, who could never get well again. In the meantime, although he felt, as he wrote to Bailey, that "Health and Spirits can only belong unalloyed to the selfish man—" he was able to add, "when I am not suffering for vicious beastliness I am the greater part of the week in spirits." And he still kept that unspeculative, happy joy in things as they are, not as they might or ought to be, which so few of us preserve beyond childhood. "I scarcely remember counting upon any Happiness," he wrote. "I look not for it if it be not in the present hour—nothing startles me beyond the Moment. The setting sun will always set me to rights or if a Sparrow come before my Window I take part in its existince and pick about the Gravel."

Perhaps he was happiest of all at these times, when he was luxuriating in "the beauty of the morning operating on a scene of Idleness—I have not read any Books—the Morning said I was right—I had no idea but of the morning, and the thrush said I was right." But there was also abundant life and pleasure and enjoyment in more mundane things.

CHAPTER VIII

*The winter of 1817-18—More quarrels among Keats's friends—
Keats as a dramatic critic—His admiration for Hazlitt.*

"I PITCHED upon another bottle of claret—Port—we
enjoyed ourselves very much were all very witty and
full of Rhyme—we played a Concert," (each member of
the party imitated vocally some musical instrument)
"from 4 o'clock till 10," he wrote to George and Tom,
and this light-hearted sentence gives something of the
keynote of the winter of 1817-18.

There were, of course, disagreeables. There were the
quarrels between Haydon, Hunt and Reynolds: "It is
unfortunate," wrote Keats. "Men should bear with
each other—there lives not the Man who may not be
cut up, aye hashed to pieces on his weakest side. The
best of Men have but a portion of good in them—a kind
of spiritual yeast in their frames which creates the
ferment of existence—by which a Man is propell'd to act
and strive and buffet with Circumstance. The sure way,
Bailey, is first to know a Man's faults, and then be
passive—if after that he insensibly draws you towards
him then you have no Power to break the link. Before
I felt interested in either Reynolds or Haydon—I was
well read in their faults yet knowing them I have been
cementing gradually with both. I have an affection for
them both for reasons almost opposite—and to both
must I of necessity cling—supported always by the hope
that when a little time—a few years shall have tried me
more fully in their esteem I may be able to bring them
together—the time must come because they have both

hearts—and they will recollect the best part of each other when this gust is overblown."

Keats himself managed to keep out of these quarrels, though his friends did their best to bring him in. "Haydon says to me Keats don't show your Lines to Hunt on any account, or he will have done half for you—so it appears Hunt wishes it to be thought. When he met Reynolds in the Theatre John told him I was getting on to the completion of 4000 Lines. Ah! says Hunt, had it not been for me they would have been 7000." What was more, when Leigh Hunt was eventually shown the poem he did not much like it. "He allows it not much merit as a whole; says it is unnatural and made ten objections to it in the mere skimming over. He says the conversation is unnatural and too high-flown for Brother and Sister—says it should be simple, forgetting do ye mind that they were both overshadowed by a Supernatural Power, and of force could not speak like Franchesca in the Rimini."

Hunt's ten objections may have been sound ones, for he was an excellent critic, but Keats was undoubtedly right when he refused to allow Pœona and Endymion to converse after the style of the *Rimini*, of which the following is a sample:

"'May I come in?' said he:—it made her start,—
That smiling voice;—she coloured, pressed her heart
A moment, as for breath, and then with free
And usual tone said, 'Oh yes,—certainly.'"

The friendship for Hunt was certainly cooling, but it is to Keats's credit that, in spite of the mischief-making and in spite of the very natural disappointment a young poet must feel at such a reception of his cherished child, he was neither weak nor touchy enough to break with Hunt. A little while previously he had written an ode to a lock of Milton's hair at Hunt's request, and three weeks after he had shown him *Endymion*, he passed another evening in the Vale of Health, writing a sonnet to the River Nile in friendly competition with Hunt and Shelley.

There were many other evening parties during this winter. Keats dined with Wordsworth, several times with Haydon, with Horace Smith and the wits of the period which he does not seem to have enjoyed very much: "These men say things which make one start, without making one feel." In addition there were one or two gay evenings with Rice and a good deal of theatre-going, since Reynolds, who had gone down to Exeter for Christmas, had turned over his post of dramatic critic on the *Champion* to Keats.

He wrote four dramatic criticisms: on Edmund Kean as a Shakespearean Actor, on Kean in *Richard of York*, on *Retribution, or the Chieftain's Daughter* and on *Don Giovanni: a Pantomime*. The opening of the first of these: "' In our unimaginative days,'—Habeas Corpus'd as we are out of all wonder, curiosity, and fear;—in these fireside, delicate, gilded days,—these days of sickly safety and comfort, we feel very grateful to Mr Kean for giving us some excitement by his old passion in one of the old plays——" plainly shows the influence of Hazlitt. Nevertheless they are not mere imitations, and even to-day they are readable. Keats had a great admiration for Kean, and he seizes on what must have been a very salient point in his acting: his power of portraying a character in the round. Kean, partly because of his physical disabilities, his lack of inches, brought a new style of acting into the theatre. He revolted against the classical tradition upheld by John Kemble at Covent Garden. He was what the critics of the day called "naturalistic." He was not really so, of course. A contemporary wrote of his farewell speech in *Othello*: "It ran on the same tones and semitones, had the same rests and breaks, the same forte and piano, the same crescendo and diminuendo, night after night, as if he spoke it from a musical score." But to his audiences Kean gave the impression of a character who really existed, who had a past and a future. "When he says in *Othello* ' Put up your bright swords for the dew will rust them,' we feel that his throat had commanded where swords were as thick as reeds," writes Keats. And again: "Although so many times he has lost the battle of Bosworth Field, we can easily conceive him really expectant of victory, and a different termination of the piece."

Keats's enormous admiration for Kean is understandable, for they are not unalike. Cowden Clarke says that in his schoolboy days Keats was fond of imitating the great actor, and that physically there was a strong resemblance between them. Certainly they were both small men, since Kean was only five foot four, and both had, according to contemporary testimony, extremely mobile, expressive faces. They were both sensitive, fierily proud and of undaunted courage. Both had an unassuming, implicit belief in their own genius and both were in their early days cruelly assaulted by the world. Kean's success, it is true, came in his own lifetime—his was the true fairy-story of the theatre, the young provincial actor, for the first time at Drury Lane, playing Shylock to a half-empty house, and taking that handful of audience by storm, so that the next day he woke to assured fame and potential riches, but in his way he was as unhappy or unhappier than the poet who died obscure and neglected. He had none of Keats's magnanimity of soul and sweetness of nature. How could he have, the son of a prostitute and a lunatic, dragged up in the gutters of Drury Lane and Covent Garden? However unhappy he might be, there was behind John Keats the background of that safe home at Edmonton, where he was the favourite child of his mother, where his kind, sensible grandmother baked rich, dark cakes, and his baby sister tumbled on the lawn.

Keats had one quality supremely necessary to a dramatic critic. He loved the theatre. "The play is a fine amusement," he wrote, "as a friend of mine once said to me—' Do what you will,' says he, ' a poor gentleman who wants a guinea cannot spend his two shillings better than at the playhouse.'" He wrote this after having seen what he considered an uncommonly bad play, "made up of a virtuous young woman, an indignant brother, a suspecting lover, a libertine prince, a gratuitous villain, a street in Naples, a Cypress grove, lilies and roses, virtue and vice," (a curious pre-echo of Swinburne,) "a bloody sword, a spangled jacket," etc., etc. And here is his description of "behind the scenes" at a "private" theatre: "There was not a yard wide all the way round for actors, scene-shifters and interlopers to move in; for ' Nota Bene ' the Green Room was under the stage and there was I, threatened over and over again to be turned out by the oily scene-shifters—— There did I hear a little painted Trollop own, very candidly, that she had failed in Mary, with a ' damned if she'd play a serious part again, as long as she lived,' and at the same time she was habited as the Quaker in the Review—There was a quarrel, and a fat good-natured looking girl in soldiers' Clothes wished she had only been a man for Tom's sake—One fellow began a song, but an unlucky finger-point from the Gallery sent him off like a shot. One chap was dressed to kill for the King in Bombastes, and he stood at the edge of the scene in the very sweat of anxiety to show himself, but alas the thing was not played. The sweetest morsel of the night moreover was, that the Musicians began pegging and fagging away at an overture—never did you see faces more in earnest, dropping all kinds of correctness and still did not the curtain draw up—Well then they went into a country-dance, then into a region they well knew, into their old boonsome Pothouse, and then to see how pompous o' the sudden they turned; how they looked about and chatted; how they did not care a damn; was a great treat——" It is all written in the affectionate, derisive, intimate style of a real lover of the theatre.

Whether Keats would have been a great dramatic author had he lived is one of those questions to which there is no answer. Certainly it was in his mind. "One of my ambitions," he wrote to Bailey in 1819, "is to make as great a revolution in modern dramatic writing as Kean has done in acting——" And in Kean he would have found an interpreter after his own heart, while no other playwright of the day could write plays in which the great little actor could display his intense emotional power; Kean's great successes were all in Shakespeare and the Elizabethan dramatists. It might have been . . .

The influence of Hazlitt on Keats's style as a dramatic critic, which we have just passingly glanced at, is not to be wondered at, since he was one of the best, possibly the best, writer on the theatre of his day. But his influence on the younger man was of greater extent than that.

All this winter, Keats was diligently attending Hazlitt's lectures on the English poets at the Surrey Institute. He missed the first one, being an hour late, but he probably read it later. Certainly some of the ideas it contained were strikingly similar to his own. "The poetical character," he wrote, as we have seen, to Woodhouse, ". . . has no self—it is everything and nothing—

It has no character—it enjoys light and shade; it lives
in gusto, be it foul or fair, high or low, rich or poor,
even or elevated." And "Fear is poetry, hope is poetry,
love is poetry, hatred is poetry; contempt, jealousy,
remorse, admiration, wonder, pity, despair, or madness,
are all poetry," said Hazlitt in this lecture. "Gusto"
morover, is one of Hazlitt's words. He wrote a paper
on it for the *Examiner* in 1816, which Keats must have
seen. It contains this passage on the Greek statues:

"It seems enough for them *to be*, without acting or
suffering. Their forms are ideal, spiritual. Their beauty
is power. By their beauty they are raised above the
frailties of pain or passion; by their beauty they are
deified."

The wind bloweth where it listeth, and who can say
from whence a poet takes his material, but this passage
does chime in very strangely with the idea underlying
the *Ode to the Grecian Urn*.

"Fair youth, beneath the trees, thou canst not leave
    Thy song, nor ever can those trees be bare;
    Bold Lover, never, never canst thou kiss,
    Though winning near the goal—yet, do not grieve;
    She cannot fade, though thou hast not thy bliss,
    For ever wilt thou love, and she be fair!"

Hazlitt's whole character, his "dark soul bent upon
truth," the maturity of his mind, and, clouded as it was
by disappointment, bitterness and chronic indigestion,
his abundant love of living, would have attracted,
obviously did attract, Keats.

But their relationship is something of a puzzle.
That Keats admired him enormously is evident. In one
of his earliest letters he wrote to Reynolds: "How is
Hazlitt? We were reading his Table" (*the Round Table*)
"last night. I know he thinks himself not estimated by

ten People in the World—I wish he knew he is." And a few months later he wrote to Haydon: "I am convinced that there are three things to rejoice at in this Age—The Excursion, Your Pictures, and Hazlitt's depth of Taste." He copies out enormously long extracts from Hazlitt's lectures and articles for his brother and sister-in-law in America, always with some admiring comment: "The manner in which this is managed: the force and innate power in which it yeasts and works itself up—the feeling for the costume of society; is in a style of genius—He hath a demon, as he himself says of Lord Byron." He records punctually every time he sees Hazlitt, but the curious thing is that he, who is such a good reporter of conversations, never says what passed on these occasions. Sometimes if the meeting took place with others present, there is some allusion: "The topic was the Duke of Wellington very amusingly pro and con'd," when they were alone we have no idea what they talked of: "I called on Hazlitt the day I went to Romney St." . . . "On thursday I walked with Hazlitt as far as Covent Garden: he was going to play Rackets." That is all we know.

"I . . . shall learn Greek and very likely Italian," wrote Keats from Teignmouth, "and in other ways prepare myself to ask Hazlitt in about a year's time the best metaphysical road I can take." But we have no knowledge that he ever did. Hazlitt must have been intimidating, with his lean, lined face, his bright, piercing eyes, and his well-known bitterness of tongue. Perhaps Keats walked beside him down to Covent Garden in silence, unable to bring forth those questions, that eager flood of talk which he would have liked to pour out. Haydon says that he never could get Hazlitt to appreciate Keats's poetry during the latter's life-time, but it is not always safe to believe Haydon. Certainly

Hazlitt gave it full appreciation after his death, though this may have been partly because it was a handy stick with which to beat his adversary, Mr Gifford, the editor of the *Quarterly*. It is true that in this famous, castigatory review in which Hazlitt speaks of Keats being "hooted out of the world," there is one curious mistake, which may illustrate up to a point the relations between them. "Mr Keats," writes Hazlitt, "died when he was scarce twenty." I do not think that although the sentence is used to score a point against Gifford, that Hazlitt can wittingly have made such an obvious mistake. Keats must have left on him the impression of a *very* young man.

CHAPTER IX

Two neighbours and intimate friends—Charles Dilke—Charles Brown—Keats and his brothers now living in Hampstead—George and Tom go to Teignmouth—George's engagement and decision to go to America—Keats joins Tom at Teignmouth—The end of the happy period of Keats's life—Miss Jeffrey.

AFTER the Christmas pantomime of 1817, his review of which contains one charming and very true sentence, "Be it good or bad, a child should write a critique on it," Keats walked home with two companions, who had already become intimate friends. It was a long walk from Drury Lane to Hampstead, but the presence of Brown and Dilke must have made it seem considerably shorter, for as he wrote to his brothers, "We are very thick . . . I don't think I could stop in Hampstead but for their neighbourhood"

Mr. and Mrs. Charles Dilke and Charles Brown shared a house which was very close to Keats's lodgings in Well Walk. Dilke and Brown had built it together in 1816 and it was called Wentworth Place after a name hereditary in the Dilke family.

Dilke was a clerk in the Navy Pay Office by profession, but by taste he was a man of letters and a critic. He was a contributor to reviews and was, in future days, to become the editor and saviour of the *Athenæum*. He was only six years senior to Keats, but somehow he gives the impression of being much older, possibly because he had married at twenty, and was the very devoted, over-devoted in Keats's opinion, father of an only son. When the boy went to school at Westminster the Dilkes removed from Hampstead in order to be near him, on which Keats comments as follows: "I cannot help thinking what a shame it is that poor Dilke should give up his comfortable house and garden for his Son—whom he will certainly ruin with too much care—The boy has nothing in his ears all day but himself and the importance of his education. Dilke has continually in his mouth, 'My Boy.' This is what spoils princes: it may have the same effect with Commoners . . . Eve(r)y one has some wear and tear—One would think Dilke ought to be quiet and happy—but no—this one Boy makes his face pale, his society silent and his vigilance jealous—. He would I have no doubt quarrel with any one who snubb'd his boy—With all this he has no notion how to manage him." The last sentence comes out with the blithe assurance of the bachelor, and it should be recorded in fairness to Dilke that he by no means ruined his boy, who, judging by their later correspondence, returned his father's affection and was the great happiness in his life. Keats, however, being still young and intolerant, merely comments: "Dilke is entirely swallowed up in his boy: 'tis really lamentable to see what a pitch he carries parental mania." And again a little later: "He (Dilke) thinks of nothing but 'Political Justice' and his Boy." The subsequent sentences in this letter show very clearly the difference between Dilke's mind and that of Keats, and though possibly they may be unfair to the former, they give another very good picture of that great quality of openness of mind, which was one of the foundations of Keats's character. Keats describes Dilke as a Man "who cannot feel that he has a personal identity unless he has made up his Mind about everything. The only means of strengthening one's intellect is to let the mind be a thoroughfare for all thoughts. Not a select party. The genus is not scarce in the population. All the stubborn arguers you meet

with are of the same brood. They never begin upon a
subject they are not preresolved on. They want to
hammer their nail into you and if you turn the point,
still they think you are wrong." Keats concludes with
a very happy phrase. "Dilke," he says, "will never come
at a truth as long as he lives; because he is always trying
at it." It is in this letter that he describes him as a
"Godwin-Methodist," and in another he sums him up
as a "Godwin perfectibility Man," which is to say that
Dilke subscribed to the opinions of Shelley's father-in-
law, who held heterodox but highly serious tenets about
the ultimate perfection of the human race. Dilke toyed
with the idea, which sounds somehow strangely modern,
that America will be the country to take up the torch
when the civilization of Europe is extinguished, but
there once more Keats disagrees with him; in a passage
comparing Washington and Franklin to Milton and the
two Sidneys he says: "The Americans are great but
they are not sublime Man—the humanity of the United
States can never reach the sublime."

But in spite of these differences of opinion and tempo,
Keats got on well with Dilke, who was a most intelligent,
cultivated man. He borrowed books from him (both
the first letter and the last he wrote him are apropos of
this), took over his papers and copied out *Endymion*
at Dilke's house, and it was when having "not a dispute
but a disquisition with Dilke on various subjects," that
"several things dove-tailed in his mind" and that he
was struck with the idea of Negative Capability already
quoted. Nor was all their intercourse on an intellectual
level: they went frequently to the play (this very discussion took place walking back from the Christmas
pantomime), there was a dance at Dilke's house, and a
little later when Keats was living with Brown in the
other half of the Hampstead house, Mrs. Dilke would

knock on the wall to bid them to tea, where at least on
one occasion she and Keats "had a battle with the celery
stalks." Moreover, the Dilkes were kind to Keats in a
way that must have touched him more than any other,
since for his sake they were extremely good to Fanny
Keats, frequently inviting her to stay, so that she might
have the pleasure of being near her brother.

Perhaps the best proof of the terms they were on is
to quote a part of a long, facetious letter that Keats and
Charles Brown wrote jointly to the Dilkes in January,
1819. The quotation is also interesting as showing
what excruciatingly bad puns Keats and his friends
could make. Punning was the habit in the early
nineteenth century, all the Hunt coterie indulged in it.
Keats, on at least two occasions, complained of the bad
puns that Hunt and his friends inflicted on him, but if
they were worse than his own imagination boggles——!
It is very difficulty to make head or tail of the puns in
their letter, though perhaps it may be a little help to
state they were both staying at Bedhampton near
Chichester with a Mr. John Snook. The letter is in the
most part from Brown, but in the absence of the latter
Keats apparently read it and added a page of his own,
giving the Dilkes the information that a young lady
had persuaded Brown to shave his whiskers, so that he
came down to breakfast looking "like the Sign of the
Full Moon," and that he himself had been metamor-
phosed by another "young 'ooman" persuading him
"to wear my shirt collar up to my eyes," so that he
"cannot now look sideways." He concludes: "Your's if
possible J. Keats." And Brown takes up the running
again.

"This is abominable! I did but go upstairs to put
on a clean and starched handkerchief, & that over-

weening rogue read my letter & scrawled over one of
my sheets, [1]*and given him a counterpain,*—I wish I could

blank-it all over *and beat him with a* ⌠k *certain rod,* &
have a fresh one bolstered up, *Ah! he may dress me as he
likes but he shant tickle me pillow the feathers,*—I would
not give a tester for such puns, *let us ope brown* (erratum—
a large B—*a Bumble B.*) *will go no further in the Bedroom*
& not call Mat snook a relation to Matt-rass—*This
is grown to a conclusion—I had excellent puns in my head
but one bad one from Brown has quite upset me* but I am
quite set-up for more, but I'm content to be conqueror.
Your's in love, Chas. Brown.

N.B.   *I beg leaf to withdraw all my Puns—they are all
        wash, an base uns——*"

Presumably Keats and Brown did not find this
lamentable exhibition really witty, but they probably
giggled over it a good deal, roused to more and more
laughter by the very badness of the jokes. And it is a
happy way in which to introduce Charles Brown, who
was to become Keats's most intimate friend. For besides
his never-failing kindness and intense affection, Brown
had this great charm for Keats, he could make him
laugh, in a way that Reynolds, who was apt himself to
suffer from the "blue devils," and most certainly Bailey,
could not. Rice had the gift, but then Rice was ill
himself, always suffering and hiding his weakness with
a joke with an effort that Keats could estimate only too
well. But Brown was never ill; he was strong and
healthy; he loved the good things of life; he had a
coarse, earthy streak, he ate prodigiously, he enjoyed
drink and he liked women. He was on the side of life,
and he bolstered up Keats's will to live. All through
the two last terrible years, through the pains of con-

----

[1]Keats's insertions are *in Italics.*

sumption and the torments of love, Keats clung to Brown.

Charles Brown was nine years older than Keats. He inherited the business of a merchant trading with Russia, but this failing, because of "the substitution of fringed whalebone for bristles and the anticipation of a war with Russia," he wound up his business in Petersburg when he was still quite a young man and came back to London and after a hard struggle inherited enough to live on from his brother and devoted himself to literature.

He was not unsuccessful. He wrote a comic opera called *Narensky* which was produced at Drury Lane in 1814, of which the *Champion* wrote that: "It would be unmerciful to give a minute detail of the plot, as our readers will think, when we tell them it was made up of a cave, a band of robbers, an imprisoned lady and a lover who effects her deliverance . . . We do not recollect any production of which the comic scenes are so utterly guiltless of a joke, the serious so barren of pointed sentiment, the songs so far from poetry."

Probably the *Champion* was rather hard on *Narensky*; the lyrics are quite as good as those of any modern Drury Lane production:

> "The summer gale that gently blows
> Joys not to meet the balmy rose
> As I delight in thee, love,"

And so forth and so forth. Anyway, it was good enough to earn Brown £300 and a silver medal which gave him admission to Drury Lane for life.

Brown was a queer person. He was a man of terrifically strong prejudices, an agnostic and a radical. He taught his son never to say "sir" and he himself never employed the then common address of "my lord," except on one occasion to Byron, who it is said noted the concession with a sidelong glance. His dislikes were hearty and unredeemable, and he expressed them with great force and pithiness. "I never met with a more affected fool—ugly to boot," he wrote of one of his own nieces, and of Dilke, with whom he quarrelled after Keats's death, he wrote to his son: "If he should accidentally meet with you, and civilly accost you—spit in his face." "Nor," continues Brown later in the same letter, "with his piggish son ought you to exchange a salutation." It was a sad ending to a friendship that had started in schooldays and it arose out of another salient feature of Brown's character: his fierce, protective loyalty towards those whom he loved. Brown thought, as we shall see later, that George Keats cheated his brother out of part of their inheritance, and no words or deeds were too bad for what he considered this piece of villainy. Dilke, who went into the affair and took George's part, was overwhelmed with the same avalanche of scorn and indignation.

Brown's bust, which now stands in Wentworth Place, gives a very good idea of his character, with its air of resolute energy, its bushy eyebrows, and the pugnacious, jutting-out lower lip. He must have looked older than his years, for he was both bald and fat, a fact glanced at sarcastically by Keats, in some comic verses in the manner of Spenser. The stanzas begin:

"He is to weet a melancholy Carle
Thin in the waist, with bushy head of hair."

They go on in friendly mockery to his love of good food and drink and conclude:

"The slang of cities in no wise he knew
Tipping the wink to him was heathen greek
He sipped no olden Tom nor ruin blue
Or nantz or cherry brandy drank full meek
By many a damsel hoarse and rouge of cheek;
Nor did he know each aged watchman's beat,
Nor in obscured purlieus would he seek
Fur curled Jewesses, with ankles neat,
Who as they walk abroad make tinkling with
    their feet."

How much of this is poetic licence it is of course impossible to say, Keats still chaffing Brown, who was looking over the letter, wrote to Dilke: "When I come to town I shall have a little talk with you about Brown and one Jenny Jacobs . . ." so that the "curled Jewesses" seem to be a long-established joke possibly with a foundation in fact. In any case from what we know of Brown, it seems that he liked women, but from a purely material standpoint. He regarded them neither as romantic beings nor as companions; they were necessities, and that was all. Abigail O'Donaghue, the girl whom he seduced and subsequently married seems to have meant little or nothing in his emotional life. And it is strange to contrast his kindly but flippant allusions to her with the tender and constant affection which he bestowed on John Keats.

"The interval between writing this sheet and the day I put this supplement to it, has been completely filled with generous and most friendly actions of Brown towards me," wrote Keats to his brother in September, 1819. "How frequently I forget to speak of things which I think of and feel most." And indeed Brown was very good to him; he was a rock to lean on, a continual supply of inexhaustible good-humour and kindness. He

supplied money as a matter of course, he encouraged
Keats in his writing, he nursed him in his illness, he
watched over him like an old nurse. There is a quaint
recollection of one of Brown's nephews, written down
over seventy years later: "One easter holyday I remember I was staying there" (with Charles Brown at Wentworth Place) "and I recollect Keats coming down to
breakfast and sitting opposite to me looking very ill
and dejected." (The dejection may have owed something
to the very presence of the chronicler—"The servant has
come for the little Browns this morning," wrote Keats
on the occasion of this Easter visit, "they have been a
tooth-ache to me which I shall enjoy the riddance of—
Their little voices are like wasp stings.") "I have a
perfectly clear recollection," James Brown continues,
"of his solemn, sad eyes and my Uncle pressing him to
take a cup of Arrowroot."

The "solemn, sad eyes," if they were not due to the
"voices like wasp stings," may possibly have owed
something to a later knowledge of events on the part
of the writer, but the "cup of arrowroot" bears the
stamp of unromantic truth!

Keats must have started to become intimate with
Brown and Dilke in the summer of 1817. Brown's
account of it is that he was anxious for Keats's friendship
from the first, but that he did not press himself forward:
"I succeeded in making him come often to my house
by never asking him to come oftener; and I let him feel
himself at perfect liberty there chiefly by avoiding to
assure him of the fact. He quickly became intimate."
On which statement in later days Dilke tartly comments:
"As to the soul of sympathy which united Brown to
Keats on their first meeting, why it was not till long
after they had met and met often that Brown would
consent to become intimate with him—He says truly,

I

though with an odd inferential consequence, that 'he never asked him to come to the house.' The facts are that the Keats, John, George and Tom, were with me three times a week and often three times a day and Brown and Keats were drawn together by force of circumstance and position."

There is no coming at the relative truth of these two accounts, but at least it is clear that when John and Tom joined George at Well Walk, after their trip to Margate and Canterbury in June, 1817, the three boys came often to Wentworth Place.

They were very close, since they were now living in Well Walk, having all removed to Hampstead early in 1817. Why they chose Hampstead is not known; possibly because it was near Leigh Hunt; also, it was probably cheaper, the higher air may have done Tom's cough good, and they were used to living on the north side of London. They lodged with a postman, named Bentley, whose wife seems to have been a kind, friendly woman, who was very good to the young Keats brothers, especially to the poor, ill Tom. She probably looked on them with a motherly eye, since she had plenty of children of her own, "the young carrots," as Keats dubbed them, who made a great deal of noise and who wore worsted stockings which smelt of damp wool when the weather was wet.

But all this winter John had been alone. "In this World," he wrote to Bailey in October, 1817, "there is nothing but teasing and snubbing and vexation—my brother Tom look'd very unwell yesterday and I am for shipping him off to Lisbon—perhaps I ship there with him." It was the prevalent belief that consumption benefited from a milder, warmer climate. The idea of Lisbon was abandoned, but Tom and George some time in November went to Teignmouth in Devon, and now at the beginning of March John was to go down there and take George's place as nurse and companion, since George, who had lately come of age, had decided to collect his patrimony, buy 1,400 acres from the American Government and try his fortune across the sea.

"This," writes John, "for many reasons has met with my entire consent—and the chief one is this—he is of too independent and liberal a Mind to get on in trade in this Country—in which a generous Man with a scanty recourse must be ruined. I would sooner he should till the ground than bow to a Customer—there is no choice with him; he could not bring himself to the latter. I would not consent to his going alone—no; but that objection is done away with—he will marry before he sets sail a young Lady he has known some years—of a nature liberal and highspirited enough to follow him to the Banks of the Mississipi."

The young lady was Georgiana Augusta Wylie, and she must have been liberal and high-spirited indeed. What is even more surprising is the liberalism of her family. Young ladies in the early nineteenth century must have had their own way in certain cases just as much or more than they do in the twentieth. That the Wylie family should permit a much-cherished daughter of seventeen to marry a young man of twenty-one, with a total fortune of £1,100, who had shown no particular business ability, and who was to take her to America, then a half-savage continent reached by a sailing ship after a voyage of three to four weeks, is almost incredible. We must suppose that Georgiana Wylie twisted her family around her little finger. She certainly knew herself what she wanted. "To see an entirely disinterrested Girl quite happy is the most pleasant and extraordinary thing in the world," comments her future brother-in-law.

He was very fond of the "Nymph of the downward smile and sidelong glance," as he called her in a sonnet. His long journal letters to America, which give us such a breathing, speaking, moving picture of him, are addressed as much to her as to George. "If you were here my dear Sister," he wrote her once, "I could not pronounce the words which I can write to you from a distance; I have a tenderness for you, and an admiration which I feel to be as great and more chaste than I can have for any woman in the world. You will mention Fanny—" (his sister, Fanny Keats), "her character is not formed, her identity does not press upon me as yours does. I hope from the bottom of my heart that I may one day feel as much for her as I do for you—I know not how it is but I have never made any acquaintance of my own—nearly all through your medium my dear Brother—through you I know not only a sister but a glorious human being."

Meanwhile Miss Wylie was asking George to come to town and John went down to Devonshire, bearing a sheaf of songs and sonnets to be read aloud, and leaving the thrushes in Hampstead singing "as if they would speak to the winds," to be with Tom. Much has been written of John Keats's goodness to his sister, but less of his unselfish devotion to Tom, which was at least as remarkable. When he went down to Teignmouth he seems to have given up all thoughts of his own preferences. "Tom has taken a fancy to a physician here, Dr. Turton, and I think is getting better—therefore I shall remain here some Months," he wrote as if it were the most natural thing in the world, and yet it must have been a sacrifice for him to give up his friends, his cheerful life in London and to remain as Tom's sick nurse in a little country town.

Teignmouth is in itself a delightful place, though it

has that faint atmosphere of indefinable melancholy that hangs about all places designed for pleasure resorts. It stands on a narrow peninsula with the sea on one side and the broad tidal river on the other. It is surrounded by woods climbing green hills, and steep red cliffs running down into the sea. The town itself in 1818 must have been charming, with tall, curving crescents of plaster houses bordering an open space of grass, known as the Den, on the other side of which was the sea.

It is a curious thought, incidentally, that Keats during his whole life probably never saw an ugly thing. Ugly people he must have seen in plenty, especially in his medical days, many more of them than he would have seen in this century, rickety, hydrocephalous children, pock-marked women, men with deformed limbs and strange skin diseases. But the houses in which he lived, the streets he walked through, the furniture he sat on, the table-silver he used, the china he ate off, must all have been, if not beautiful, at least harmonious and graciously proportioned.

The house he stayed in at Teignmouth is still standing. It is in a quiet street and it is very small and unpretentious, three storeys high, of white plaster, with bow-fronted windows and black, shining front door, with fluted jambs and a classical pediment surmounting its rounded arch. The small paned windows of the sitting-rooms look down a narrow opening on to the estuary, where small white-sailed boats dance up and down in the bobbing waves, and the gulls hover round the fishermen's nets, wailing in hoarse, melancholy voices. On a sunny day it would be delightful; but, alas! there were almost no sunny days while John and Tom were in Devonshire. The continual dropping of the cold, mizzling West Country rain runs like a refrain through all the letters of this time. It must have been a very dreary five weeks. Tom had a bad relapse with blood-spitting as soon as John arrived, and after that they were mewed up day after day in their little sitting-room, with the windows tightly shut, according to the hygienic notions of the day, with Tom, feverish and unhappy, coughing his lungs away, occasionally putting his handkerchief to his mouth and bringing it back stained with the bright arterial red. There were no hygienic precautions in those days, there was nothing to prevent the tubercular bacilli from the lungs of one brother settling in those of the other. And all the time the rain "beat against the window as if the roots of the Earth were rotten cold and drench'd." It was no wonder that when John went to bed at night he lay awake and listened to it "with a sense of being drown'd and rotted like a grain of wheat."

His letters at this time are not happy. In spite of the nonsense verses about "Bishop's teign and King's teign and Coomb at the dear teign head," and the Devon maids with their baskets, and Dawlish Fair, and the cumulative nonsense, in a style of which Keats was rather fond, written to Rice, there is a strain of melancholy which is not to be wondered at. "What I complain of," he wrote to Reynolds, "is that I have been in so uneasy a state of mind as not to be fit to write to an invalid." (Reynolds was ill at the time.) "I cannot write at any length under a disguised feeling. I should have loaded you with an addition of gloom, which I am sure you do not want."

In fact, the weeks at Teignmouth mark more or less the ending of the happy period of John Keats's life. "Another time," he wrote to Taylor, "I shall be more bent to all sort of troubles and disagreeables—young Men for some time have an idea that such a thing as happiness is to be had and therefore are extremely impatient under any unpleasant restraining—in time however, of such stuff is the world about them, they know better and instead of striving from Uneasiness greet it as an habitual sensation, a pannier which is to weigh upon them through life." It is as well that we cannot see into the future and John Keats could not know that in his case what he wrote was literally true.

He is searching all this time for some solution to the "burden of the mystery." Sometimes he thought that it might lie in knowledge or philosophy—(they are in Keats's language curiously interchangeable terms; for instance Lamb and Keats had once agreed that Newton "had destroyed all the poetry of the rainbow by reducing it to prismatic colours," and in *Lamia* the unweaving of the rainbow is attributed to the "mere touch of cold philosophy")—and he wrote once more to Reynolds: "An extensive knowledge is needful to thinking people— it takes away the heat and fever; and helps, by widening, speculation, to ease the Burden of the Mystery. . . . The difference of high Sensations with and without know- ledge appears to me this—in the latter case we are falling continually ten thousand fathoms deep and being blown up again without wings and with all (the) horror of a bare shouldered creature—in the former case our shoul- ders are fledge, and we go thro' the same air and space without fear." And again he wrote, this time to Taylor: "I find that I can have no enjoyment in the World but continual drinking of Knowledge,—I find there is no worthy pursuit but the idea of doing some good for the world."

Keats was continually to come back to this idea, it is the root cause of his remodelling of *Hyperion*, and as continually to be brought up sharply against his other conviction that we cannot know—that on this Earth,

God or the Eternal Being, or whatever one may choose to call that mysterious Power, will only reveal himself in snatches, infinitesimal glimpses, and that consecutive, or "consequitive," as Keats spelt it, reasoning, will never lead man anywhere, that it is better to keep one's heart open and to seek for God where He will show Himself to us, in beauty or poetry or "the holiness of the heart's affections."

> "Things cannot to the will
> Be settled,"

wrote Keats at this time,

> "but they teare us out of thought.
> Or is it that Imagination brought
> Beyond its proper bound, yet still confined,—
> Lost in a sort of Purgatory blind,
> Cannot refer to any standard law
> Of either earth or heaven?—It is a flaw
> In happiness to see beyond our bourn—
> It forces us in Summer skies to mourn:
> It spoils the singing of the Nightingale."

Meanwhile while all this speculation and thought and imagery was passing through one young poet's head, the life of Teignmouth, the small seaside town, went on in an uneventful, Jane Austenish Chronicle. Round the tea-tables ladies still lamented the sad death of Princess Charlotte in child-birth. The little sailing boats bobbed up and down in the estuary. A nest of robins hatched on the roof. In the evenings the tightly trousered young men with high collars to their coats gave their arms to young ladies in bonnets and muslin frocks, to walk up and down beside the sea. The Captain paid court to the "stony-hearted" Miss Mitchell, and the two Keats brothers went and took tea with Mrs. Jeffrey

and her four daughters, and on the very few fine days
lounged with them on the Den.

One of the daughters named Marian must have much
resembled her namesake in *Sense and Sensibility*, and there
is a local tradition that Keats more or less filled the
part of her Willoughby. Certain it is that in 1830 when
she was married to Colonel Brandon, otherwise Mr.
I. S. Prowse, a gentleman of Torquay, she published a book
of poems, among which the following verses are tradi-
tionally supposed to have been addressed to John Keats:

"If thou canst bear to say adieu,
To her who loves so warm, so true;
If thou canst think thou mayst depart,
Yet leave unbroken the young heart,
Which gave to thee its earliest vow
And lives but in thy presence now;
Then quit thy love, thy bride—but know
Si deseris, ah! pereo.

"Yet dearest go; the pang will be
Soon o'er; I shall not live to see
Thy look of love; which is my heaven
My happiness—to others given;
'Tis best we part; I could not bear
Thy coldness—nor the sick despair
Of love decaying; go then, go,
Si deseris, ah! pereo.

"I had a foolish hope—'tis gone:
I thought thou might'st have lov'd alone
The simple heart which clung to thee
With more than Woman's constancy:—
'Tis over—but I murmur not
Nor dare I wish a happier lot—
To thee, to life farewell—for oh
Si deseris, ah! pereo!"

Whether Keats really was the object of this romantic outpouring, and, if he was, how much he had encouraged the young lady, we shall never know. When he returned to Hampstead he wrote a joking letter, full of rattling nonsense, addressed to both the Miss Jeffreys, which may have been written in pure brotherly friendliness or may have been an awkward masculine way of putting finis to an over-romanticized episode. Six days later he was writing to Bailey: "My Love for my Brothers from the early loss of our parents and even for earlier misfortunes has grown into an affection 'passing the Love of Women'—I have been ill temper'd with them I have vex'd them—but the thought of them has always stifled the impression that any woman might otherwise have made upon me——" Which sounds somehow as if he had a particular case in his mind. When he writes to Miss Jeffrey (probably, though not certainly, Marian), over a year later, to ask her to find him lodgings near Teignmouth it is in a grave, confiding style quite different from the nonsensical rattle of 1818.

"Now I find I must buffet it—I must take my stand upon some vantage ground and begin to fight—I must choose between despair and Energy—I choose the latter—though the world has taken on a quakerish look with me, which I once thought was impossible—

'Nothing can bring back the hour
Of splendour in the grass and glory in the flower.'

I once thought this a Melancholist's dream—

"But why do I speak to you in this manner? No believe me I do not write for a mere selfish purpose—the manner in which I have written of myself will convince you. I do not do so to Strangers."

Miss Jeffrey writes twice in answer to this letter. If she were in love with him, how excited she must have

been at the thought of having him in a small Devonshire
village among the overhanging green lanes and the
clear streams of that almost over-picturesque county
for a whole summer! But her hopes were dashed. Keats
wrote again to tell her that he was going to the Isle
of Wight with Rice. He thanks her for her "very wise
advice," about sticking to poetry rather than going as a
ship's surgeon on an Indiaman. He goes on to say that
"One of the greatest reasons that the English have
produced the finest writers in the world is that the
English world has ill-treated them during their lives
and foster'd them after their deaths." A singularly
true comment.

I suspect that the sentence Miss Jeffrey cherished most
in the whole of this long letter was the concluding one:
"Give my love to your Mother with the assurance that
I can never forget her anxiety for my Brother Tom.
Believe also that I shall ever remember our leave taking
with *you*."

And that is the whole of that innocent, somewhat
one-sided little romance, if romance it was.

CHAPTER X

THE episode of Marian Jeffrey brings up the whole question of Keats's attitude towards women, which provides something of a psychological puzzle. With that calm, lucid good sense which is almost astonishing to find in a person as temperamental as Keats, he himself once discussed it in a letter to Bailey:

"I am certain I have not a right feeling towards Women—at this moment I am striving to be just to them but I cannot—Is it because they fall so far below my Boyish imagination? When I was a Schoolboy I thought a fair Woman a pure Goddess, my mind was a soft nest in which some one of them slept, though she knew it not—I have no right to expect more than their reality. I thought them etherial above Men—I find them perhaps equal—great by comparison is very small. Insult may be inflicted in more Ways than by Word or action—one who is tender of being insulted does not like to think an insult against another—I do not like to think insults in a Lady's Company—I commit a crime with her which absence would not have known. Is it not extraordinary? When among men I have no evil thoughts, no malice, no spleen—I feel free to speak or to be silent—I can listen and from every one I can learn—my hands are in my pockets—I am free from all suspicion and comfortable. When I am among Women I have evil thoughts, malice spleen—I cannot speak or

be silent—I am full of Suspicions and therefore listen
to nothing—I am in a hurry to be gone—You must be
charitable and put all this perversity to my being disappointed since Boyhood. Yet with such feelings I am
happier alone among Crowds of men, by myself or with
a friend or two—With all this trust me Bailey I have
not the least idea that Men of different feelings and
inclinations are more short-sighted than myself—I never
rejoiced more than at my Brother's Marriage and shall
do so at that of any of my friends—. I must absolutely
get over this—but how? The only way is to find the
root of evil, and so cure it ' with backward mutterings
of dissevering Power.'" (Keats was anticipating Professor
Freud's theory by nearly a century.) "—that is a difficult
thing; for an obstinate Prejudice can seldom be produced
but from a gordian complication of feelings, which
must take time to unravell and care to keep unravelled.
I could say a good deal more about this but I will leave
it in hopes of better and more worthy dispositions—
and also content that I am wronging no one, for after all
I do think better of Womankind than to suppose they
care whether Mister John Keats five feet high likes
them or not."

How much the "five feet high" had to do with it is
a matter of conjecture. Many men who are very small
feel themselves at a disadvantage in the presence of
women, especially if they be as sensitive as Keats. On
the other hand, his lack of inches was never a sore
subject or a secret canker. He refers to it with a good-
humoured ruefulness which is very endearing. "When
it is two feet in length," he wrote to George and
Georgiana, referring in this somewhat off-hand way to
his baby niece, "I shall not stand a barley corn higher.
That's not fair—one ought to go on growing as well
as others." "I heard," he wrote to the same correspon-

dents, "that Mr L. Said a thing I am not at all contented with—Says he ' O, he is quite the little Poet' now this is abominable—you might as well say Buonaparte is quite the little Soldier—You see what it is to be under six foot and not a lord——" One cannot help feeling that if the poetical lord to whom Keats is obviously referring had been only five feet high there would have been a far greater to-do about the matter. Still, the heart knoweth its own bitterness, and Keats may have minded more about his stature than his common sense would allow him to show.

He was very easily stirred by the physical beauty of women. Indeed, his poems, especially his early ones with their frequent, often rather tasteless, references to creamy breasts, dove-like bosoms, plump shoulders, dark violet eyes, etc., prove as much; there was a time when, as he wrote himself, "even a bit of ribband was a matter of interest with me." In very early days, before he was introduced to Leigh Hunt, Keats and his brother George had quite a little circle of feminine friends, for whom John provided poems either on his own behalf or on that of his brother. There was, for instance, Mary Frogley, who transcribed many of his early poems in her album and to whom that shockingly bad effusion, "Hadst thou lived in days of old," was addressed as a Valentine. It seems to have been composed by John and presented by George, who, being of an economical turn of mind, later used it up on his fiancée, Georgiana Wylie. His other Valentine:

"O come Georgiana the rose is full blown,"

also provided for him by John, stood originally as:

"O come my dear Emma the rose is full blown,"

and seems to have referred to a Miss Emma Mathews but to which brother she was adjured to give her hand,

"with love-looking eyes and with voice sweetly bland,"

is quite uncertain.

There were also the Misses Ann and Caroline Mathew, cousins of George Felton Mathew, to whom in Moore-like metre Keats addressed two poems entitled respectively: *To Some Ladies*, and *On Receiving a Curious Shell and a Copy of Verses from the Same Ladies*, eulogizing them as "elegant, pure and aerial minds."

Poor Caroline Mathew! We get a small glimpse of her two years later when Keats writes to his brother mentioning, among other items of gossip, that he has heard from a friend called Kirkman, a cousin of the Mathews, of "the abominable behaviour of Archer to Caroline Mathew—Archer has been living at the Mathews these two years; he has been amusing Caroline all this time—and now he has written a Letter to Mrs. M. declining on pretence of inability to support a wife as he would wish all thoughts of marriage. What is the worst is, Caroline is 27 years old—It is an abominable matter." Keats's honest indignation at the abandoning of the ageing Miss Mathew is charming; it is one of the very few reminders we get that he was a contemporary of Jane Austen. "Lord," cried Lydia Bennet in *Pride and Prejudice*, "how ashamed I should be of not being married before three-and-twenty! My aunt Philips wants you so to get husbands you can't think."

Whether Keats's interest in bits of ribband ever took him beyond the Valentines and small flirtations with girls of his own class is not known. Some of his biographers have alleged, on the strength of the following passage in one of his letters, that he contracted a venereal

disease when he was staying at Oxford with Bailey.
"The little Mercury that I have taken has corrected the
Poison and improved my Health—though I feel from
my employment that I shall never be again secure in
Robustness." But in the early nineteenth century
mercury was a very common remedy and was used for
every sort of ill, and the latter half of the sentence
seems to imply that Keats was dosing himself for something that was caused by his sedentary fashion of living;
and though he may well at one time or another have
slipped up when going round the town with Brown,
Rice or Reynolds, such a circumstance does not fit in
with all we know of the Oxford visit, when he was busy
and tranquil, with the religious-minded Bailey as a
companion.

His attitude towards sex in general was, however, far
from being the natural uninhibited pagan one that
some of his modern admirers seem to think. He was,
up to a point, like so many of the greatest English poets,
hag-ridden and obsessed with it. One has only to read
this note scribbled in the margin of Burton's *Anatomy
of Melancholy*: "Here is the old plague spot; the pes-
tilence, the raw scrofula. I mean that there is nothing
disgraces me in my own eyes so much as being one of
a race of eyes nose and mouth beings in a planet call'd
the earth who all from Plato to Wesley have always
mingled goatish winyish lustful love with the abstract
adoration of the deity. I don't understand Greek—is the
love of God and the Love of woman expressed by the
same word in Greek? I hope my little mind is wrong—
if not I could—Has Plato separated these loves? Ha!
I see how they endeavour to divide—but there appears
to be a horrid relationship."

Why he suffered from this distorted feeling towards
sex, this "gordian complication of feelings," as he

called it himself, we do not know. I think it possible
that his trouble may have been Hamlet's. His father had,
after all, been only buried for two months when his
mother married again. It is true that William Rawlings,
her second husband, deserted her within the year and
did not remain to trouble his step-children, but the
"o'er hasty marriage" must have been a great shock to
a little boy of eight years old who adored his mother.

However it may be, it is certain that his instinct was
to adore and to idealize women, yet to suspect and
fear them and to despise himself for being so much
attracted to them. It was not a state of mind likely to
lead to much happiness in love. Nor did it; love, when
it came to him, came accompanied by acute suffering,
partly owing to circumstances, but partly owing to his
own temperament, his over active and inflamed imagination. How passionate and active that imagination could
be is shown by an encounter which took place in Vauxhall Gardens in which he never even spoke to the lady,
yet which does indicate a capacity for feeling and for
suffering which were to be only too greatly fulfilled.

He glimpsed the lady and wrote three poems to her
which are worth quoting in full in order to understand
something of Keats's character. The first stanzas were
written directly after the encounter in August, 1814.

> " Fill for me a brimming bowl
>   And let me in it drown my soul;
>   But put therein some drug designed
>   To Banish Women from my mind."

(Or as he was to write five years later: " O for a draught
of vintage.")

> "For I want not the stream inspiring
>   That fills the mind with fond desiring,

K

"But I want as deep a draught
  As e'er from Lethe's wave was quaff'd;
From my despairing heart to charm
The Image of the fairest form
That e'er my reveling eyes beheld,
That e'er my wandering fancy spell'd.

"In vain! away I cannot chace
The melting softness of that face,
The beaminess of those bright eyes,
That breast—earth's only Paradise.
My sight will never be more blest;
For all I see has lost its zest;
Nor with delight can I explore
The Classic page, or Muse's lore.

"Had she but known how beat my heart,
  And with one smile reliev'd my smart
I should have felt a sweet relief,
I should have felt ' the joy of grief.'
Yet as a Tuscan mid the snow
Of Lapland thinks on sweet Arno,
Even so for ever shall she be
The Halo of my memory."

So might any poet of eighteen have written with
his imagination stirred by a lovely unknown, but what
is curious is that, three and a half years later, Keats
wrote the following two sonnets still, according to
Woodhouse, harping on the same strangely persistent
memory:

"When I have fears that I may cease to be
  Before my pen has glean'd my teeming brain,
Before high piled books, in charact'ry,
  Hold like rich garners the full-ripen'd grain;

When I behold, upon the night's starr'd face,
　　Huge cloudy symbols of a high romance,
And think that I may never live to trace
　　Their shadows, with the magic hand of chance;
And when I feel, fair creature of an hour!
　　That I shall never look upon thee more,
Never have relish in the faery power
　　Of unreflecting love!—then on the shore
Of the wide world I stand alone and think
Till love and fame to nothingness do sink."

"Time's sea hath been five years at its slow ebb;
　　Long hours have to and fro let creep the sand;
Since I was tangled in thy beauty's web,　　·
　　And snar'd by the ungloving of thine hand.
And yet I never look on midnight sky,
　　But I behold thine eyes' well memoried light;
I cannot look upon the rose's dye,
　　But to thy cheek my soul doth take its flight;
I cannot look on any budding flower,
　　But my fond ear, in fancy at thy lips,
And hearkening for a love-sound, doth devour
　　Its sweets in the wrong sense:—Thou dost eclipse
Every delight with sweet remembering,
And grief unto my darling joys dost bring."

Well, that is certainly the effect of the imagination,
and it may be, as his standard biographer says, that it
is "rather a fine Shakesperian exercise than an expression
of profound feeling." And yet there is a strange sincerity
in the lines and a curious foreshadowing of a mood in
which he was to write a little later: "I do not know
how elastic my spirit might be, what pleasure I might
have in living here and breathing and wandering as free
as a stag about this beautiful Coast if the remembrance
of you did not weigh so upon me."

The lady of Vauxhall was not the only unknown fair in Keats's life; there was also the more prosaic affair of the lady from Hastings. This is such a tantalizingly inexplicable little episode that I will give the whole of it in Keats's own words.

In October, 1818, he wrote to George and Georgiana Keats: "Since I wrote thus far I have met with that same Lady again, whom I saw at Hastings and whom I met when we were going to the English Opera. It was in a Street which goes from Bedford Row to Lamb's Conduit Street—I passed her and turned back—she seemed glad of it; glad to see me and not offended at my passing her before. We walked on towards Islington where we called on a friend of her's who keeps a Boarding School. She has always been an enigma to me—she has been in a Room with you and with Reynolds and wishes we should be acquainted without any of our common acquaintance knowing it. As we went along, sometimes through shabby, sometimes through decent Streets I had my guessing at work, not knowing what it would be and prepared to meet any surprise—First it ended at this House at Islington: on parting from which I pressed to attend her home. She consented, and then again my thoughts were at work what it might lead to, tho' now they had received a sort of genteel hint from the Boarding School. Our Walk ended in 34 Gloucester Street, Queen Square—not exactly so for we went up stairs into her sitting room—a very tasty sort of place with Books, Pictures a bronze statue of Buonaparte, Music, aeolian Harp; a Parrot, a Linnet—a case of choice Liquers &c. &c. &c. She behaved in the kindest manner—made me take home a Grouse for Tom's dinner—Asked for my address for the purpose of sending me more game. As I had warmed with her before and kissed her—I thought it would be living backwards not to do it again—she had a better taste: she perceived how much a thing of course it was and shrunk from it—not in a prudish way but as I say a good taste. She contrived to disappoint me in a way which made me feel more pleasure than a simple Kiss could do—She said I should please her much more if I would only press her hand and go away. Whether she was in a different disposition when I saw her before—or whether I have in fancy wrong'd her I cannot tell. I expect to pass some pleasant hours with her now and then: in which I feel I shall be of service to her in matters of knowledge and taste: if I can I will. I have no libidinous thought about her— she and your George" (his sister-in-law Georgiana, to whom he often referred as "little George") "are the only women à peu près de mon age whom I would be content to know for their mind and friendship alone."

That was one of the major troubles of his relations with women: he did not like them unless he was attracted by them, and if he were attracted, suspicion, jealousy and sex antagonism were certain to creep in. The only women he knew well from a brotherly stand-point were Jane and Mariane, the sisters of John Hamilton Reynolds, and of them he quickly wearied. Why, it is not quite clear. I think it possible from the trend of the letters that Jane Reynolds may have been a little in love with him, a feeling which he would certainly have been unable to reciprocate—or it may have been simply that he found them tiresome. "I seldom go to Little Britain" (where the Reynoldses lived), "because the Ennui always seizes me there," he wrote in 1818, "and John Reynolds is very dull at home."

It was a pity. If Fanny Keats had been older, if Georgiana Keats had stayed in England, and he had been able to have a deeply intimate yet unsentimental relation-ship with some woman, things might have turned out easier for him. Meanwhile, he was waiting to fall in love. Consciously or unconsciously his imagination and his senses were both urging him towards it. There was to be one more false start and then "the wind on the mountain falling on the oaks."

CHAPTER XI

"THEY say we are all (that is our set) mad at Hampstead.
There's George took unto himself a Wife a Week ago
and will in a little time sail for America—and I with a
friend am preparing for a four Months Walk all over
the North—and belike Tom will not stop here—he has
been getting much better—Lord what a Journey I had
and what a relief at the end of it—" (Tom had been
taken with bad blood-spitting at Bridport on the return
journey from Teignmouth.) "I'm sure I could not have
stood it many more days. Hampstead is now in fine
order." So wrote Keats to the Misses Jeffrey, on June
4th, 1818.

Endymion was finished, copied, and gone to press. For
the original, somewhat aggressive preface had been
substituted, partly owing to Reynolds, the short, moving,
eminently dignified foreword, which now stands at the
head of the poem.

"Knowing within myself the manner in which this
Poem has been produced, it is not without a feeling of
regret that I make it public.

"What manner I mean, will be quite clear to the
reader, who must soon perceive great inexperience,
immaturity, and every error denoting a feverish attempt,

rather than a deed accomplished. The two first books, and indeed the two last, I feel sensible are not of such completion as to warrant their passing the press; nor should they if I thought a year's castigation would do them any good;—it will not: the foundations are too sandy. It is just that this youngster should die away: a sad thought for me, if I had not some hope that while it is dwindling I may be plotting and fitting myself for verses fit to live.

"This may be speaking too presumptuously, and may deserve a punishment: but no feeling man will be forward to inflict it: he will leave me alone, with the conviction that there is not a fiercer hell than the failure in a great object. This is not written with the least atom of purpose to forestall criticisms of course, but from the desire I have to conciliate men who are competent to look, and who do look with a zealous eye, to the honour of English literature.

"The imagination of a boy is healthy, and the mature imagination of a man is healthy; but there is a space of life between, in which the soul is in a ferment, the character undecided, the way of life uncertain, the ambition thick-sighted: thence proceeds mawkishness, and all the thousand bitters which those men I speak of must necessarily taste in going over the following pages.

"I hope I have not in too late a day touched the beautiful mythology of Greece, and dulled its brightness: for I wish to try once more before I bid it farewell.
"*Teignmouth, April 10th 1818.*"

Thus was the preface written, and the men who should have looked "with a zealous eye to the honour of English literature," but who were, in fact, blinded by politics and the pettiness of party spites, did not begin their "punishment" until September. In the meantime, there was an interim, and Tom was a little better, and George was leaving for America; and in spite of a terrible fit of black depression, (he wrote to Bailey: "I was in hopes some little time back to be able to relieve your dullness by my spirits—to point out things in the world worth your enjoyment—and now I am never alone without rejoicing there is such a thing as death,") and a slight indisposition, John started out with Charles Brown for the north.

They were to accompany George and Georgiana as far as Liverpool, and on June 22nd all four of them took coach from the Swan and Two Necks in Lad Lane. They stopped at Redbourne for dinner and there called on Henry Stephens, John's old medical comrade, who had a practice in that small country town.

Mr. Stephens, with his usual observant eye, noted that Georgiana Keats was "rather short, not what might strictly be called handsome, but looked like a being whom any man of moderate sensibility might easily love." She was, moreover, "somewhat singular or girlish in her attire," which might have been due, he thought, to the taste of "the Poet, the presiding genius of the family." Henry Stephens had never much approved of Keats's poetical carelessness in dress. "He used to go," he remembered, "with his neck nearly bare à la Byron. The collar turned down and a ribbon tied round his neck without any neckerchief. He also let his moustachios grow occasionally." From the phrase the "presiding genius of the family," one gathers that he is remembering those days in St. Thomas' St., when the two younger brothers sat looking at John perched on the window-seat as if he were the seventh wonder of the world, something to the annoyance of his fellow-medical students, who found "little Keats," with his pretensions as a poet, rather ridiculous and conceited.

However, Stephens ends up on a kindlier note. "There was something original about her," he concludes, "and John seemed to regard her as a being whom he delighted to honour, and introduced her to me with an evident satisfaction."

Then the little glimpse of a happy family life ends. Mr. Stephens steps back into his surgery and the coach rolls on along the dusty, white roads, between June hedges starred with wild roses, to Liverpool.

There George and Georgiana, twenty-one and seventeen, were left to begin their new life together, and Keats and Brown departed to Lancaster.

Their walking tour did not begin auspiciously. They got up at four in the morning and a heavy downpour kept them within doors till seven. They whiled away the time reading Milton, with Brown "preaching patience" out of Samson Agonistes. Milton must have been Brown's contribution to literary resources, since Keats took only one book, Cary's *Dante*, in three small volumes. By seven the rain had dwindled to a drizzle, and they set out. Lancaster on a grey, dripping morning is not cheerful, and after the long wait on empty stomachs, they must have felt they richly deserved the comment made by a labourer, as they left the town: "There go a couple of gentlemen!—having nothing to do, they are finding out hard work for themselves!"

They looked a strange "couple of gentlemen" as they trudged along the northward road. They both carried knapsacks, Brown wore a white hat, a tartan coat and trousers, while Keats sported a fur cap. It was no wonder that a drunken man reeled up to Keats in Glasgow, exclaiming that: "He had seen all foreigners, bu-u-ut he had never seen the like o' him!"

The north country was at that moment in the throes of an election. That pert, brilliant young man with the turned-up nose, Henry Brougham, had had the impertinence to come down and challenge the great family of Lowther in their own stronghold. Consequently, when the two travellers stopped for dinner and asked at the Green Dragon, "What could we have?" they were met by the discouraging reply of: "Nothing! You can have nothing here!" Which was amplified by the landlady of the King's Arms into a complaint, which still sounds pathetic: "Ah! Gentlemen, the soldiers are upon us! The Lowthers have brought 'em here to be in readiness . . . at this election time to have soldiers upon us, when we ought to be making a bit of money. Not to be able to entertain anybody! There was yesterday—I was forced to turn away two parties in their own carriages; for I have not a room to offer, nor a bed for any one. You can't sleep here, gentlemen; but I can give you a dinner. Dear, dear me! It goes to my heart—my spirits are quite down—to be forced to turn away two such parties! Oh! It's the Lowthers as I suspect—but that's only one's own mind—that brought 'em in."

Owing to the bad weather they could not make Kendal that night, so they put up at a little pub at a place called End Moor. The house was, their landlady informed them "in a squeer with whitewashing," and she looked doubtfully at the knapsacks, inquiring if they provided their own eating. But on hearing they did not she promised them accommodation, and with true north country exactitude took something off the bill when she found they did not take sugar in their tea.

They were sitting in the parlour-kitchen, discussing the election with a pleasant discharged soldier, who had served in the American and in the Napoleonic wars, when an old drunkard staggered out of a corner, in an attitude "something like a bear," according to Brown, or, as

Keats described it, with a memory of the crabbed figure used in medical prescriptions, "in the shape of a ℥," and thrusting his face into Brown's and making a grab at his knapsack, asked if they sold spectacles and razors, appearing to take Brown's glasses for the sign in the front of the shop.

Next morning they passed through Kendal and had their first view of the lake and the mountains of Windermere. Keats had never seen anything like this, and they made a very great impression on him. Indeed, it is hard to estimate nowadays the impression that would be made on a sensitive, intelligent adult mind by mountains, lakes and scenery of which he had never seen a photograph, a picture-postcard or a moving picture. "How can I believe in that? Surely it cannot be!" was his exclamation when the lake lay before him, and in his letter to Tom he wrote: "The two views we have had of it are of the most noble tenderness—they can never fade away—they make one forget the divisions of life; age, youth, poverty and riches; and refine one's sensual vision into a sort of north star which can never cease to be open lidded and stedfast over the wonders of the great Power."

Nevertheless, it is interesting to note that Keats never lets himself go into the stock raptures so common among writers of the period. Brown, though he can be amusing enough when writing of personalities, has the whole romantic vocabulary at his finger-tips: "The mountains completely surpassed all our expectations. . . . You may hear people talk eloquently of these scenes; you may see them portrayed by the best painters—language and art are equally inefficient. The reality must be witnessed before it can be understood. What is it while moving on, at times unconscious of feet, and incapable of uttering more than sudden tokens of wonder—that so presses on the brain, with such awe, with such intense delight? Can it be that the intellect is then susceptible of the sublimest poetry, is throbbing under its influence while bereaved of the power of clothing it in words? Differ as we may on the cause, all will acknowledge the effect." But here is Keats on the same subject: "June 26—I merely put pro forma, for there is no such thing as time and space, which by the way came forcibly upon me on seeing for the first hour the Lake and Mountains of Winander—I cannot describe them—they surpass my expectation—beautiful water—shores and islands green to the marge—mountains all round up to the clouds." It is true that Keats is writing a letter and Brown a newspaper article, so that he may have been afflicted with a rush of journalese to the pen, but the contrast is striking.

Even in those days Windermere was afflicted with tourists. Brown was picked up at Ambleside by a young gentleman from Oxford anxious to show off his classical quotations, his uncle's carriage, and his genealogy traced from Edward I; and Keats complained of the "miasma of London." "The border inhabitants," he writes, "are quite out of keeping with the romance about them, from a continual intercourse with London rank and fashion. But why should I grumble? They let me have a prime glass of soda water—O they are as good as their neighbors. But Lord Wordsworth, instead of being in retirement, has himself and his house full in the thick of fashionable visitors quite convenient to be pointed at all the summer long."

This petulant allusion to Wordsworth was due to something of the Lost Leader feeling. Wordsworth was canvassing for the Lowthers, for the Tories against Reform. "What think you of that?" wrote Keats. "Wordsworth versus Brougham! Sad—sad—sad—and yet," he adds with his usual justice of mind, "the family has been his friend always."

Wordsworth was, in fact, at Lowther Hall, when Keats and Brown climbed up to visit him at Rydal Mount, so that there was nothing to be done but to write a note and stick it up over Dorothy Wordsworth's portrait and to admire the view from the parlour window.

Earlier that morning they had visited the waterfall at Ambleside, which gave Keats "a pleasant twinge." Then after a "Monstrous Breakfast" came the call on Wordsworth, and they turned their faces north once more. They passed Rydal and Grasmere, observing the "ancient woman seated on Helm crag," and slept the night at Wytheburn, where it began to drizzle, and there were fleas in the beds. It was too wet next morning to go up Helvellyn, so they went on to Keswick, where they were much struck with the approach to Derwent Water, with its "nest" of wooded mountains.

This must have been an exceedingly energetic day, for they walked eight miles into Keswick for breakfast, after which they did a complete circuit of Derwent Water, which is about ten or twelve miles. Here they visited the Falls of Lodore, which Keats describes as oozing "out from a cleft in perpendicular rock, all fledged with Ash and other beautiful trees," an expression which he used later in the *Ode to Psyche*:

> "Far, far around shall those dark-cluster'd trees
>   Fledge the wild ridged mountains steep by steep."

Keats must have been quite fairly athletic at this time. Brown records that he scrambled down the waterfall at Ambleside "lightly and quickly," adding ruefully, "but I never was a sure-footed beast." And at Lodore he endeavoured to reach the summit, which is no mean climb. "I had an easy climb among the streams, about the fragments of Rocks," he writes to Tom, "and should have got I think to the summit, but unfortunately I was damped by slipping one leg into a squashy hole." Undeterred by a twenty-mile walk and the visit to Lodore, when they once more reached Keswick, they set out again to see the "Druid Temple," about two miles out along the road to Penrith. After which they went to bed rather fatigued, but got up at four in order to climb Skiddaw before breakfast. There is a pleasant mixture of romantic poetry and matter-of-fact prose in Keats's description: "All felt, on arising into the cold air, that same elevation which a cold bath gives one. I felt as if I were going to a Tournament."

From Keswick they walked on to Ireby, a small market town hidden in the folds of the Cumberland hills. There they chanced upon a village dancing class, where the little sons and daughters of the neighbouring farmers were jumping and twirling away in the energetic north-country dances, taking no notice of the two strange gentlemen from London. "There was as fine a row of boys and girls as you ever saw;" wrote Keats, "some beautiful faces and one exquisite mouth. I never felt so near the glory of Patriotism, the glory of making by any means a country happier. This is what I like better than scenery."

After a night at Carlisle they took the coach to Dumfries, where they dined, saw Burns's tomb and had their first taste of whisky, which in those days does not seem to have penetrated to the south. "Very smart stuff it is—" comments Keats, "mixed like our liquors, with sugar and water, 'tis called toddy; very pretty drink and much praised by Burns."

But, apart from the whisky, Scotland did not make a very favourable impression on him.

"The town, the churchyard, and the setting sun,
    The Clouds, the trees, the rounded hills all seem
    Though beautiful, cold—strange—as in a dream,"

are the opening lines of his sonnet on Burns's tomb, and
he adds: "This Sonnet I have written in a strange
mood half-asleep. I know not how it is, the Clouds, the
Sky, the Houses, all seem anti-Grecian and anti-Charle-
magnish." "Keats," writes Brown, "has been for five
hours abusing the Scotch and their country. He says
that the women have large, splay feet, which is too true
to controvert, and that he thanks Providence he is not
related to a Scot, nor any way connected with them."
Since Brown himself was of Scotch extraction, Keats was
presumably teasing him, and as for the "large splay
feet," he certainly retracted his opinion a little later, for
when Brown objected to the Scotch women not wearing
shoes and stockings, he adds: "Keats was of the opposite
opinion, and expatiated on the beauty of the human
foot that had grown without natural restraint, and on
the beautiful effect of colour when a young lassie's foot
was on the green grass."

The two travellers had much pleasure in the lovely
country of the Lowlands as they travelled slowly on
from Dumfries to Dalbeattie, to Kirkcudbright, to
Newton Stewart, and to Stranraer. They were both
particularly struck with the view of Kirkcudbright as
they approached it, and indeed, with its blue bay, its
distant hills and the fresh, young green of the valley
cornfields, it is a singularly lovely one. As they walked,
Brown told Keats the story of *Guy Mannering*, which the
latter had never read, and when they sat down to a picnic
breakfast in a little spot close to the path, "among
fragments of rock, and brambles and broom . . . most
tastefully ornamented with a profusion of honeysuckle,

wild-roses, and fox-glove, 'Here,' exclaimed Keats, 'must Meg Merrilees often have boiled her kettle!'" He pulled his pen and ink and paper out of his knapsack after breakfast, and in his letter to his little sister Fanny he wrote the impromptu ballad beginning:

> "Old Meg she was a Gipsey
> And lived upon the Moors
> Her bed it was the brown heath turf
> And her home was out of doors"

to be followed a day later by the charming nonsense lines:

> "There was a naughty Boy
> A naughty boy was he
> He would not stop at home
> He could not quiet be."

Both he and Brown were beginning to find more good in the Scotch. "For two days," writes Brown, "we had been admiring the people's neatness of attire, their civility, and their intelligence, both in feature and speech—for I conversed with all I could." But Keats's opinion of Scotland was not wholly favourable. For instance, he writes from Ireland, to which he and Brown crossed over from Portpatrick for a very short time: "I can perceive a great difference in the nations from the Chambermaid at this nate Inn kept by Mr. Kelly. She is fair, kind and ready to laugh, because she is out of the horrible dominion of the Scotch Kirk. A Scotch girl stands in terrible awe of the Elders—poor little Susannas—They will scarcely laugh—they are greatly to be pitied and the Kirk is greatly to be damn'd. These Kirkmen have done Scotland good (Query?) they have made Men, Women, Old men, Young Men, old Women, young women, boys, girls and infants all careful." (Keats was perhaps thinking of an incident which took

L

place at Dalbeattie, a small town near Dumfries, recorded by Brown as follows: "A chubby urchin stared in alarm at the strangers, and, when called a 'fat pig,' he cried and screamed till he brought out an old 'wifie' upon us. She was 'nae pleased to see bairns made game of.' Atonement was made by sixpence in the child's hand— his plump fingers closed over it with a true Scotch grasp, tight as the claw of a lobster; and off he went to take his place in a formal circle of children, who were amusing themselves by sitting down with their hands before them, in perfect silence—no wonder they grow up to be such staid men and women.") "They are formed into regular Phalanges of savers and gainers," Keats's letter continues, "such a thrifty army cannot fail to enrich their Country and give it a greater appearance of comfort than that of their poor irish neighbours— There Kirkmen have done Scotland harm—they have banished puns and laughing and Kissing (except in cases where the very danger and crime must make it very fine and gustful.) I shall make a full stop at Kissing for after that there should be a better paren*t* thesis: and go on to remind you of the fate of Burns. Poor unfortunate fellow—his disposition was Southern—how sad it is when a luxurious imagination is obliged in self defence to deaden its delicacy in vulgarity, and not in things attainable that it may not have leisure to go mad after things which are not. No Man in such matters will be content with the experience of others—It is true that out of suffrance there is no greatness, no dignity; that in the most abstracted Pleasure there is no lasting happiness: yet who would not like to discover over again that Cleopatra was a Gipsey, Helen a Rogue and Ruth a deep one? I have not sufficient reasoning faculty to settle the doctrine of thrift—as it is consistent with the dignity of human Society—with the happiness of Cottagers—

All I can do is by plump contrasts—Were the fingers made to squeeze a guinea or a white hand?—Were the lips made to hold a pen or a Kiss? And yet in Cities Man is shut out from his fellows if he is poor, the Cottager must be dirty and very wretched if she be not thrifty—The present state of society demands this and this convinces me that the world is very young and in a very ignorant state—We live in a barbarous age. I would sooner be a wild deer than a Girl under the dominion of the Kirk, and I would sooner be a wild hog than be the occasion of a Poor Creatures pennance before those execrable elders."

Returning from Ireland, which they found too expensive, they wound their way up the West Coast, through the Vale of Glenap, till, emerging from it, they suddenly beheld Ailsa Rock, fifteen miles out to sea. "It came upon us like something supernatural," wrote Brown. And Keats, in his simple and more striking language: "Ailsa struck me very suddenly—really I was a little alarmed." It was raining when they saw it and there was the white line along the horizon, which gives Ailsa the peculiar effect of being perched a foot or two above sea-level. It gave Keats, as he says, "the complete Idea of a deluge," and moved him to write the sonnet on Ailsa Rock:

"Hearken thou craggy ocean pyramid,
 Give answer by thy voice the Sea fowl screams,"

which he considers "is the only Sonnet of any worth I have of late written." They slept at Ballantrae, where they had a very uncomfortable night (for the good reason that the landlord of the inn had just been arrested for robbing the Paisley Bank), and then went on to Ayr, which was one of the great objectives of Keats's pilgrimage, since it was Burns's native place. They crossed the Doon and stood some time on the narrow, grey-stone bridge, looking down the brown, transparent, shallow water, and taking a pinch of snuff on the keystone. They passed through Kirk Alloway and went on to the thatched one-storey crofter's cottage in which Burns was born. Here they drank a dram to the poet's memory with an old man who said he knew Burns, and whose presence and anecdotes depressed and disillusioned Keats. "One song of Burns's is of more worth to you," he wrote to Reynolds, "than all I could think of for a whole year in his native country.—His Misery is a dead weight upon the nimbleness of one's quill—I tried to forget it—to drink Toddy without any Care—to write a merry Sonnet—it won't do—he talked with Bitches— he drank with blackguards, he was miserable." "I wrote a sonnet," he says in the same letter, "for the mere sake of writing some lines under the Roof—they are so bad I cannot transcribe them." They are bad, but to such as have wandered through Wentworth Place, perhaps fingering the window sashes, or leaning on the mantel-piece and thinking, "Here his hands must have touched, here his elbow must have rested," there is a curious fascination to think of Keats in the low white-washed room of Burns's cottage writing:

"Yet can I stamp my foot upon thy floor,
     Yet can I ope thy window sash to find
The meadow thou hast tramped o'er and o'er."

Even in 1818 there were too many tourists on Loch Lomond. "Steam Boats on Loch Lomond and Barouches on its sides," wrote Keats, "take a little from the Pleasure of such romantic chaps as Brown and I." Nevertheless he found the blue-silvered water and the sun setting behind the dark purple mountains very lovely, and drew for Tom a quite recognizable little sketch of "that blue place among the Mountains," where he was "worldly enough to wish for a fleet of chivalry Barges with Trumpets and Banners just to die away before" him.

The following morning they again rose at four (all through this trip they kept the most horribly early hours; one is relieved to find Keats, back in Hampstead, still in bed at ten in the morning), and trudged ten miles up a "tremendous Glen." The "Rest and Be Thankful" was marked on their map, and they took it to be an inn at which they intended to breakfast, but when they reached the summit they found only a stone seat, with "Rest and Be Thankful" carved on it, which must have been a disillusioning experience.

The physical discomforts of the tour were beginning to take their toll. Brown's feet were hurting him badly and Keats was tormented with gad-fly stings. What was worse, the fare and accommodation were very coarse and poor. They lived chiefly on eggs and oatcake, the last of which they both disliked intensely. "I cannot manage the cursed Oatcake," writes Keats to Tom, and: "As for the Oat-cakes," writes Brown, "I was once in despair about them. I was not only too dainty, but they absolutely made me sick. With a little gulping I can manage them now."

The west of Argyllshire is even now an open and barren country; and in those days it must have been deserted indeed. "It's a far cry to Loch Awe," used to be the Campbell boast, when they challenged their enemies to follow them into their green hill stronghold. Keats notices what is still characteristic of the Highlands: the intense, pure silence, only broken by the sound of running water. He also gives a vivid picture of passing through Glencroe on a misty morning and hearing the sounds of shepherds, sheep and dogs on the heighths close above them, yet seeing nothing "till two came in sight creeping among the Craggs like Emmets."

In 1773 Boswell gave a description of an inn in the Highlands: "The house here was built of thick turfs and thatched with thinner turfs and heath. It had three rooms in length, and a little room projected. Where we sat, the side walls were *wainscotted*, as Dr Johnson said, with wands very well plaited. . . . The rooms had some deals laid as a kind of ceiling. There were two beds in the room. A woman's gown was hung on a rope to make a curtain of separation between them. . . . We had much hesitation whether to undress or lie down with our clothes on. I said at last, ' I'll plunge in! I shall have less room for vermin to settle about me when I strip! ' "

It is interesting to compare this account with Keats's written forty-five years later: "I cannot give you a better idea of Highland Life than by describing the place we are in—The Inn or public is by far the best house in the immediate neighbourhood—It has a white front with tolerable windows—the table I am writing on surprises me as being a nice flapped Mehogany one; at the same time the place has no watercloset nor anything like it." ("It is strange how rare that convenience is amongst us," comments Boswell wistfully, whereat Mr. Johnson "laughed heartily and said, ' You take very good care of one end of a man, but not of the other.' ") "You may," continues Keats, "if you peep see through the floor chinks into the ground rooms. The old Grandmother of the house seems intelligent though not over clean, N.B. No snuff being to be had in the village she made us some. The Guid Man is a rough looking hardy stout Man who I think does not speak so much English as the Guid wife who is very obliging and sensible and moreover though stockingless has a pair of old Shoes—

Last night some Whisky Men sat up clattering Gaelic
till I am sure one o'Clock to our great annoyance—
There is a Gaelic testament on the Drawers in the next
room—White and blue China ware has crept all about
here. Yesterday there passed a Donkey laden with tin-
pots—opposite the Window there are hills in a Mist—a
few Ash trees and a mountain stream at a little distance—
They possess a few head of Cattle—If you had gone
round to the back of the House just now—You would
have seen more hills in a Mist—some dozen wretched
black Cottages scented of peat smoke which finds its way
by the door or a hole in the roof—a girl here and there
barefoot. There was one little thing driving Cows down
a slope like a mad thing—there was another standing
at the cowhouse door rather pretty fac'd all up to the
ankles in dirt."

But the discomforts of the mainland were as nothing
to those of the island of Mull. They had thought at
first to abandon their plan of visiting Staffa and Iona,
as the seven guineas it cost was beyond their slender
means, but they were persuaded to do it a cheaper way,
by ferrying over to Mull and walking the thirty-seven
miles across the lower half of that island. It must have
been a terrific walk: "Thirty-seven miles of jumping and
flinging over great stones along no path at all, up the
steep and down the steep, and wading thro' rivulets up
to the knees, and crossing a bog, a mile long, up to the
ancles," is how Brown describes it. They slept the night
in their clothes in a shepherd's cottage, where the peat-
smoke filled every cranny, and the next morning set off
in bad weather for the islands of Iona and Staffa.

They came first to Iona, where they must have looked
nearly as queer a pair of travellers as those two who had
landed forty-five years previously: the gallant, corpulent,
twitching old gentleman, who refused to be carried to

shore by the boatmen, but dashed valiantly into the sea, and the short, dapper little Scotch lawyer who insisted on shaking hands cordially after they landed, thinking to himself: "What an addition was it to Icolmkill to have the Rambler upon the spot!"

Keats and Brown, who were very conscientious sight-seers (there is hardly an abbey or a castle that they missed on their tour), were duly shown round by the tiny little schoolmaster, Allan Maclean, and saw the nunnery, the Cathedral, the crosses with their curious, intricate, curving designs, and the burying-place of the sixty-one kings; and Keats, like Boswell, picked up some of the Icolmkill pebbles in order to take them back to his sister Fanny, who had a liking for stones and pebbles, imitation gems and pretty seals.

There was luckily a break in the bad weather which enabled them to land at Staffa, which he describes to Tom as follows: "One may compare the surface of the Island to a roof—this roof is supported by grand pillars of basalt standing together as thick as honey-combs. The finest thing is Fingal's Cave—it is entirely a hollowing out of Basalt Pillars. Suppose now the Giants who rebelled against Jove had taken a whole Mass of black Columns and bound them together like bundles of matches—and then with immense Axes had made a cavern in the body of these columns—of course the roof and floor must be composed of the broken ends of the Columns—such is Fingal's Cave except that the Sea has done the work of excavations and is continually dashing there—so that we walk along the sides of the cave on the pillars which are left as if for convenient Stairs—the roof is arched somewhat gothic wise and the length of some of the entire side pillars is 50 feet—About the island you might seat an army of Men each on a pillar. The length of the Cave is 120 feet and from its

extremity the view into the sea through the large Arch
at the entrance is very grand—the colour of the columns
is a sort of black with a lurking gloom of purple therein—
For solemnity and grandeur it far surpasses the finest
Cathedrall—At the extremity of the Cave there is a
small perforation into another cave, at which the waters
meeting buffetting each other there is sometimes produced a report as of a cannon heard as far as Iona which
must be 12 Miles."

The "Giants who rebelled against Jove" are the first
mention we have of the subject of *Hyperion*, and perhaps
the description of Enceladus's voice:

> "The ponderous syllables, like sullen waves
>   In the half-glutted hollows of reef-rocks
>   Came booming thus,"

is a reminiscence of the sound of the waters in Fingal's
Cave. It is certainly an onomatopœic description of them.

Keats caught a bad cold "bog-trotting in Mull,"
which turned into a feverish sore throat which was to
haunt him for many months. Whether this was the
beginning of his consumption is a difficult question. He
must have absorbed the tubercle bacilli from his brother
Tom, but whether he had already done so at Teignmouth
and the hardships and strain of this tour helped to
develop them, or whether he, coming back to Tom
feverish and under par, was then a ready prey for the
bacilli, which must have been only too contagious in
the small rooms they shared at Hampstead, it is impossible to say. From the healthy state he was in at the
beginning of the tour and the amount of exertion he
was able to undergo, it does not seem very likely that he
was already infected. The general opinion is that the
tuberculosis began with this "haunting sore throat."
But one leading medical authority who has made a

special study of Keats's health disagrees with this diagnosis.[1] He thinks that the sore throat may have been due to inflammation in or around the teeth. Keats certainly, on his return to London, complained of "a confounded toothache." But whatever the cause of his ailment, it left him too unwell and feverish to continue the tour. He had strength enough to climb Ben Nevis, though in speaking of the descent he says: "I felt it horribly. 'Twas the most vile descent—shook me all to pieces." And when they reached Inverness the physician there thought him "too thin and fevered to proceed."

There were letters waiting for him at Inverness. There was one from his sister Fanny, telling him she did not wish to leave her school, that her canary was dead and that she wanted a flageolet; and, more important, one from Dilke saying that Tom was much worse. Keats, therefore, took ship at Cromarty, and after a voyage of nine days—twice as long as it now takes to cross the Atlantic—he arrived in London. Mrs. Dilke records that: "John Keats arrived here (at Wentworth Place) last night, as brown and as shabby as you can imagine; scarcely any shoes left, his jacket all torn at the back, a fur cap, a great plaid, and his knapsack. I cannot tell what he looked like." He sank into a stuffed chair, exclaiming: "Bottom, Bottom, how thou art translated!"

This tour really marks a division in John Keats's life. Hitherto there had been suffering, discouragement and melancholy. "I scarcely remember counting upon any happiness," he wrote to Bailey, and:

> "To Sorrow
> I bade good morrow
> And thought to leave her far away behind,

[1] *See* Appendix II.

> But cheerly, cheerly,
> She loves me dearly—
> She is to me so constant and so kind—
> I would deceive her
> And so leave her—
> But Ah! she is too constant and too kind."

But the hues of life had not been entirely sombre. He had had health and strength, good friends, a large capacity for enjoyment, a knowledge of his own genius and hope for the future. No young poet is ever happy, but he was as happy as most—at times happier. But from this time onward it is all dark.

His first sorrow was the death of Tom. The poor boy was very ill when he got back. He lingered on from the middle of August till the end of November. He was weak and in the intensely nervous state that is a symptom of tuberculosis. He could hardly bear his sister to visit him; it upset him even to speak of George and Georgiana and of their future child. "Tom is rather more easy than he has been," John wrote to them, "but is still so nervous that I cannot speak to him of these Matters—indeed it is the case I have had to keep his Mind aloof from feelings too acute that has made this Letter so short a one—I did not like to write before him a Letter he knew was to reach your hands—I cannot even now ask him for any Message—his heart speaks to you."

His brother John, who nursed him with tender, unremitting devotion, was his only comfort, all these three months he scarcely left him.

"My Brother Tom gets weaker every day," he wrote to Mr. Richards in October, "and I am not able to leave him for more than a few hours." But it was a terrible strain on the elder boy, who was, though he did not know it, already ill himself. "I wish I could say Tom was any better," he wrote to Dilke. "His identity presses upon me so all day that I am obliged to go out—and although I intended to have given some time to study alone I am obliged to write, and plunge into abstract images to ease myself of his countenance his voice and feebleness—so that I live now in a continual fever—it must be poisonous to life although I feel well."

At last the end came. There was a warning note to Fanny at school, ending: "Keep up your spirits for me my dear Fanny—repose entirely in Your affectionate Brother, John." But by the time she received it, the youngest brother, the one who looked most like her and had been her playmate at Edmonton, had loosened his frail hold on life. Tom died early in the morning of December 1st. "The last days of poor Tom were of the most distressing nature," Keats wrote to George and Georgiana, "but his last moments were not so painful and his very last was without a pang. I will not enter into any parsonic comments on death—yet the common observations of the commonest people are as true as their proverbs. I have scarce a doubt of immortality of some nature or other—neither had Tom."

That cold December morning John Keats walked the few hundred yards between Well Walk and Wentworth Place and came into Brown's bedroom, awakening him by pressing his hand. Brown's warm and living grasp, his silence and the knowledge of his rock-like affection must have been a comfort to Keats then. At last Brown spoke and said, with characteristic common sense: "Have nothing more to do with those lodgings—and alone too! Had you not better live with me?" And from that time Keats came to live at Wentworth Place.

The project may have been discussed before, since Brown often took paying guests, but it was a fortunate circumstance for Keats. His nerves were very shattered by Tom's illness and the constant attendance on him. Shortly after Tom's death Dilke shot a white rabbit in the garden (the sporting proclivities of the Hampstead set must have been fascinating; on another occasion Keats went out shooting on the Heath and accounted for a tomtit. "There were as many guns abroad as Birds," he records). Keats, according to Dilke, insisted so strongly that this rabbit was Tom's spirit come back to visit him, that not only did he not partake of it himself, but when it came up at the dinner-table no one else was able to touch it. This is really very unlike the essentially sane-minded Keats. He was, in fact, suffering from a nervous breakdown; and aggravated as they were by ill-health and emotional excitement, his nerves never recovered their stability again.

It makes all the more remarkable to read of the firmness with which he was enabled to meet the attacks which, at this time, just before Tom's death, were launched in the press.

CHAPTER XII

The press of the early nineteenth century—Political passions—
Attacks on Leigh Hunt—"Blackwood's" attack on Keats—The
"Quarterly's" attack on Keats—Keats's attitude to the reviews.

NEWSPAPER attacks were, in no case, mere milk and water
affairs, in the early part of the Nineteenth Century. We
have seen what Leigh Hunt's comments on the Regent
could be like and here are a few sentences from the
article in which he takes on Sheridan:

"We laugh at the idolatries of a mob of heathens,
who could worship an insect, an onion or a stone; but
here is a man, a polished man in a polished country, a
wit, a senator, nay, a public satirist, who has bartered
his liberty like the veriest slave on the coast of Guinea
for something that turns his head; who has passed his
whole life in worshipping a red liquor enclosed in a
coarse kind of glass; and for the pleasure of being
slapped on the shoulders and called 'a mad wag' has
sacrificed the last comfort and honour of his old age."

Hazlitt, writing on Southey, is even more vitriolic:

"As some persons bequeath their bodies to the surgeons to be dissected after their death, Mr. Southey
publicly exposes his mind to be anatomised while he is
living. He lays open his character to the scalping knife,
guides the philosophic hand in its painful researches,
and on the bald crown of our petit tondu, in vain concealed under withered bay-leaves and a few contemptible grey hairs." (It is interesting that Keats, certainly
more civilized than his contemporaries, wrote in a letter
to Hunt: "I must mention Hazlitt's Southey, O that he
had left out the 'grey hairs!'") you see the organ of
vanity triumphant—sleek, smooth, sound, perfect, pol-

ished, horned and shining, as it were in a transparency. This is the handle of his intellect, the index of his mind; ' the guide, the anchor of his purest thoughts, and soul of all his moral being; ' the clue to the labyrinth of all his tergiversations and contradictions; the medius terminus of his political logic."

"Political logic," that was the trouble; it was not Sheridan the playwright that Hunt was attacking, but Sheridan the friend of the Prince Regent; it was not Southey's poetry that Hazlitt was holding up to scorn, though he thought little enough of that, but his anti-revolutionary principles, his advocacy of Legitimacy and the cause of the Allied Sovereigns. Keats got into the trouble with the reviewers, not because his poetry was new and strange and romantic, but because he was a friend and so-called disciple of Leigh Hunt, and Leigh Hunt was a Liberal. It was as simple as all that.

The position, in 1818, was as follows. The chief Whig periodical in Scotland was the *Edinburgh Review*, published by Constable, and edited by Jeffrey. Its Tory rival was the *Quarterly*, also published by a Scotsman, but a Scotsman who had, in Johnson's phrase, found the "fairest prospect in Scotland the high road to London," John Murray. In 1817, William Blackwood, bookseller in Edinburgh, started another Tory review, with the intention both of upholding his party colours, and of rivalling his trade competitor, Constable. It started under the title of the *Edinburgh Monthly Magazine*, but after it had been threatened with failure, Blackwood changed his editors, placed his own name on the cover, and ran it under a sort of triple control of himself, John Wilson, and John Gibson Lockhart.

Wilson and Lockhart were both able and quite un-scrupulous literary satirists, and the first number of *Blackwood's* opened with an extraordinary virulence. It

contained a savage attack on Coleridge, the "Chaldee
Manuscript," which was a biting satire on contemporary
Edinburgh society in mock Biblical language, and the
first of a series of articles on the "Cockney School of
Poetry," i.e., Leigh Hunt and his friends, signed by an
anonymous Z, and headed by a quotation from one,
Cornelius Webb:

" Our talk shall be (a theme we never tire on)
  Of Chaucer, Spenser, Shakespeare, Milton, Byron,
  (Our England's Dante)—Wordsworth, Hunt, and Keats,
  The Muses' son of promise, and what feats
  He yet may do——"

 .The article contained the following passage: "The
extreme moral depravity of the Cockney School is
another thing which is for ever thrusting itself upon the
public attention, and convincing every man of sense
who looks into their productions, that they who sport
such sentiments can never be great poets. How could
any man of high original genius ever stoop publicly,
at the present day, to dip his fingers in the least of those
glittering and rancid obscenities which float on the
surface of Mr. Hunt's *Hippocrene*? His poetry is that of a
man who has kept company with kept-mistresses. He
talks indelicately like a tea-sipping milliner girl. Some
excuse for him there might have been, had he been
hurried away by imagination or passion. But with him
indecency is a disease, as he speaks unclean things from
perfect inanition. The very concubine of so impure a
wretch as Leigh Hunt would be to be pitied, but alas!
for the wife of such a husband! For him there is no
charm in simple seduction; and he gloats over it only
when accompanied with adultery and incest."

This attack was not only disgusting but outrageously
silly, for Hunt's private life was of the most blameless,

while the story of *Rimini* is a most milk and watery affair, summed up neatly enough by Z's own phrase, as a "genteel comedy of incest;" (it was only sister-in-law and brother-in-law at that!). Hunt retorted by publishing, in the *Examiner*, the following advertisement: "To Z. The writer of the article signed Z in *Blackwood's Edinburgh Magazine* for October 1817 is invited to send his address to the printer of the *Examiner* in order that Justice may be executed on the proper person." But the libellers were not going to come into the open, they retained their anonymity and continued to attack Hunt, who wisely declared he would take no further notice. Why this special savagery was directed against Hunt is not altogether clear. His own friends thought that it was because of his slighting treatment of Scott in the *Feast of the Poets*, which, in their infatuated loyalty, Scott's supporters were vindictively anxious to revenge. In any case, it was clear that not only Leigh Hunt, but any tarred with the same brush, were not likely to escape Blackwood's abuse. Not only were the names of Keats and Hunt printed in large type in the quotation from Cornelius Webb, but in the issue of May, 1818, in a letter from Z to Leigh Hunt, "King of the Cockneys," he is expressly referred to. Hunt is first ridiculed for the "ivy crown," "shed nodding over the eyes as it was fixed there by the delicate hand of young Mister Keats," an allusion to the "intercoronation" episode, and later, reference is made to that "magnificent chamber of yours at Lisson Grove, where amiable but infatuated bardling, Mister John Keats, slept on the night when he composed his famous Cockney Poem of :

'Him of the rose, the violet, and the spring,
    The social smile, *the charm for freedom's sake*,'

and other mighty masters of the Lyre."

M

Some efforts were made to prevent the attack. Lockhart's friend, Christie, who was working in London, met Keats in January, 1818, and wrote to Lockhart that he had been favourably impressed by him, to which Lockhart replied: "What you say of Keats is pleasing, and if you like to write a little review of him, in admonition of his ways and in praise of his natural genius I shall be greatly obliged to you." Later, Bailey, who was in Scotland, met Lockhart, and took the opportunity of explaining Keats's circumstances to him, his poverty, his former profession, and the fact that his friendship with Hunt was purely personal and not political. He ended up by asking Lockhart that none of this confidence should be used against Keats. Lockhart replied that it certainly should not be so used by *him*. Three weeks later the famous article appeared. Possibly Bailey, with his pomposity, was not an ideal advocate; perhaps Lockhart may have known of Keats's circumstances from other sources, but Bailey's confidences must have been fresh in his memory. In any case, to taunt a young man with having been an apothecary, and with being poor, seems to fall hardly into the domain of decent breeding, common humanity, or literary criticism.

Beginning by deploring the general prevalence of verse-writing: "our very footmen compose tragedies and there is scarcely a superannuated governess in the island that does not leave a roll of lyrics behind her in her band-box," *Blackwood's* goes on to attack Keats in particular. "This young man appears to have received from nature talents of an excellent, perhaps even of a superior order—talents which, devoted to the purposes of any useful profession, must have rendered him a respectable, if not an eminent citizen. His friends, we understand, destined him to the career of medicine, and he was bound apprentice some years ago to a worthy apothecary in town. But all has been undone by a sudden attack of the malady to which we have alluded. Whether Mr. John had been sent home with a diuretic or composing draught to some patient far gone in the poetical mania, we have not heard. This much is certain, that he has caught the infection, and that thoroughly. For some time we were in hopes, that he might get off with a violent fit or two; but of late the symptoms are terrible. The phrenzy of the '*Poems*' was bad enough in its way; but it did not alarm us half so seriously as the calm, settled, imperturbable drivelling idiocy of '*Endymion*.'"

And the review concludes as follows: "We venture to make one small prophecy, that his bookseller will not a second time venture £50 upon anything he can write. It is a better and wiser thing to be a starved apothecary than a starved poet; so back to the shop Mr. John, back to 'plasters, pills and ointment boxes,' &c. But, for Heaven's sake, young Sangrado, be a little more sparing of extenuatives and soporifics in your practice than you have been in your poetry."

Yet, in spite of the galling personalities of *Blackwood's*, or perhaps because of them, the *Quarterly's* is the more damaging review of the two. *Blackwood's* is so personal, and so obviously determined to have its fling at Hunt, that its bitter satire seems suspect. John Wilson Croker, the writer of the *Quarterly* review, does not indulge in the light-hearted pleasantries of *Blackwood's*, but pulls *Endymion* to pieces as if it were a grammatical exercise sent up to a pedantic headmaster. Neither reviewer can see anything of the richness, the abundance and the gleams of real, if immature, poetry that illuminate the verse. Croker, moreover, attempts to turn the avowals of the preface against Keats, an error which one might have thought could have been avoided by any critic of the most ordinary taste and sensibility. Nevertheless,

his criticism, while totally devoid of imagination, has
yet justice enough to be extremely damaging.

"Of the story," writes Mr. Croker, "we have been
able to make out but little. It seems to be mythological,
and probably relates to the loves of Diana and Endymion;
but of this, as the scope of the work has altogether
escaped us, we cannot speak with any degree of certainty,
and must therefore content ourselves with giving
examples of its diction and versification. And here again
we are perplexed and puzzled. At first it appeared to us
that Mr. Keats had been amusing himself and wearying
his readers with an immeasurable game at bouts rimés;
but, if we recollect rightly, it is an indispensable condition at this play that the rhymes, when filled up, shall
have a meaning; and our author, as we have already
hinted, has no meaning. He seems to us to write a line
at random, and then he follows not the thought excited
by this line, but that suggested by the *rhyme* with which
it concludes. There is hardly a complete couplet enclos-
ing a complete idea in the whole book. He wanders
from one subject to another, from the association, not of
ideas, but of sounds; and the work is composed of hem-
stichs which, it is quite evident, have forced themselves
upon the author by the mere force of the catchwords on
which they turn.

"We shall select, not as the most striking instance, but
as that least liable to suspicion, a passage from the opening of the poem.

> ' Such the sun, the moon,
> Trees old and young, sprouting a shady boon
> For simple sheep; and such are daffodils,
> With the green world they live in; and clear rills
> That for themselves a cooling covert make
> 'Gainst the hot season; the mid-forest brake

Rich with a sprinkling of fair musk rose blooms,
And such too is the grandeur of the dooms
We have imagined for the mighty dead,' etc.

Here it is clear that the word and not the idea, *moon*,
produces the simple sheep and their shady *boon*, and that
' the *dooms* of the mighty dead' would never have
intruded themselves except for the 'fair musk—rose
blooms.'"

The effect that these attacks had on Keats has been
the cause of much controversy. The prevailing opinion
of the time, fostered by *Adonais* and the couplet in *Don
Juan*, was that they killed him. What is more, all his
friends shared that belief, even those of them, such as
Brown, who knew his whole inner history and the
depression that his unhappy love wrought in his spirits.

Of course, the answer to the accusation is a simple
one. No newspaper article, however virulent, can produce tubercular bacilli in the lung. Nor does he appear
from his correspondence to have attached any weight to
these critical opinions. He wrote to Hessey his publisher
to thank him for a copy of the *Chronicle*, which included
a most excellent and well-judged letter, signed J.S.,
speaking of the *Quarterly* article as "an act of malice and
gross injustice." Keats refers to the letter as follows:
"I cannot but feel indebted to those Gentlemen who have
taken my part—As for the rest I begin to get a little
acquainted with my own strength and weakness.—
Praise or blame has but a momentary effect on the man
whose love of beauty in the abstract makes him a severe
critic on his own Works. My own domestic criticism has
given me pain without comparison beyond that what
Blackwood or the *Quarterly* could possibly inflict, and also
when I feel I am right, no external praise can give me
such a glow as my own solitary reperception and rati-

fication of what is fine. J.S. is perfectly right in regard to the slip-shod *Endymion*. That it is so is no fault of mine. —No!—though it may sound a little paradoxical. It is as good as I had power to make it—by myself. Had I been nervous about its being a perfect piece, & with that view asked advice, & trembled over every page, it would not have been written; for it is not in my nature to fumble—I shall write independantly.—I have written independantly *without Judgement*.—I may write independantly, & *with Judgement* hereafter. The Genius of Poetry must work out its own salvation in a man: It cannot be matured by law and precept, but by sensation and watchfulness in itself. That which is creative must create itself—In *Endymion*, I leaped headlong into the Sea, and thereby have become better acquainted with the Soundings, the quicksands, and the rocks, than if I had stayed upon the green shore, and piped a silly pipe, and took tea & comfortable advice.—I was never afraid of failure; for I would sooner fail than not be among the greatest."

Richard Woodhouse also wrote to him burning with righteous indignation: "God help the Critic, whoever he be!" he writes. "He is as ignorant of the rudiments of his own craft as of the Essentials of English poetry." To which Keats answered:

"MY DEAR WOODHOUSE,—Your letter gave me a great satisfaction; more on account of its friendliness, than any relish in that matter in it which is accounted so acceptable in the ' genus iritabile.' "

He then goes on to outline his views on the poetical character, which have been already quoted, and continues:

"In the second place I will speak of my views, and of the life I purpose to myself. I am ambitious of doing the world some good: if I should be spared that may be the work of maturer years—in the interval I will assay to reach to as high a summit in Poetry as the nerve bestowed upon me will suffer. The faint conceptions I have of Poems to come brings the blood frequently into my forehead. All I hope is that I may not lose all interest in human affairs—that the solitary indifference I feel for applause even from the finest Spirits, will not blunt any acuteness of vision I may have. I do not think it will —I feel assured I should write from the mere yearning and fondness I have for the Beautiful even if my night's labours should be burnt every morning, and no eye ever shine upon them."

Finally, he wrote to George and Georgiana: "There have been two letters in my defence in the *Chronicle* and one in the *Examiner*, coppied from the *Alfred Exeter* paper and written by Reynolds." (Reynolds wrote a warm defence of Keats's poetry, which was published in the *Alfred*, a West Country newspaper. Leigh Hunt rightly judging that he would do Keats's cause more harm than good by his support, confined himself to reprinting part of Reynolds's article in the *Examiner*.)—"I don't know those in the *Chronicle*—This is a mere matter of the moment—I think I shall be among the English Poets after my death. Even as a Matter of present interest the attempt to crush me in the *Quarterly* has only brought me into notice and it is a common expression among book men ' I wonder the *Quarterly* should cut its own throat.' It does me not the least harm in Society to make me appear little and rediculous: I know when a Man is superior to me and give him all due respect—he will be the last to laugh at me and as for the rest I feel that I make an impression upon them which insures me personal respect while I am in sight whatever they may say when my back is turned."

This is obviously genuine. Keats was proud, and

might well have endeavoured to conceal his humiliation from his friends had he felt humiliated, but he is speaking from a plane far above such considerations. He speaks with the consciousness of the artist who knows the value of his own work and to whom anything else is utterly indifferent. It is a pride almost above any other, and it echoes, without blasphemy, the words of the Jewish God: "I am that I am." In his correspondence he hardly ever mentions the reviews again. He is said once, when he was very ill, to have said to Reynolds or to Brown: "If I die you must ruin Lockhart," but we do not know the intonation with which the words were spoken; it may even have been a grim little jest. None the less, I do not think we can assume that the reviews had no effect on him. No artist, no man, can like to feel himself completely misunderstood, even if he never loses faith in himself. From another point of view it crippled his hopes of depending on literature as a livelihood. In spite of his brave words to George, the reviews had a most damaging effect on his sales, and for a young man with little money, a young man, moreover, anxious to marry, the prospect was a gloomy one. Above all, it shut away from him an avenue of escape During the next two years things were to go very badly for Keats, and wherever he looked there was gloom and disappointment. His health, his love, his financial affairs, what pleasure were there in these? And though he could, for a little, escape on the "viewless wings of poesy," *Blackwood's* and the *Quarterly* had effectually poisoned all the environs, the attendant thoughts and hopes that might have encouraged him in pleasant speculations. "O," he wrote from Naples, about three months before he died, "that something fortunate had ever happened to me or my brothers!—then I might hope,—but despair is forced upon me as a habit."

*

CHAPTER XIII

*Falling in love—" Charmian"—Fanny Brawne—Keats's attitude
towards her—Her character and her feelings for him—" La Belle
Dame sans Merci."*

THE reviews were, however, very far from being Keats's
chief preoccupation in the winter of 1818-19 When he
returned from his Scottish tour, in spite of Tom's illness,
in spite of his absorption in *Hyperion*, which he had
begun to work on, Keats was ripe for falling in love.
Any chance encounter with a beautiful woman stirred
him profoundly. Almost as soon as he got back he went
to call on the Reynolds, and there met their cousin, a
Miss Jane Cox, an heiress from India, by whom he was
immediately and powerfully attracted to the annoyance
and chagrin of the Misses Reynolds.

" She is not a Cleopatra," he wrote, describing Miss Cox
to Georgiana Keats, "but she is at least a Charmian. She
has a rich eastern look; she has fine eyes and fine manners.
When she comes into a room she makes an impression the
same as the Beauty of a Leopardess. She is too fine and
too conscious of her Self to repulse any Man who may
address her—from habit she thinks that nothing *particular*. I always find myself more at ease with such a
woman; the picture before me always gives me a life
and animation which I cannot possibly feel with anything inferior—I am at such times too much occupied in
admiring to be awkward or on a tremble. I forget myself entirely because I live in her. You will by this time
think I am in love with her; so before I go any further
I will tell you I am not—she kept me awake one Night
as a tune of Mozart's might do—I speak of the thing as

a passtime and an amuzement than which I can feel none deeper than a conversation with an imperial woman the very ' yes ' and ' no ' of whose Lips is to me a Banquet. I don't cry to take the moon home with me in my Pocket nor do I fret to leave her behind me. I like her and her like because one has no *sensations*—what we both are is taken for granted—You will suppose I have by this had much talk with her—no such thing—there are the Miss Reynoldses on the look out—They think I don't admire her because I do not stare at her—They call her a flirt to me—What a want of knowledge? She walks across a room in such a manner that a Man is drawn towards her with a magnetic Power. This they call flirting! they do not know things. They do not know what a Woman is. I believe tho' she has faults—the same as Charmian and Cleopatra might have had. Yet she is a fine thing speaking in a worldly way: for there are two distinct tempers in which we judge of things—the worldly, theatrical and pantomimical; and the unearthly, spiritual and etherial—in the former Buonaparte, Lord Byron and this Charmian hold the first place in our Minds; in the latter John Howard, Bishop Hooker rocking his child's cradle and you, my dear Sister are the conquering feelings. As a Man of the world I love the rich talk of a Charmian; as an eternal Being I love the thought of you. I should like her to ruin me, and I should like you to save me."

He wrote also to Reynolds on the same subject: "I never was in love—yet the voice and the shape of a Woman has haunted me these two days—at such a time when the relief, the feverous relief of Poetry seems a much less crime." ("At such a time" refers to Tom's grave illness.) "—This morning Poetry has conquered— I have relapsed into those abstractions which are my only life—I feel escaped from a new, strange, and threatening sorrow. And I am thankful for it—There is an awful warmth about my heart like a load of Immortality. Poor Tom—that woman—and Poetry were ringing changes in my senses."

But he was not to escape that new, strange, and threatening sorrow for long. Almost directly after he had encountered Miss Cox he went to the Dilkes's home and there met a Mrs. Brawne and her daughter Fanny. Mrs. Brawne was a widow, a charming, good hearted, motherly woman with two daughters and a son. While Charles Brown was in Scotland she had rented his house, and she was still a very near neighbour, since she was living at Elm Cottage, one of a block of four newly-built, plastered houses, looking out on what was then known as "the Road" and is now Rosslyn Hill. Her elder daughter, Fanny, was aged eighteen. She was a tiny creature, very graceful in all her movements, with a long pale face, attractive almond-shaped eyes and a gay, lively, flirtatious manner. She was nothing very extraordinary on the surface—just a pleasant, well-brought up girl of the middle class. She was not stupid, she read a great deal, although she thought but little of her attainments: "You may rate your powers that way as low as you please," she wrote to Fanny Keats, "but as I consider mine only worth three halfpence I dare say you won't think them lower than that—Don't suppose I ever open my lips about books before men at all clever and stupid men I treat too ill to talk to at all." In fact, from her letters, she seems to have had something of the same shrewd, lively, humorous intelligence that is characteristic of Jane Austen's nicest heroines. She seems to have had the same leisurely occupations, too; dressmaking: "Margaret" (her sister) "and I are red-hot to make a *chinks* gown apiece;" basket-work: "Heaven knows how you have got on with the allum

baskets but I am annoyed to death—I sent to a lady to
know the quantity of logwood I ought to put and her
answer was that she had never in her life mentioned
logwood to me but that cochineal would have the
same effect;" and pigeon-rearing: "I am quite in
despair about my pigeons, I believe they are the most
refractory pair in the Kingdom—they never lay more
than one egg and never make anything of that." Above
all, she had, as Miss Austen's heroines also had, her feet
firmly planted on the soil of this earth. She possessed
intelligence, a refreshing common sense, and deep feelings, but she was not romantic, neither in the worst or
the best sense of that much abused word. She could not
have had much comprehension of the Keats who wrote:
"I feel more and more every day, as my imagination
strengthens, that I do not live in this world alone but
in a thousand worlds. No sooner am I alone than shapes
of epic greatness are stationed around me, and serve my
Spirit the office which is equivalent to a King's body-
guard—then ' tragedy with scepter'd pall, comes sweep-
ing by.' According to my state of mind I am with
Achilles shouting in the Trenches, or with Theocritus
in the Vales of Sicily." Nevertheless, his subjugation
was instant and complete.

"Mrs. Brawne who took Brown's house for the
Summer still resides in Hampstead" he wrote to George
and Georgiana in December, 1819, "she is a very nice
woman—and her daughter senior is I think beautiful
and elegant, graceful, silly, fashionable and strange,
we have a little tiff now and then—and she behaves a
little better, or I must have sheered off." And again:
"Shall I give you Miss Brawne? She is about my height—
with a fine style of countenance of the lengthen'd sort
—she wants sentiment in every feature—she manages
to make her hair look well—her nostrils are fine—

though a little painful—her mouth is bad and good—
her Profil is better than her full-face which indeed is not
full but pale and thin without showing any bone—
Her shape is very graceful and so are her movements—
her Arms are good her hands badish—her feet tolerable
—she is not seventeen" (a mistake, she was actually
eighteen), "but she is ignorant—monstrous in her
behaviour flying out in all directions, calling people
such names—that I was forced lately to make use of the
term *Minx*—that is I think not from any innate vice but
from a penchant she has for acting stylishly. I am however tired of such style and shall decline any more of it.
She had a friend to visit her lately—you have known
plenty such—Her face is raw as if she was standing out
in a frost—her lips raw and seem always ready for a Pullet
—she plays the Music without one sensation but the feel
of the ivory at her fingers—She is a downright Miss
without one set off—We hated her and smoked her and
baited her, and I think drove her away—Miss B—thinks
her a Paragon of fashion, and says she is the only woman
she would change persons with—What a Stupe—She is
superior as a Rose to a Dandelion—When we went to bed
Brown observed as he put out the taper what an ugly old
woman that Miss Robinson would make—at which I
must have groan'd aloud for I'm sure ten minutes."

It is a pathetically revealing passage. Georgiana, at
least, should have diagnosed his condition from it. The
minute catalogue of looks and charms, with the painful
effort to appear unbiassed; the cavalier assumption of
free-will: "I am however tired of such style and shall
decline any more of it;" the jealousy of the unfortunate
female friend. Actually Keats fell head over ears in love
with Fanny Brawne at first sight. "I have, believe me,"
he wrote to her, "not been an age in letting you take
possession of me; the very first week I knew you I wrote

myself your vassal; but burnt the Letter as the very next time I saw you I thought you manifested some dislike to me. If you should ever feel for Man at the first sight what I did for you I am lost." After that events moved quickly. On December 22nd, he wrote a note of really unparalleled clumsiness to Mrs. Reynolds, excusing himself for not accepting her invitation for Christmas Day. He had only accepted another invitation, he wrote, because he had thought he would be in Hampshire, otherwise he would have kept in mind his old friends. "I will not speak of the proportion of pleasure I may receive at different Houses—that never enters my head—you may take it for a truth that I would have given up even what I did see to be a greater pleasure for the sake of old acquaintanceship—time is nothing—two years are as long as twenty——" He was plainly very agitated, and no wonder, for Mrs. Brawne's was the other house at which he dined, and it was probably on Christmas Day that he became engaged to Fanny. "Three years ago," she wrote to Keats's sister at Christmas, 1821, "was the happiest day I had ever then spent."

However happy Fanny may have been, her immediate circle looked on the event with gloom. "It is quite a settled thing between John Keats and Miss Brawne," wrote Dilke. "God help them. It's a bad thing for them. The mother says she cannot prevent it, and that her only hope is that it will go off. He don't like anyone to look at or to speak to her." It is hardly likely that Mrs. Brawne could have approved of her daughter getting engaged to a mercurial and unsuccessful young poet, with indifferent health and no money, but the general air of foreboding and ill-omen that hung over their engagement is curious. They were, after all, of suitable ages, of the same circle in society, and they were in love. Yet from the very first there were signs of strain and unhappiness. Unfortunately, we have very little evidence about what actually did occur and the relations between Keats and Fanny during the first year of their love. They were living extremely close to one another, so there is no correspondence between them, and since the engagement was kept the deepest secret, there are no direct references to it in Keats's other letters. Yet, from what we can read between the lines, it does not appear that he was as happy as a young man who has just been accepted by the girl he loves should be.

From the very first he did not accept love easily. The references that he makes to women in general in his letter to America, written directly after he became engaged, are not happy ones. (It must be remembered that he said nothing of his love to George and Georgiana, but in his letters it is often possible to deduce his particular state of mind from his general observations.) "The more we know," he wrote, less than a week after he had dined with Mrs. Brawne on Christmas Day, "the more inadequacy we discover in the world to satisfy us. . . . This same inadequacy is discovered (forgive me little George you know I don't mean to put you in the mess) in Women with few exceptions." And again: "I never forget you except after seeing now and then some beautiful woman—but that is a fever—the thought of you both is a passion with me but for the most part a calm one." This reads as if he thought himself an unwilling captive to Fanny's beauty. He thought of her as he had thought of Charmian, she evoked in him the temper of mind which he called "worldly, theatrical and pantomimical."

"I should like her to ruin me," he wrote of Charmian, and that is what he thought of Fanny Brawne; and since things are what we think them, he laid up a great store of unhappiness for himself.

He felt himself trapped, not so much by Fanny, but by love, and by his own nature. The "little thing" that he "wrote off to some Music as it was playing," whether consciously or unconsciously well illustrates his state of mind:

"I had a dove and the sweet dove died;
    And I have thought it died of grieving:
O what could it grieve for! it was tied
    With a silken thread of my own hands weaving;
Sweet little red-feet! why did you die—
    Why would you leave me, sweet dove! why?
You liv'd alone on the forest tree,
    Why, pretty thing! could you not live with me?
I kiss'd you oft, and gave you white peas,
    Why not live sweetly, as in the green trees?"

He loved her but he resented his own love. He saw her as a captor and himself as a victim; the thread by which she held him was a silken one but he was a captive none the less.

As for Fanny, we have not the slightest clue as to what her feelings were. It is difficult altogether to estimate what she was like. For one thing, we have no contemporary letter of hers. We do not know what she wrote to her lover or what she wrote about him. All we have is a packet of letters which, after Keats had left England, she wrote over a period of years to that little sister, also called Fanny, whom she was prepared to love for his sake. These letters show something of her character, but necessarily they do not show all. They are written to a girl much younger than herself, who was not very mature either in mind or character. We should have a very incomplete picture of John Keats if all we possessed were his letters to his sister.

The only other letter we have of Fanny Brawne's is the

draft of that famous one she wrote to Charles Brown when, in 1829, he wrote to ask her permission to publish the poems addressed to her by Keats. It has long been held against her, especially the one sentence: "I fear the kindest act would be to let him rest for ever in the obscurity to which unhappy circumstances have condemned him." Till the letters to Fanny Keats were discovered, Fanny Brawne was adjudged, on this letter, by many, to be hard and unloving; but even on this letter alone it seems to me a most harsh and presumptuous judgment. It is a most curious composition, written evidently in great agitation and distress of feeling, as if the secret of her love had been so locked up within herself, that the most gentle, the most ordinary approach to it shook her more than she could bear. It is the letter of a woman of very deep but inhibited feelings, such as are often found beneath that lively and flirtatious manner which is at once an attraction and a barrier to the outside world.

"I assure you," she writes, "I should not have hinted that your wishes were painful to me did I not feel the suffering myself to be even alluded to was a want of pride. So far am I from possessing overstrained delicacy that the circumstance of its being a mere love story is the least of my concern, on the contrary had I been his wife I should have felt my present reluctance would have been so much stronger that I think I must have made it my request that you would relinquish your intention. The only thing that saves me now is that so very few can know I am in any way implicated and that of those few I may hope the greatest number may never see the book in question. Do then entirely as you please and be assured that I comply with your wishes rather because they are yours than with the expectation of any good that can be done. I fear the

N

kindest act would be to let him rest for ever in the obscurity to which unhappy circumstances have condemned him. Will the writings that remain of his rescue him from it? You can tell better than I, and are more impartial on the subject for my wish has long been that his name, his very name could be forgotten by everyone but myself, that I have often wished most intensely. . . . Without claiming too much constancy for myself I may truly say that he is well-remembered by me and that satisfied with that I could wish that no one but myself knew he had ever existed but I confess as he was so much calumniated and suffered so much from it, it is perhaps the duty of those who loved and valued him to vindicate him also, and if it can be done, all the friends that time has left him and I above all must be deeply indebted to you."

Keats was also very reserved in certain ways, particularly about his engagement. "My friends have behaved well to me in every instance but one," he wrote to Fanny, "and there they have become tattlers, and inquisitors into my conduct: spying upon a secret I would rather die than share it with anybody's confidence." But there is a great difference in the quality of their reserve. Keats could hide a particular fact but he never attempted to hide himself. Fanny, except when sudden strong emotion literally forces her defences, seems to conceal her feelings even from herself. Witness the extreme inhibition of her way of expressing herself to Brown: "Without claiming too much constancy for myself, I may truly say he is well remembered by me." Keats, on the other hand is almost completely articulate, he has a singular gift of being able to recognize and to communicate his feelings, without false shame or affectation.

Yet it is remarkable that in all the letters which he

wrote to Fanny, of her personality we get not the slightest glimpse. It is significant of their relations that from thirty-nine letters written to her without any reserve we cannot form the faintest idea of what she was like. Keats loved her, but he loved her with the desperately selfish love of a very young man. To her he poured out everything, his hopes, his dreams, his fears, his passions, his thoughts and feelings, and he never thought of her feelings at all. Such selfishness in an older person would be repellant but in a young man of Keats's age it is natural and almost right. He is desperately trying to find himself and until he has done that he cannot think about her. The young cannot give, for they do not know what they have, instinctively and rightly they fear to part with something vital. A man must build his own character and discover himself before he has the right or the strength to be unselfish, and the more there is to discover the longer the process takes. From all ordinary standpoints Keats treated Fanny Brawne very badly but it was impossible for him not to do so.

His difficulties were increased by his suspicion and mistrust of women, and by conviction that she did not love him as he loved her. He may have been right. That she came to love him is unquestionable. "Dear Fanny," she wrote to his sister, three months after his death, "no one but you can feel with me—All his friends have forgotten him, they have got over the first shock, and that with them is all. They think I have done the same, which I do not wonder at, for I (have) taken care never to trouble them with any feelings of mine, but I can tell you who next to me (I must say *next* to me) loved him best, that I have not got over it and never shall— It's better for me that I should not forget him but not for you, you have other things to look forward to—and I would not have said anything about him for I was

affraid of distressing you but I did not like to write to
you without telling you how I felt about him and
leaving it to you whether the subject should be mentioned in our letters."

But at the beginning it was different. He must have
attracted her since she accepted him. She was doubtless
intrigued by him. She must have heard a great deal
about him from the Dilkes before she met him, and he
had the advantages of being revered in her own immediate circle and persecuted by the world at large, thus
satisfying the double feminine need of admiration for
her choice and desire to run counter to something. But
she had not his imaginative capacity; the wild anguished
passion he felt for her was not within the scope of a girl
of eighteen and perhaps at first she did not love him
very much.

The only outside account we have of her are the
reminiscences of a cousin who, as a young boy, used
to frequent Mrs. Brawne's house: "Miss Fanny
Brawne was very fond of admiration. I do not think
she cared for Keats, although she was engaged to him.
She was very much affected when he died because she
had treated him so badly. She was very fond of dancing,
and of going to the opera and to balls and parties. Miss
Brawne's mother had an extensive acquaintance with
gentlemen, and the society in which they mingled was
musical and literary. Through the Dilkes, Miss Brawne
was invited out a great deal, and as Keats was not in
robust health enough to take her out himself (for he
never went with her), she used to go with milatary men
to the Woolwich balls and to balls in Hampstead; and
she used to dance with those milatary officers a great
deal more than Keats liked. She did not seem to care
much for him. Mr Dilke . . . admired her very much
in society, and although she was not a great beauty she

was very lively and agreeable. I remember that among
those frequenting Mrs Brawne's house in Hampstead
were a number of foreign gentlemen. Keats could not
talk French as they could, and their conversation with
his fiancée in a language he could not understand was
a source of continual disagreement between them.
Keats thought that she talked and flirted and danced too
much with them, but his remonstrances were all unheeded by Miss Brawne."

No outside person can possibly say with confidence
what is the inner tempo of a love affair, especially in the
case of a girl like Fanny Brawne, determined instinctively,
at all costs, to conceal her feelings. And it would be
absurd to take the testimony of a boy of sixteen or
seventeen on that point; but the surface content of the
passage is probably true enough. The account of Fanny's
liveliness and animation tallies with all the descriptions
given of her including Keats's own two little pen
portraits. As for the foreign gentlemen there must have
been quite a little set of them. Fanny Keats eventually
married a Spaniard to whom she was introduced at the
Brawnes', and Fanny Brawne's own husband, whom she
married in 1832, was Louis Linden or Lindo, of Portuguese extraction. There is evidence, too, of the dancing,
not only in the *Ode to Fanny*:

"Save it for me, sweet love! though music breathe
 Voluptuous visions into the warm air;
 Though swimming through the dance's danger-
  ous wreath;"

but in the letter which, in February, 1819, he wrote to
Fanny Keats:—a letter which must strike one as pathetic
when the facts that lie behind it are known.

"Keep on reading and play as much on the music and
the grass plot as you can. I should like to take possession

of those Grass plots for a month or so . . . for I want
you to teach me a few common dancing-steps—and I
would buy a Watch box to practise them in by myself."

Poor Keats! It was the beginning of a long Purgatory,
but it was not Fanny's fault. She was only eighteen, and
he must have seemed and been extraordinarily unreason-
able. We have Dilke's testimony that: "He don't like
anyone to look at her or to speak to her." She can have
had no conception of the racking torment of physical
jealousy. If he had been older and more experienced he
might have known that, and have known that the more
innocent were her pleasures, the less likely she would be
to allow herself to be forced to give them up. But he did
not know it and he mistrusted her and love. It was the
April of this year that he wrote:

> "I met a lady in the meads,
>   Full beautiful—a færy's child,
> Her hair was long, her foot was light,
>   And her eyes were wild.
>
> "I made a garland for her head,
>   And bracelets too, and fragrant zone;
> She look'd at me as she did love,
>   And made sweet moan.
>
> "I set her on my pacing steed,
>   And nothing else saw all day long,
> For sidelong would she bend, and sing
>   A færy's song.
>
> "She found me roots of relish sweet,
>   And honey wild and manna dew,
> And sure in language strange she said—
>   ' I love thee true.'

"She took me to her elfin grot,
    And there she wept and sigh'd full sore,
And there I shut her wild wild eyes
    With kisses four.

"And there she lulled me asleep,
    And there I dream'd—Ah! woe betide!
The latest dream I ever dream'd
    On the cold hill side.

"I saw pale Kings and princes too,
    Pale warriors, death pale were they all;
They cried—'La Belle Dame sans Merci
    Hath thee in thrall.'"

CHAPTER XIV

*Life at Wentworth Place—The Brawnes come to live next door
—1819, the year of great poetry—The " Vale of Soul-making."*

WHEN the Dilkes left Hampstead for Westminster, in
order to be nearer their precious boy, Mrs. Brawne once
more moved into Wentworth Place, this time into the
larger half of the house, so that for many months Keats
and Fanny were under the same roof. She was still never
mentioned in the apparently unreserved affectionate
letters which he wrote to his brother and others at this
time, though reading between the lines one can occasionally infer her presence and Keats's preoccupation with her.
"The fifth canto of Dante pleases me more and more,"
he wrote in April, 1819—"it is the one in which he
meets with Paulo and Francesca—I had passed many
days in rather a low state of mind, and in the midst of
them I dreamt of being in that region of Hell. The
dream was one of the most delightful enjoyments I ever
had in my life—I floated about the whirling atmosphere
as it is described with a beautiful figure to whose lips
mine were joined as it seemed for an age—and in the
midst of all this cold and darkness I was warm—even
flowery tree-tops sprung up and we rested on them
sometimes with the lightness of a cloud till the wind
blew us away again—I tried a Sonnet upon it—there are
fourteen lines but nothing of what I felt—O that I could
dream it every night."

But it is only in sidelights like this that we gain a
glimpse of Keats's inner life. For the most part we have
only a placid chronicle of outside events, from which we
can reconstruct something of the life that went on in

that pleasant unpretentious two-storied house. In Keats's time Wentworth Place had a view right across to the Heath, to the hills of Highgate. One approaches the house across a green lawn on which still grows an ancient mulberry tree. The door directly facing one is up two or three steps, and on each side of it are long French windows, opening on to wrought-iron balconies, one of which was Mrs. Brawne's sitting-room and the other that of Charles Brown. To call on the Brawnes one would have mounted the steps to this front door and rapped on the shining brass knocker. To call on Mr. Brown or Mr. Keats one would have gone round to the left side of the house, where there was another outside door opening on to a narrow passage. Mr. Brown's sitting-room was on the right, Mr. Keats's on the left, with his picture of Shakespeare over the fireplace, ornamented by the tassels that his sister-in-law had embroidered for it. In the summer you might have found him by the long window opening on to the garden, sitting on one chair and propping his arm on another, reading "all day like a picture of somebody reading"; or in the winter, by the light of a wax taper, with a long snuff on it, sitting with his back to the nearly-extinguished fire, "with one foot rather askew upon the rug and the other with the heel a little elevated from the carpet," writing to George and Georgiana on a copy of the *Maid's Tragedy* by Beaumont and Fletcher, with two volumes of *Chaucer*, and *Tom Cribb's Memorial to Congress* strewn about on the untidy table; or perhaps you would have found him and Brown in the same room, "authorizing at different ends of the table." "Brown has been walking up and down the room a breeding," wrote Keats on one occasion, "now at this moment he is being delivered of a couplet—and I dare say will be as well as can be expected—Gracious— he has twins!"

It was, on the surface, a peaceful and uneventful existence, though there are occasional glimpses of suffering, as in the sonnet: "*Why did I laugh to-night?*" which he sent to George, with the comment that it was "written with no Agony but that of ignorance; with no thirst of anything but Knowledge when pushed to the point though the first steps to it were through my human passions—they went away and I wrote with my Mind—and perhaps I must confess a little bit of my heart."

The two lines of this sonnet:

"Verse, fame and Beauty are intense indeed
But Death intenser—Death is Life's high mead,"

show the preoccupation with the thought of death as "easeful" and a release, which now began to take hold of him. The will to die was slowly making itself felt, probably in consequence of his bodily health. He was stricken, though he did not know it. That disinclination for any kind of exertion which is one of the first symptoms of tuberculosis had already seized on him. "You will judge of my 1819 temper when I tell you that the thing I have most enjoyed this year has been writing an *Ode to Indolence*," he wrote to Miss Jeffrey; and to George and Georgiana: "Neither Poetry, nor Ambition, nor Love have any alertness of countenance as they pass by me: they seem rather like three figures on a Greek vase—a Man and two women whom no-one but myself could distinguish in their disguisement."

Nevertheless, in spite of disease, this year was the year of his flowering. In spite of disease, and yet perhaps because of it. It seems almost as if the combined play of circumstances, the seeds of weakness in himself, the scorn of the world, the experience of love, worked in him to produce a forced, unnatural but perfect blossoming 1819 was an unusually fine summer. "This is the third of May," he wrote, "and everything is in delightful forwardness; the violets are not withered before the peeping of the first rose." And the summer of his poetry resembled the summer of the year. Surely scarcely ever in the annals of poetry has there been such a blossoming. In January he wrote the *Eve of St. Agnes*, in February *The Eve of St. Mark*, in April *La Belle Dame sans Merci*, the *Ode to Psyche* and the *Ode to a Grecian Urn*. In May, lying out on the grass-plot under the plum-tree at Wentworth Place, he wrote the *Ode to a Nightingale*. Between July and September he wrote *Lamia*, in September the *Ode to Autumn*, and from September to December the greater part of the *Fall of Hyperion*.

It is not within the province of this book to discuss Keats's poetry from a technical point of view. Besides, as he wrote when he enclosed *Fancy* and *Bards of Passion* to George and Georgiana: "They will explain themselves—as all poems should do—without comment." Nevertheless, if it should be the feeling of any readers, as it is the feeling of many in this generation, that they are out of touch with the romantic poets, that there is something in the luxuriance of epithet, the conventionality of phrasing, the wealth of classical allusion, that does not strike home to them, that does not "bite" —let them take the 1820 volume of Keats's poetry and read the Odes over aloud. The *Eve of St. Agnes*, lovely as it is, may seem touched with sham mediævalism; *Isabella* may strike them, as it struck Keats, with being "mawkish" and "smokeable;" *Lamia*, technically perfect, may seem lacking in feeling, above all we may find it difficult to enjoy in these days the "poem that tells a story"; but in the odes we have, clear and untouched, a quality of sheer beauty, of pure poetry which leaves us marvelling.

With the composition of the odes Keats entered into a new phase of his poetical career. "The following poem," he writes, referring to the *Ode to Psyche*, "the last I have written is the first and only one with which I have taken even moderate pains. I have for the most part dash'd off my lines in a hurry. This I have done leisurely—I think it reads the more richly for it and will I hope encourage me to write other things in even a more peaceable and healthy spirit." In view of the numberless corrections and revisions shown on the manuscript of the *Eve of St. Agnes*, written four months before the *Ode to Psyche*, the statement that the latter was the first and only poem with which he had taken even moderate pains may seem surprising. There is scarcely a line in the *Eve of St. Agnes* which does not have some correction, but all these revisions and fresh starts were interpolated in hot blood as the poem was written. It seems probable that in the *Ode to Psyche* he had, for the first time, reached the second stage of creative art. In his extreme youth the artist depends almost entirely on inspiration; the things that come to him, the expression of those things seems to be almost beyond his control. It is as if some Power were working through him, and the result is often a curious mixture of good and bad, of strength and weakness. His best work at such a period may be incredibly good, and may be touched with a freshness and brilliance that is surprisingly moving, but if he is a true artist he will find the second stage infinitely more satisfactory. Then he is in command of his material. He can allow himself to pause between inspiration and expression. Envisaging what he has to achieve he knows that he bears within himself the power to achieve it. It is no more question of hit or miss but a slow steady bending of ability to reach a desired and certain goal.

Some critics have questioned whether his meeting

with Fanny Brawne, and his love for her encouraged or
retarded the growth of his great genius. Yet surely the
question answers itself when we see that he wrote all his
greatest poems in the year after he met her, most of them
when he was seeing her every day, living side by side
under the same roof. Nor did his nascent love affair
affect only his poetry. The experience of suffering,
perhaps the prescience of tragedy, were producing in
him a true spiritual maturity.

The following passage, in one of his American letters,
is the richest and the most philosophical sheaf of thoughts
that we ever are to have from him. It shows a spacious-
ness of mind and a nobility of intelligence which are
rare enough in any man. Age has perhaps little to do
with the ripening of the soul but it may be noted that
at this time he was only twenty-three.

"Man," he writes, "is originally ' a poor forked
creature ' subject to the same mischances as the beasts of
the forest, destined to hardships and disquietude of some
kind or other. If he improves by degrees his bodily
accommodations and comforts—at each stage at each
ascent there are waiting for him a fresh set of annoy-
ances—he is mortal and there is still a heaven with its
Stars above his head. The most interesting question that
can come before us is, How far by the persevereing
endeavours of a seldom appearing Socrates Mankind
may be made happy—I can imagine such happiness
carried to an extreme—but what must it end in?—
Death—and who could in such a case bear with death—
the whole troubles of life which are now frittered away
in a series of years, would then be accumulated for the
last days of a being who instead of hailing its approach,
would leave this world as Eve left Paradise. . . . The
common cognomen of this world among the misguided
and superstitious is ' a vale of tears ' from which we are

to be redeemed by a certain arbitrary interposition of God and taken to Heaven—What a little circumscribed straightened notion! Call the world if you Please ' The vale of Soul-Making.' Then you will find out the use of the world (I am speaking now in the highest terms for human nature admitting it to be immortal which I will here take for granted for the purpose of showing a thought which has struck me concerning it.) I say ' *Soul making* ' Soul as distinguished from an Intelligence —There may be intelligences or sparks of the divinity in millions—but they are not Souls till they acquire identities, till each one is personally itself. Intelligences are atoms of perception—they know and they see and they are pure, in short they are God—How then are Souls to be made? How then are these sparks which are God to have identity given to them—so as ever to possess a bliss peculiar to one's individual existence? How, but by the medium of a world like this? This point I sincerely wish to consider because I think it is a grander system of salvation than the chrystian religion—or rather it is a system of Spirit-creation—This is effected by three grand materials acting the one upon the other for a series of years. These three materials are the *Intelligence* —the *human heart* (as distinguished from intelligence or Mind) and the *World* or *Elemental space* suited for the proper action of *Mind and Heart* on each other for the purpose of forming the *Soul* or *Intelligence destined to possess the sense of Identity*. I can scarcely express what I but dimly perceive—and yet I think I perceive it—that you may judge the more clearly I will put it in the most homely form possible—I will call the *world* a School instituted for the purpose of teaching little children to read—I will call the *human heart* the *horn Book* used in that School—and I will call the *Child able to read, the Soul* made from that *School* and its *hornbook*. Do you not see

how necessary a World of Pains and troubles is to school
an Intelligence and make it a Soul? A Place where the
heart must feel and suffer in a thousand diverse ways!
Not merely is the Heart a Hornbook, it is the Minds
Bible, it is the Minds experience, it is the teat from
which the Mind or intelligence sucks its identity. As
various as the Lives of Men are—so various become their
Souls, and thus does God make individual beings,
Souls, Identical Souls of the Sparks of his own essence."

It seems to us, reading of this brief life, a tragedy that
pain and weakness and the heart's sufferings should have
been able to conquer a spirit like this. Yet if we meet
him on his own plane, who shall dare say what is or is
not necessary for the making of a soul?

CHAPTER XV

Keats and Rice spend the summer at Shanklin—Keats works at "Lamia" and "Otho the Great"—His letters to Fanny—His effort to escape from love—Financial troubles—Keats and Brown at Winchester.

ON the 8th of June, 1819, James Rice called upon Keats and suggested that they should spend a month in the Isle of Wight together. Keats, who had been waiting to get away to work both at *Lamia* and *Otho the Great*, agreed, and by the beginning of July they were installed at Shanklin.

The holiday was not a great success, though Rice was in many ways a delightful companion. There is a charming little description of him, given by Keats in a letter to his sister, where he writes: "He has a greater tact in speaking to the people of the village than I have, and in those matters is a great amusement as well as a good friend to me. He bought a ham the other day for says he 'Keats, I don't think a Ham is a wrong thing to have in a house.'" Unfortunately, Rice was in bad health, and this fretted Keats, whose nerves were not at all strong. Moreover, Shanklin did not suit him. "You should live in a dry, gravelly, barren elevated country, open to the currents of air," he wrote to his publisher, John Taylor, after he had removed to Winchester. "The neighbourhood of a rich inclosed fulsome manured arrable Land especially in a valley and almost as bad on a flat, would be almost as bad as the smoke of Fleet Street. Such a place was this Shanklin only open to the south east, and surrounded by hills in every other direction. From this south east came the damps from the sea which having no egress the air would for days together take on an unhealthy idiosyncrasy altogether enervating and weakening as a city Smoke—I felt it very much—Since I have been at Winchester I have been improving in health—it is not so confined—and there is on one side of the city a dry chalky down where the air is worth sixpence a pint." There are pages more in the same strain. The poor diseased lungs knew better than the doctors of that day; it is pathetic to read of them gasping for the mountain air which they needed and were never to have.

But the chief cause of his unhappiness was the parting from Fanny Brawne. In one of his own favourite phrases he "ached" to be near her; and yet he felt within himself traces of resentment that she had such power to make him unhappy. All men have a moment when they feel that they are trapped, when they first yield their independence to a woman, but a poet feels it above all. "I hope I shall never marry," Keats had written in the October of the previous year just after the episode of the lady from Hastings. "Though the most beautiful Creature were waiting for me at the end of a Journey or a Walk; though the carpet were of Silk, the Curtains of the morning Clouds; the chairs and Sofa stuffed with Cygnet's down; the food Manna, the Wine beyond Claret, the Window opening on Winander mere, I should not feel—or rather my happiness would not be so fine, as my Solitude is Sublime. Then instead of what I have described, there is a Sublimity to welcome me home. The roaring of the wind is my wife and the Stars through the window pane are my children."

Even now, as his love took stronger and stronger hold on him, we find these two threads continually twisted in it.

"I have never known any unalloy'd Happiness for

o

many days together;" he wrote in his first letter from Shanklin, "the death or sickness of some one has always spoilt my hours—and now when none such troubles oppress me, it is you must confess very hard that another sort of pain should haunt me. Ask yourself my love whether you are not very cruel to have so entrammelled me, so destroyed my freedom." It is written half jokingly and yet the basis of what he says he means for truth. And much as he longs for her—"I am miserable when you are not with me; or rather breathe in that dull sort of patience that cannot be called life,"—yet the thought of matrimony and of the ordinary routine of married life does not come easily to him. "I almost wish we were butterflies and live'd but three summer days," he wrote in his first letter; and again: "You absorb me in spite of yourself—you alone: for I look not forward with any pleasure to what is call'd being settled in the world; I tremble at domestic cares—yet for you I would meet them, though it would leave you the happier I would rather die than do so. I have two luxuries to brood over in my walks, your Loveliness and the hour of my death. O that I could have possession of them both in the same minute. I hate the world: it batters too much the wings of my self-will, and would I could take a sweet poison from your lips to send me out of it."

Fanny seems to have objected to this letter, perhaps she thought it exaggerated, but in the next, though it is calmer in tone, there is another reference to the same subject: "We might spend a pleasant year at Berne or Zurich—if it should please Venus to hear my 'Beseech thee to hear us O Goddess.' And if she should hear god forbid we should what people call, *settle*—turn into a pond, a stagnant Lethe—a vile crescent, row or buildings. Better be imprudent moveables than prudent fixtures. Open my Mouth at the Street Door like the Lion's head

at Venice to receive hateful cards Letters messages. Go
out and wither at teaparties; freeze at dinners; bake at
dances, simmer at routs. No my love, trust yourself to
me and I will find you nobler amusements, fortune
favouring."

He was more than right, of course—"settling" was
not for him; but he must have been a difficult lover for
an ordinary, well-brought-up girl of the middle-class.
Things were not going altogether well between them.
Keats wrote in this letter: "So you intend to hold me to
my promise of seeing you in a short time. I shall keep
it with as much sorrow as gladness: for I am not one of
the Paladins of old who lived upon water grass and smiles
for years together." Fanny seems to have resented this, for
in the next letter we find: "You seem offended at a little
simple, innocent, childish playfulness in my last. I did
not seriously mean to say that you were endeavouring
to make me keep my promise." Keats is writing dis-
ingenuously here. The first letter was not playful; he
saw Fanny as a temptation, a far too sweet temptation

> "The fly that sips treacle is lost in the sweets
> And he who tastes Woman, Woman, Woman,
> Ruin meets."

That was his attitude towards her and indeed in his next
letter to Taylor he uses a very similar phrase to Mac-
heath's. "I equally dislike," he writes, "the favour of
the public with the love of a woman—they are both a
cloying treacle to the wings of independance."

From this time onwards, during his sojourn at
Winchester, from the last week in August to the middle
of October, he was doing his best to free himself from
love and to cling to poetry. If Fanny loved him it must
have been very hard for her. He does not seem to have
considered her point of view at all. This may have

partly arisen from a kind of humility, whatever may have been the true case he certainly thought that she did not love him anything like as much as he loved her. "Though I could centre my Happiness in you, I cannot expect to engross your heart so entirely—indeed, if I thought you felt as much for me as I do for you at this moment I do not think I could restrain myself from seeing you again to-morrow for the delight of one embrace," and again: "You cannot conceive how I ache to be with you: how I would die for one hour—for what is in the world? I say you cannot conceive; it is impossible you should look with such eyes upon me as I have upon you: it cannot be."

Nevertheless, in his unhappiness he had no time for her feelings. Between the 16th of August and the 11th of October, when he saw her again, he seems not to have written at all except for one letter written from London. "Am I mad or not?" he writes, "I came by the Friday night coach and have not yet been to Hampstead. Upon my soul it is not my fault. I cannot resolve to mix any pleasure with my days: they go one like another undistinguishable. If I were to see you to-day it would destroy the half comfortable sullenness I enjoy at present into downright perplexities. I love you too much to venture into Hampstead, I feel it is not paying a visit, but venturing into a fire. Que feraije as the french novel writers say in fun, and I in earnest: really what can I do? Knowing well that my life must be passed in fatigue and trouble, I have been endeavouring to wean myself from you: for to myself alone what can be much of a misery? As far as they regard myself I can despise all events: but I cannot cease to love you. This morning I scarcely know what I am doing. I am going to Waltham-stow. I shall return to Winchester to-morrow; whence you shall hear from me in a few days. I am a Coward,

I cannot bear the pain of being happy: 'tis out of the question: I must admit no thought of it.

> Yours ever affectionately
> JOHN KEATS."

They were strange letters for a girl of eighteen to receive. It is tantalizing that we have no idea what effect they had on her. Did she weep over them? or did she feel irritated at this obstinate desire on the part of her love to break away from her? or did she smile a little over them and shake her head knowing, with the "wisdom in women that is more than they have known," that all his efforts would be in vain?

It was after this visit that he wrote wryly to George: "Nothing strikes me so forcibly with a sense of the rediculous as love. A man in love I do think cuts the sorryest figure in the world."

Another effort on Keats's part to escape from his love was his determination not to return to Hampstead. "I like . . . , and I cannot help it," he wrote to Charles Brown, (Brown suppresses the name, but it is obviously Fanny). "On that account I had better not live there." He determined to settle in Westminster, and wrote to Dilke to find him some cheap rooms there.

Certainly, the prospect of living under the same roof with the object of a passion so devouring as Keats's was, would not be very conducive to steady work, and he felt strongly he should, as he wrote, "set myself doing something, and live no longer upon hopes," since not only was he troubled by his love and by his health, but "shabby glutinous cares," as he disdainfully called them, were crowding in upon him. In fact, the financial situation was exceedingly gloomy.

Keats had always been bad about money. From his earliest letters onward there are continual passing references to money and bills. He hated anything to do with that side of life. "I shall have a little trouble in procuring the Money and a great deal to go through——" he wrote once. "No trouble indeed to anyone else—or ordeal either. I mean I shall have to go to town some thrice, and stand in the Bank an hour or two—to me worse than any thing in Dante."

He had, moreover, an incurably generous nature, and was always anxious to share and give away what little he had. "I wish he could be cured of the vice of lending —for in a poor man it is a vice," wrote Woodhouse very reasonably. In the beginning of the year 1819 Keats had lent £30 to Haydon, which considerably crippled his very slender resources. The whole transaction admirably illustrates the wisdom of Polonius's advice. It began on a very high plane: "I will turn to a thing I have thought on more," writes Keats, ". . . your means till your Picture be finished: not only now but for this year and a half have I thought of it. Believe me Haydon I have that sort of fire in my Heart that would sacrifice everything I have to your service—I speak without any reserve —I know you would do so for me—I open my heart to you in a few words—I will do this sooner than you should be distressed: but let me be the last stay—ask the rich lovers of art first—I'll tell you why—I have a little money which may enable me to study and to travel three or four years.—Try the long purses—but do not sell your drawing or I shall consider it a breach of friendship."

To which Haydon replied: "I approve most completely your plan of travels and study and should suffer tortures if my wants interrupted it—in short they shall not my dear Keats—I believe you from my soul when you say you would sacrifice all for me; and when your means are gone, if God gives me means my heart and house and home and everything shall be shared with you."

(Haydon's tiresomeness is extremely well exemplified in this letter: " Can I bear the thousandth part of a day's hesitation?" he inquires grandiloquently, " the searching scrutiny of an apprehension of insincerity, the musing hum of a *sounding* question; the prying, petty, paltry whining doubt, that is inferred from a request *for a day to consider*!—Ah Keats this is sad work for one of my soul and Ambition. The truest thing you ever said of mortal was that I have a touch of Alexander in me!")

Keats had some difficulty in raising the money. Taylor, to whom he first applied, seems to have refused it, and it was always extremely difficult for the Keats children to get any of their own money out of Abbey. However, Haydon pursued him with requests, still in the same high-flown style, and by April was addressing him with downright reproaches, which Keats answered very patiently. After that the money seems to have been handed over, for in July, Keats, being unable to draw any more money of his own, owing to a tiresome Chancery suit instituted by his aunt, applied for its return. The final, depressing conclusion of the matter is contained in a letter to George: " I have a few words to say about Haydon. Before this Chancery threat had cut off every legitimate supply of cash from me I had a little at my disposal: Haydon being very much in want I lent him £30 of it. Now in this see-saw game of Life I got nearest to the ground and this chancery business rivetted me there so that I was sitting in that uneasy position where the seat slants so abominably. I applied to him for payment—he could not—that was no wonder; but good man Delver, what was the wonder then, why marry, in this, he did not seem to care much about it— and let me go without my money with almost nonchalance when he ought to have sold his drawings to supply me. I shall perhaps still be acquainted with him, but for friendship that is at an end."

The chancery suit arose from the difficulties springing from Mr. Jennings's will. He had left more money than his will provided for, and his survivors had, very foolishly, allowed the estate to get into the hands of the lawyers. It is very difficult to follow exactly what course the affair did take, since Richard Abbey, though not dishonest, seems to have been both muddle-headed and incompetent. After Keats's death, when Fanny Keats came of age, it took Dilke, who was her trustee, several months hard work to extract her portion from Abbey and to disentangle the financial muddle in which the Keats children's affairs had been left.

Meanwhile, in this summer of 1819, ready money was painfully short, and in August, Keats and Brown found themselves stranded at Winchester without a penny. Keats was forced once more to have recourse to his publisher, in a long letter, at the end of which his pride and his just disappointment and bitterness break out in a scornful diatribe against the public and the literary world.

". . . I shall ever consider them (People) as debtors to me for verses, not myself to them for admiration—which I can do without. I have of late been indulging my spleen by composing a preface *at* them: after resolving never to write a preface at all. 'There are so many verses,' would I have said to them, 'give me so much means to buy pleasure with as a relief to my hours of labour'—You will observe at the end of this if you put down the Letter 'How a solitary life engenders pride and egotism!' True:—I know it does—but this Pride and egotism will enable me to write finer things than anything else could—so I will indulge it.

Just so much as I am humbled by the genius above my grasp, am I exalted and look with hate and contempt on the literary world—A Drummer boy who holds out his hand familiarly to a field marshall—that Drummer boy with me is the good word and favour of the public. Who would wish to be among the commonplace crowd of the little-famous—who are each individually lost in a throng made up of themselves? is this worth louting or playing the hypocrite for? To beg suffrages for a seat on the benches of a myriad-aristocracy of Letters? This is not wise—I am not a wise man—'Tis Pride. I will give you a definition of a proud Man—He is a Man who has neither vanity nor wisdom—one fill'd with hatreds cannot be vain—neither can he be wise."

Taylor seems to have been rather disturbed by the receipt of this fiery letter, for he sent it to Woodhouse for his opinion. From the first Woodhouse had been one of the most ardent admirers of Keats's, he copied and recopied his poems with unwearied diligence. In the November of the previous year Keats had received an anonymous £25 note, accompanied by a sonnet, the sextet of which runs:

" And there breathe now who dote upon thy fame,
  Whom thy wild numbers wrap beyond their being,
Who love the freedom of thy harp—their aim
  Above the scope of a dull tribe unseeing—
And there is one whose hand will never scant
From his poor store of fruits all *thou* canst want."

There is some ground for believing that the sender of this was Woodhouse, and in his reply to Taylor he shows the same generosity and enthusiasm, tempered with an excellent good sense.

" MY DEAR JOHN,"—he wrote—" Though I have let a

post elapse, I apprehend this letter which will go in a parcel to you, will reach you as soon as Keats's answer— I have read his letter; and I did it before I read yours, and with my usual disposition to understand his terms in the sense in which he uses them.—Now I apprehend his word pride to mean nothing more than literary Pride —that disposition which arises out of a Consciousness of superior and improving poetical Powers, and which would keep him even in his present state of comparative imperfectness, from writing so as to minister to the depraved state of the age.—It is not in my opinion personal pride, but literary pride which his letter shews; —That he has some of the former also I believe; But his letter does not evince it, further than as it displays a solitary spirit . . . I agree with you in every syllable you say about Pride. But I do not think it applies to Keats, as he shews himself in his letter. And if you were (to) cull out a person upon whom to fit your summary of the whole (neither self love nor Man's praise can turn the scale either way,—nor can unmerited neglect or censure weigh a feather) I think as far as poetry is concerned that very man would be Keats as evidence in his letter.

"Having complied with your wish of telling you what I thought of his letter, I come now to his request. —I doubt whether he will want so much as you mention. I apprehend £50 or £60 would suffice him, but this his next letter will shew. I think I mentioned to you how I was situated as to Cash; that I had scraped all I could together, to pay my Father, whose two calls lately had run him close. That I expected nothing till Winter, and had made my calculations upon wanting little till that time. Under these circumstances I could not command £100. But I can spare £50 which shall be at your disposal at what time and place you think proper—You are well acquainted with my good wishes towards Keats, as well as with their complete disinterestedness. Whatever People regret they could not do for Shakespeare or Chatterton, because he did not live in their time, that I would embody into a Rational principal and (with due regard to certain expediencies) do for Keats. But one's means are not unlimited, and one would not wish to give rise to expectations which should end in disappointment, nor would one like to have the oats eaten by other cattle. I wish he could be cured of the Vice of lending for in a poor man it is a vice. . . . I can say nothing about what is best to be done for.—I am tempest tost on the subject, and even with the light of his next letter I may be as much in the dark. I think (and you need not make a bow for the compliment) that you are the prudenter man of the two, to judge in this case—But take this with you—1st I really can't spare more, ' cas in presenti ' than the sum I have named. And 2nd my friendship for the poor fellow wd. willingly go, if need is, greater lengths than merely lending your money to lend him."

The upshot was that Hessey, Taylor's partner, sent Keats a bank-bill for £30 which he acknowledges cheerfully, saying: "This morning I hear that some unknown part of a Sum due to me . . . had been sent to Chichester by mistake. Brown has borrow'd money of a friend of his in Hampshire—A few days we had but a few shillings left and now between us we have £60 besides what is waiting in the Chichester post office. To be a complete Midas I suppose some one will send me a pair of asses ears by the waggon." A joke which tickled Woodhouse so much that he wrote to Taylor: "I roared aloud over it, to the astonishment of some female and male ' natives ' who were buying in the back shop."

But Keats, unlike Haydon, was not wholly unmindful of his friends' money: "Though of my own money I should be careless; of my Friends' I must be spare," he wrote to Fanny Brawne; and he was determined to achieve some measure of financial independence.

The tragedy of *Otho the Great*, was an effort to do this. Brown, as has been seen, gained £300 from his opera at Drury Lane and he had proposed to Keats that, in order to earn money, they should collaborate on a tragedy, Brown to supply the plot and dramatic action and Keats to clothe it in blank verse. The result was *Otho the Great*, which was composed in the following curious way, Brown telling the story as he went along, and Keats turning the dialogue into verse, without any idea of the outcome or of the future events. It was not a very satisfactory way to work, and Keats felt it, for he insisted on completing the 5th act by himself. And, later on, when Brown suggested the subject of King Stephen for a tragedy and started to outline a possible plot, Keats stopped him, exclaiming: "No, no. I have been in leading strings long enough." It proves his growing interest in the theatre and, indeed, the fragment of Stephen is better than anything in *Otho*, but whether 1820 was not already late for heroic dramas in blank verse is a moot question. In any case, *Otho* was finished and actually accepted by Elliston, the manager of Drury Lane. But the theatrical profession is notoriously uncertain and Kean, for whom the chief part was written, chose this moment to make an American tour. It was essentially a part for Kean, who excelled in portrayals of hysterical emotion; (in one of his celebrated parts, Sir Giles Overreach, he fell down in a fit after a terrific mad scene, and on his first night terrified the company as well as the audience.) Keats had found some relief, as artists can, by endowing Ludolph, the lover in *Otho the*

Great, with the torments of jealousy and of hysterical love that he was striving to subdue in himself. "The Lover is madder than I am," he wrote to Fanny, "I am nothing to him—he has a figure like the Statue of Maleager and double distilled fire in his heart." Kean not being available to present this unfortunate sufferer, Elliston decided to put off production for another season. Being much in want of ready money, Brown and Keats therefore withdrew *Otho* from Drury Lane and sent it to Covent Garden, where it was, in process of time, incontinently rejected.

Meanwhile, Keats, with admirable resolution, determined not to wait for the issue of the tragedy. He determined to try to do some journalistic hack-work, possibly dramatic criticism and, with that end in view, he wrote to Dilke that he purposed living in a "cheap lodging in town, that I may be in reach of books and information, of which here there is a plentiful lack."

He had not disliked Winchester, though he had been unhappy there. The "temperate sharpness" of the air and the warm tones of the stubble-fields had inspired the *Ode to Autumn*, and the "excessively Maiden ladylike" side streets, with "doorsteps always fresh from the flannel," and a "very staid, serious nay almost awful quietness" about the knockers, had given him that feeling of "Town quietude," which led him to write the lovely opening to the unfinished *Eve of St. Mark*:

> "Upon a Sabbath day it fell;
>   Twice holy was the Sabbath bell,
>   That call'd the folk to evening prayer;
>   The city streets were clean and fair
>   From wholesome drench of April rains;
>   And, on the western window panes,

The chilly sunset faintly told
Of unmatured green vallies cold,
Of the green thorny bloomless hedge,
Of rivers new with spring-tide sedge,
Of primroses by sheltered rills,
And daisies on the aguish hills.
Twice holy was the Sabbath-bell:
The silent streets were crowded well
With staid and pious companies,
Warm from their fire-side orat'ries;
And moving, with demurest air,
To even-song, and vesper prayer.
Each arched porch, and entry low,
Was fill'd with patient folk and slow,
With whispers hush, and shuffling feet,
While played the organ loud and sweet."

"I think," he wrote to George, "it will give you the Sensation of walking about an old country Town in a coolish evening."

CHAPTER XVI

*Keats returns to Hampstead—His love for Fanny—His grow-
ing unhappiness—Charles Brown's affair with Abby—George
returns from America and borrows money.*

RESOLUTIONS are all too easily broken. Keats knew himself only too well when he wrote to Fanny: "I love you
too much to venture to Hampstead, I feel it is not paying
a visit, but venturing into a fire." He was at College
Street, Westminster, for barely a fortnight, of which
three days were occupied by a visit to Wentworth Place.
As soon as he saw Fanny he fell under her spell once more.
She was kind to him, he had made her suffer and she may
have loved him the more for it. When, at last, they met,
she gave him a "thousand kisses," and perhaps threatened
to break from him, if, as he had kept writing, he felt it
better for him. In any case he writes to her the day after
their meeting: "If you should ever carry your threat
yesterday into execution—believe me 'tis not my pride,
my vanity or any petty passion would torment me—
really 'twould hurt my heart—I could not bear it." He
concludes his letter with the moving little postscript :
"Ah hertè mine."

In his next letter written two days later he seems to
give himself utterly to his love.

"MY DEAREST GIRL,—This moment I have sent myself
to copy some verses out fair. I cannot proceed with any
degree of content. I must write you a line or two and
see if that will assist me in dismissing you from my Mind
for ever so short a time. Upon my Soul I can think of
nothing else. The time is passed when I had power to
advise and warn you against the unpromising morning

of my Life. My love has made me selfish. I cannot exist
without you. I am forgetful of everything but seeing
you again—my Life seems to stop there—I see no further.
You have absorb'd me. I have a sensation at the
present moment as though I was dissolving—I should be
exquisitely miserable without the hope of soon seeing
you. I should be affraid to separate myself far from
you. My sweet Fanny, will your heart never change?
My love, will it? I have no limit now to my love—Your
note came in just here—I cannot be happier away from
you. 'Tis richer than an Argosy of Pearles. Do not
threat me even in jest. I have been astonished that Men
could die Martyrs for religion—I have shudder'd at it.
I shudder no more—I could be martyr'd for my Religion
—Love is my religion—I could die for that. I could die
for you. My Creed is Love and you are its only tenet.
You have ravish'd me away by a Power I cannot resist;
and yet I could resist till I saw you; and even since I
have seen you I have endeavoured often ' to reason against
the reasons of my love.' I can do that no more—the pain
would be too great. My Love is selfish. I cannot breathe
without you.

Yours for ever

John Keats."

So he came back to Wentworth Place, but he was
not happy. There was still the old conflict in his mind,
in which he conceived his love and his poetry to be
opposed. The following poem shows this very clearly,
and also shows a curious divided thought, for he seems
to regard his love both as his gaoler and yet as his deliv-
erer, or at least as the only thing that he really wants.

"What can I do to drive away
  Remembrance from my eyes? for they have seen
  Aye, an hour ago, my brilliant Queen!

Touch has a memory. O say, love, say,
What can I do to kill it and be free
In my old liberty?
When every fair one that I saw was fair,
Enough to catch me in but half a snare,
Not keep me there:
When, howe'er poor or particoloured things,
My muse had wings,
And ever ready was to take her course
Whither I bent her force,
Unintellectual, yet divine to me;—
Divine, I say! What sea-bird o'er the sea
Is a philosopher the while he goes
Winging along where the great water throes?

     How shall I do
     To get anew
Those moulted feathers and so mount once more
     Above, above
      The reach of flattering love,
And make him cower lowly while I soar?

.   .   .   .

"O, for some sunny spell
To dissipate the shadows of this hell!
Say they are gone,—with the new dawning light
Steps forth my lady bright!
O, let me once more rest
My soul upon that dazzling breast!
Let once again these aching arms be plac'd,
The tender gaolers of thy waist!
And let me feel that warm breath here and there
To spread a rapture in my very hair,—
O, the sweetness of the pain!
Give me those lips again!

P

Enough! Enough! it is enough for me
To dream of thee!"

But it was not enough. Part of Keats's unhappiness
at this time was due to his illness. Unknown to himself
his lungs were decaying and he suffered from all the
mental symptoms of tuberculosis, irritability, depression,
and intense nervousness. Probably, in addition, as often
happens with this illness, his physical desires were
strengthened and sharpened. He had always been
allured by the physical attractions of women, and this
feeling was intensified a thousand times when he met
Fanny. She had once told him not to mention her
beauty, and he had replied: "Why may I not speak of
your Beauty since without that I could never have lov'd
you. I cannot conceive any beginning of such love as I
have for you but Beauty. There may be a sort of love for
which, without the least sneer at it, I have the highest
respect and can admire it in others: but it has not the
richness, the bloom, the full form, the enchantment of
love after my own heart." Nor can his state of mind
have been soothed at this time by the spectacle of Charles
Brown who was complacently carrying on an affair
with their maid-servant, Abigail O'Donaghue.

She was an exceedingly pretty girl, with a quick
tongue and gift of repartee, so that while Keats was
occupied in the parlour with Miss Brawne, Brown
formed the habit of slipping off downstairs to the warm
kitchen with the round stone bread-oven, to tease and
be teased by Abby. Nor was Brown a man to content
himself with gallantries. In 1820 Abby was pregnant
and, to his credit, Brown took her over to Ireland and
married her in a Roman Catholic church.[1] Such a
marriage was not legal owing to the Catholic disabilities,

[1] Appendix iii.

but it satisfied Abby, and in December, 1820, Brown is writing to Keats in Rome:

"O—I must tell you Abby is living with me again, but not in the same capacity,—she keeps to her own bed, and I keep myself continent. Any more nonsense of the former kind would put me in an awkward predicament with her. One child is very well. She behaves extremely well, and, by what I hear from Sam" (Brawne) "my arrangements prevent the affair from giving pain next door." (To Mrs. Brawne and Fanny.) "The fact is I could not afford to allow her a separate establishment . . . In the mean time the child thrives gloriously,— but I'm not going to be fondly parental, for, between you and me, I think an infant is disagreeable,—it is all gut and squall."

But that is in the future. Meanwhile, Keats's physical desires can hardly fail to have been exacerbated by Charles Brown's successful utilitarian seduction, carried on under the same roof, of which he must have been only too fully cognizant.

The uneasy state of his mind is shown in a long letter from Woodhouse (who, of course, knew nothing about Fanny Brawne), to Taylor, interesting for many other reasons, but also showing that preoccupation with sex which was only too natural in a boy of twenty-four, for the first time passionately in love.

The excellent and admiring Woodhouse was somewhat upset by the revisions in the *Eve of St. Agnes*. "You know," he wrote, "if a thing has a decent side I generally look no further—As the Poem was orig'y written, *we* innocent ones (ladies and myself) might very well have supposed that Porphyro, when acquainted with Madeline's love for him, and when ' he arose, Etherial flush'd &c. &c. (turn to it) set himself at once to persuade her to go off with him, and succeeded and went over the

' Dartmoor black ' (now changed for some other place) to be married in right honest chaste and sober wise. But, as it is now altered, as soon as M. has confessed her love, P. winds by degrees his arm around her, presses breast to breast, and acts all the acts of a bonafide husband, while she fancies she is only playing the part of a Wife in a dream. The alteration is of about 3 stanzas; and tho' there are no improper expressions but all is left to inference, and tho' profanely speaking, the Interest on the reader's imagination is greatly heightened, yet I do apprehend it will render the poem unfit for ladies," (Woodhouse's prim concern for "the ladies" is rather charming), "and indeed scarcely to be mentioned to them among the ' things that are.' He says he does not want ladies to read his poetry: that he writes for men— and that if in the former poem there was an opening for a doubt what took place, it was his fault for not writing clearly and comprehensibly—that he sho'd despise a man who would be such a eunuch in sentiment as to leave a maid, with that character about her, in such a situation: and sho'd despise himself to write about it &c. &c. &c.—and all this sort of Keats-like rhodomontade.

"He then read me *Lamia*," Woodhouse continues, "which he has half fair copied. I was much pleased with it. I can use no other terms for you know how badly he reads his own poetry aloud." (An interesting and some-how unexpected sidelight.)

The first part of *Lamia* is strangely like what might have been the first encounters of Keats and Fanny Brawne. The enchantress determined to lure the young poet. His instant capitulation. "Her soft look growing coy, she saw his chain so sure:" Her slightly coquettish bargaining, her threat to leave him, and then in turn her capitulation, intended all along:

"The cruel lady, without any show
  Of sorrow for her tender favourite's woe,
  But rather, if her eyes would brighter be,
  With brighter eyes and slow amenity,
  Put her new lips to his, and gave afresh
  The life she had so tangled in her mesh:
  And as he from one trance was wakening
  Into another, she began to sing,
  Happy in beauty, life, and love, and every thing,
  A song of love, too sweet for earthly lyres,
  While, like held breath, the stars drew in their panting
      fires.
  And then she whispered in such trembling tone,
  As those who, safe together met alone
  For the first time through many anguish'd days,
  Use other speech than looks; bidding him raise
  His drooping head, and clear his soul of doubt,
  For that she was a woman and without
  Any more subtle fluid in her veins
  Than throbbing blood, and that the self-same pains
  Inhabited her frail-strung heart as his."

One wonders if Keats was thinking of any particular
incident when he said so gaily to Woodhouse that:
"Women love to be forced to do a thing by a fine fellow
such as this Lycius was;" or whether it was just young
man's boastfulness. In any case, it is exceedingly unlikely that he ever even asked Fanny to live with him.
She was a well-brought-up girl, sheltered under her
mother's wing, and she was only eighteen; so that he
went on living next door to her, half worn out by illness
and by passion, longing after:

"That shape, that fairness, that sweet minor zest
  Of love, your kiss,—those hands, those eyes divine,
  That warm, white, lucent, million-pleasured breast."

We have the evidence of his friends at this time as to his restless, unhappy state. "He seemed well neither in mind nor body. . . ." wrote Severn, "while alternating moods of apathetic dejection and spasmodic gaiety rendered him a companion somewhat difficult to humour." While Brown writes: "He was too thoughtful or too unquiet; and he began to be reckless of health. Among other proofs of recklessness, he was secretly taking, at times, a few drops of laudanum to keep up his spirits. It was discovered by accident, and, without delay, revealed to me." (Possibly by Abby?) "He needed not to be warned of the danger of such a habit; but I rejoiced at his promise never to take another drop without my knowledge; for nothing could induce him to break his word, when once given,—which was a difficulty. Still, at the very moment of my being rejoiced, this was an additional proof of his rooted misery."

The work he was doing at this time is another and nobler proof of the burden he was carrying. He was engaged in the recasting of *Hyperion*, and writing that new preface, in which he imagines himself, the poet, coming in a strange dream to the old, deserted temple of Saturn. Here in his dialogue with vast, shadowy Moneta he expresses something of the oppression of his soul.

"' Are there not thousands in the world,' said I,
    Encourag'd by the sooth voice of the shade,
  ' Who love their fellows even to the death;
  Who feel the giant agony of the world;
  And more, like slaves to poor humanity,
  Labour for mortal good? I sure should see
  Other men here; but I am here alone.'
  ' They whom thou spak's of are no vision'ries,'
  Rejoin'd that voice—' they are no dreamers weak,

They seek no wonder but the human face;
No music but a happy-noted voice—
They come not here, they have no thought to come—
And thou art here, for thou art less than they—
What benefit canst thou do, or all thy tribe,
To the great world? Thou art a dreaming thing;
A fever of thyself—think of the Earth;
What bliss even in hope is there for thee?
What haven? every creature hath its home;
Every sole man hath days of joy and pain,
Whether his labours be sublime or low—
The pain alone; the joy alone; distinct:
Only the dreamer venoms all his days,
Bearing more woe than all his sins deserve.'"

Occasionally his unhappiness breaks through in brief veiled comments in his correspondence. "You had best put me into your Cave of despair," he wrote to Severn, who had painted a picture with that title for the Academy Competition; and to Georgiana Keats he wrote: "If you should have a Boy do not christen him John, and persuade George not to let his partiality for me come across. 'Tis a bad name, and goes against a Man."

This letter was written while George Keats was over in England. Things had been going badly for him, too, and his financial troubles had added to John's worries in the autumn. He had purchased part of a steam-boat on the Mississippi, and it had gone to the bottom, and he was now in desperate need of ready money. He therefore came over to England to collect his share of Tom's estate.

Things had changed between the two brothers: "He was not the same being," George wrote, "although his reception of me was as warm as heart could wish, he did not speak with former openness and unreserve, he had lost the reviving custom of venting his griefs." It could hardly be otherwise after the long separation; Brown had more or less taken George's place with Keats, and George had his own affairs, his wife and his child. "We smoke George about his little girl," Keats wrote to Georgiana, "he runs the common beaten road of every father, as I dare say you do of every Mother—there is no Child like his Child—so original! original forsooth. However, I take you at your words; I have a lively faith that yours is the very gem of all Children. Ain't I its Unkle?"

George went back to America in a very short while, taking with him £700. From this circumstance arose the bitter and life-long quarrel between Brown and Dilke. Brown held that George had taken with him a large part of the money belonging to John, and that this was partly the cause of John's illness and death. Dilke, who went into the financial affairs of the Keats' family pretty carefully on behalf of Fanny Keats, held that George had taken nothing more than his rightful share. The sad thing was that certainly John thought that George had taken, or rather borrowed, his money. He was quite vague about money affairs and supposed he possessed something like £700, which certainly was not so. His depression and weakness were so great that it was difficult, well-nigh impossible, to discuss the subject with him, and George says, probably truly, that he could not bear to tell him the truth, which was that he had but £170 in the world besides what he had currently, £60 to £70. He was, therefore, left under the impression that George had borrowed a far greater sum than he had. John thought that George had borrowed something like £700, leaving him with but £60 of ready money and £80 worth of debts. "It was not fair of him, was it?" he said pathetically to Brown. It was no wonder that Brown, who adored John, should find himself bitter and suspicious about George.

Fanny Brawne, on the other hand, who might have been supposed to have even more cause for bitterness, wrote of George with a balance and a fair-mindedness which are very striking.

"In a letter you sent me some time ago," she wrote, in 1821, to Fanny Keats, "you mentioned your brother George in a manner that made me think you had been mislead about him. He is no favourite of mine, and he never liked me so that I am not likely to say too much in his favor from affection for him, but I must say I think he is more blamed than he should be. I think him extravagant and selfish but people in their great zeal make him out worse than that—soon after your brother Tom died, my dear John wrote to him offering him any assistance or money in his power. At that time he was not engaged to me and having just lost one brother felt all his affection turned towards the one that remained— George I dare say at first had no thoughts of accepting his offers but when his affairs did not succeed and he had a wife and one child to support, with the prospect of another, I cannot wonder that he should consider them first and as he could not get what he wanted without coming to England he unfortunately came. By that time your brother wished to marry himself, but he could not refuse the money. It may appear very bad in George to leave him 60 pounds when he owed 80, but he had many reasons to suppose the inconvenience would not last long. Your brother had a book of poems nearly ready to come out (which his illness kept back till the summer) he had a tragedy which Mr. Brown calculated his share of would be about two hundred pounds and he was writing a story which had he lived to finish would if the others failed make up for it at least so every one imagined."

(Fanny Brawne meant the *Cap & Bells*, a satiric fairy
tale in verse, that Keats was then writing. It was intended
for a sort of Byronic satire, and fails lamentably, being
both unfunny and second-rate. It was to be published
under the pseudonym of Lucy Vaughan Lloyd and was a
pot-boiler; but it is doubtful whether it would have had
the success anticipated for it; the talent for boiling pots
is not given to all!) "George," Fanny went on, "could
not forsee his illness—He might be a cause of the dreadful
consequences but surely a very indirect and accidental
one. . . . The person who suffered most never thought
so very badly of it, he used to say, ' George ought not to
have done this he should have recollected that I wish to
marry myself—but I suppose having a family to provide
for makes a man selfish '—They tell me that latterly he
thought worse of George, but I own I do not believe it—
One thing is against him. I don't think he could ever
have supposed it would be in his power to return the
money, at the best not for many years—his brother never
expected it at all, he always said he would not succeed."

George possibly acted in all good faith. He knew
John was, for the moment, safely provided for under
Brown's care. He had confidence that with a little
capital he could put his own affairs right and become
quickly prosperous, confidence in which he was amply
justified, since this, in spite of Fanny Brawne's fore-
bodings, is exactly what did happen. He must have
thought that this would be the best solution for them all,
John included. Whether he did actually borrow more of
John's money than he stated it is difficult to make out.
The figures as given by Dilke for George and by Brown
against him will be found in the appendix. After John's
death George paid his brother's debts fairly and scrupu-
lously, but during the remaining time that John Keats
lived in London he was entirely dependent on Brown.

CHAPTER XVII

The Valley of the Shadow—The first hæmorrhage—Conval-escence—Correspondence with Fanny—Keats leaves Hamp-stead for Kentish Town—Another hæmorrhage—Leigh Hunt takes him in at Mortimer Terrace—Keats's bitter misery.

ON Thursday, January 3rd, 1820, Keats travelled from London to Hampstead, on the outside of the coach, without his overcoat. He reeled into the warm candle-lit room at Wentworth Place "in a state," writes Brown, "that looked like fierce intoxication. Such a state in him, I knew, was impossible; it therefore was the more fear-ful. I asked hurriedly, ' What is the matter? You are fevered?' ' Yes, yes,' he answered, ' I was on the outside of the stage this bitter day till I was severely chilled,—but now I don't feel it. Fevered!—of course, a little.' He mildly and instantly yielded, a property of his nature towards any friend, to my request that he should go to bed. I entered his chamber as he leapt into bed. On entering the cold sheets, before his head was on the pillow, he slightly coughed, and I heard him say,— ' That is blood from my mouth.' I went towards him; he was examining a single drop of blood upon the sheet. ' Bring me the candle, Brown, and let me see this blood.' After regarding it steadfastly he looked up in my face with a calmness of countenance I shall never forget, and said,—' I know the colour of that blood;—it is arterial blood;—I cannot be deceived in that colour;—that drop of blood is my death-warrant;—I must die.'"

He had studied medicine, he had seen his mother die, and Tom, and if, in later months, for short moments, hope raised its flickering standard before him, he was never really mistaken. He saw it all, and on that night "when so violent a rush of blood came to my Lungs that I felt nearly suffocated—I assure you," he writes to Fanny, "I felt it possible I might not survive, and at that moment thought of nothing but you."

For the first few days he was confined to bed and Brown gives an infinitely touching description of him. "When I waited on him day and night, his instinctive generosity, his acceptance of my offices, by a glance of his eye, a motion of his hand, made me regard my mechanical duty as absolutely nothing compared to his silent acknowledgement."

In a day or two a sofa bed was made up for him in Brown's sitting-room, whence he could command the Heath and the Brawnes' front door; where he could see Fanny going in and out in her "duffle grey."

"How much more comfortable than a dull room up stairs," he writes to his sister, in the cheerful, sweet-tempered tone he nearly always uses to her, "where one gets tired of the pattern of the bed-curtains. Besides I see all that passes—for instance now, this morning, if I had been in my own room I should not have seen the coals brought in. On sunday between the hours of twelve and one I descried a Pot boy. I conjectured it might be the one o' Clock beer—Old women with bobbins and red cloaks and unpresuming bonnets I see creeping about the heath. Gipseys after hare skins and silver spoons. Then goes by a fellow with a wooden clock under his arm that strikes a hundred and more. Then comes the old french emigrant, (who has been very well to do in france) with his hands joined behind on his hips, and his face full of political schemes. Then passes Mr. David Lewis a very goodnatured, goodlooking old gentleman who has been very kind to Tom and George and me. As for those fellows the Brickmakers they are always passing to and fro. I mus'n't forget the two old maiden Ladies in well walk who have a Lap dog between them that they are very anxious about. It is a corpulent Little Beast whom it is necessary to coax along with an ivory-tipp'd cane. Carlo our Neighbour Mrs Brawne's dog and it meet sometimes. Lappy thinks Carlo a devil of a fellow and so do his Mistresses. Well they may—he would sweep 'em all down at a run; all for the Joke of it."

After the first Fanny Brawne was allowed to visit him, and they sent each other little notes nearly every day. This interlude of pain and weakness was almost the halcyon period of their love. The fever was for the moment burnt away. He was too weak to want to do more than to see her often for a few minutes at a time.— "Pray do not stop so long up stairs," he wrote to her, "it makes me uneasy—come every now and then and stop a half minute,"—to know she was there, to know she loved him. There was no more question of balls, or of foreign gentlemen, she would not even go into town since she knew it worried him. "How can you bear so long an imprisonment at Hampstead?" he asked her, "I shall always remember it with all the gusto that a monopolizing carle should. I could build an altar to you for it." And then, in an attempt to be unselfish, he sends another little note round the same evening:

"MY DEAREST GIRL,—As, from the last part of my note you must see how gratified I have been by your remaining at home, you might perhaps conceive that I was equally bias'd the other way by your going to Town, I cannot be easy to-night without telling you you would be wrong to suppose so. Though I am pleased with the one, I am not displeased with the other. How do I dare to write in this manner about my pleasures and displeasures? I will tho' whilst I am an invalid, in spite of you. Good night, Love. J.K."

At first he had some faint idea of breaking off their engagement.

"You know our situation," he wrote, "what hope is there if I should be recovered ever so soon—my very health will not suffer me to make any great exertion. I am reccommended not even to read poetry, much less write it. I wish I had even a little hope. I cannot say forget me—but I would mention that there are impossibilities in the world. No more of this. I am not strong enough to be weaned—take no notice of it in your good night.

Happen what may I shall ever be my dearest Love
Your affectionate
J— K—"

But Fanny would have none of it. Whatever prudence or friends or relations might dictate, her heart was given into his keeping.

"MY DEAREST GIRL,—how could it ever have been my wish to forget you? how could I have said such a thing? The utmost stretch my mind has been capable of was to endeavour to forget you for your own sake seeing what a chance there was of my remaining in a precarious state of health. I would have borne it as I would bear death if fate was in that humour: but I should as soon think of choosing to die as to part from you. Believe too my love that our friends think and speak for the best, and if their best is not our best it is not our fault."

"MY DEAREST FANNY,—Then all we have to do is to be patient. Whatever violence I may sometimes do myself by hinting at what would appear to any but our-

selves a matter of necessity, I do not think I could bear
any approach of a thought of losing you."

At last she had managed to show him her heart, to
convince him of her love.

"My greatest torment since I have known you has
been the fear of your a little inclining to the Cressid;
but that suspicion I dismiss utterly and remain happy
in the surety of your Love, which I assure you is as
much a wonder to me as a delight. Send me the words
' Good night' to put under my pillow.
                    Dearest Fanny,
                        Your affectionate
                                        J.K."

He writes altogether in a happier, closer, more
intimate strain than he has ever done before. He keeps
an anxious watch on her, begging her not to expose
herself to the cold, and not, alas for the hygiene of the
day! to keep the window open. He writes to her about
the little incidencts of his sick-room, and he makes small
jokes: "There last lines are . . . a little disfigured by
the smear of black-currant jelly; which has made a little
mark on one of the Pages of Brown's *Ben Jonson*, the
very best book he has. I have lick'd it but it remains
very purple—I did not know whether to write purple or
blue so in the mixture of the thought wrote purplue
which may be an excellent name for a colour made up of
those two, and would suit well to start next Spring."
"There's the Thrush again—I can't afford it—he'll run
me up a pretty Bill for Music—besides he ought to
know I deal at Clementi's." "I had nothing particular
to say to-day, but not intending that there shall be any
interruption to our correspondance (which at some

future time I propose offering to Murray) I write something."

At last, for a time, his restless doubts and jealousies and fevers ceased. Fanny had borne with them throughout and now, perhaps because she felt that there was no need for it, she was able to open her heart to him and ask, as women will, for reassurance. In answer she received one of the most perfect love letters that he, or any other man, ever wrote.

"SWEETEST FANNY,—You fear, sometimes, I do not love you so much as you wish? My dear Girl I love you ever and ever and without reserve. The more I have known you the more have I lov'd. In every way—even my jealousies have been agonies of Love, in the hottest fit I ever had I would have died for you. I have vex'd you too much. But for Love! Can I help it? You are always new. The last of your Kisses was ever the sweetest; the last smile the brightest; the last movement the gracefullest. When you pass'd my window home yesterday, I was fill'd with as much admiration as if I had then seen you for the first time. You uttered a half complaint once that I only lov'd your Beauty. Have I nothing else then to love in you but that? Do not I see a heart naturally furnish'd with wings imprison itself with me? No ill prospect has been able to turn your thoughts a moment from me. This perhaps should be as much a subject of sorrow as joy—but I will not talk of that. Even if you did not love me I could not help an entire devotion to you: how much more deeply then must I feel for you knowing you love me. My Mind has been the most discontented and restless one that ever was put into a body too small for it. I never felt my Mind repose upon anything with complete and undistracted enjoyment—upon no person but you. When you are in the room my thoughts never fly out of the window: you always concentrate my whole senses. The anxiety shown about our Loves in your last note is an immense pleasure to me: however, you must not suffer such speculations to molest you any more: nor will I any more believe you can have the least pique against me."

At last, too, the long conflict between love and poetry was in abeyance, and he was able to write of them both side by side.

"Now I have had opportunities of passing nights anxious and awake I have found other thoughts intrude upon me. ' If I should die,' said I to myself, ' I have left no immortal work behind me—nothing to make my friends proud of my memory—but I have lov'd the principle of beauty in all things, and if I had had time I would have made myself remember'd.' Thoughts like these came very feebly whilst I was in health and every pulse beat for you—now you divide with this (may *I* say it?) ' last infirmity of noble minds ' all my reflection.

God bless you, Love,

J. KEATS."

In spite of this fairly peaceful state of mind, the time seemed very long as he was getting better: "The nearer a racer gets to the Goal," he wrote, "the more his anxiety becomes, as I lingering upon the borders of health feel my impatience increase." And again, rather pathetically: "I envied Sam's walk with you to-day; which I will not do again as I may get very tired of envying."

By the end of March, however, he was up and about, though far from well, and on the 25th he was able to go to Haydon's picture-show, for Haydon records that "Keats and Hazlitt were together in a corner of the gallery, truly rejoicing." (It was on this occasion that

Mrs. Siddons saved the situation when she was asked
how she liked the Christ in the thirty feet long *Entry
into Jerusalem*, which we have already heard of as presiding at the "immortal dinner." People had been
doubtful about the picture and when the great actress
was asked for her opinion "the whole room remained
dead silent and allowed her to think. . . . After a
moment, in a deep, loud, tragic tone she said: 'It is
completely successful.'")

At the end of April Brown let his house and went off
to Scotland, whence he almost certainly continued his
journey to Ireland, in order to marry Abigail Donaghue,
now enceinte with Carlino. It must have been this
circumstance which led him to desert Keats at such a
moment, and he was probably obliged to let the house,
owing to financial straits, since they were both now
dependent on his very slender means.

It was an unfortunate necessity. There was some idea
at first of Keats making the voyage with him but he was
plainly too weak. He therefore, at the beginning of May,
moved to lodgings in Kentish Town. There he stayed
for six or seven weeks, then he was taken ill again with
blood-spitting, and Leigh Hunt very kindly took him
home to his own careless, untidy but hospitable house
at 13 Mortimer Terrace. It was very good of Leigh
Hunt, who was ill himself at the time, and it was in a
way even kinder of Mrs. Hunt, though perhaps she had
no say in the matter. Still it must have been a difficult
time for her, a consumptive herself, with Leigh Hunt
in a bilious fever that left him with "nervous pains in
the head," and Keats, who had never liked her, suffering
from hæmorrhage and deep nervous depression.

There is little doubt that these weeks in Kentish
Town were the unhappiest of Keats's life. Not even the
terrible voyage in the *Maria Crowther* was so utterly

miserable. Here, after the blood-spitting, he knew that he was dying and he did not want to die. He knew now that every hope was vain and the sweetness he had enjoyed in his love and the sweetness he had hoped to enjoy mocked him. He had written to her: "How horrid was the chance of slipping into the ground instead of into your arms—the difference is amazing Love. Death must come at last; Man must die, as Shallow says; but before that is my fate I feign would try what more pleasures than you have given, so sweet a creature as you can give." Life and love were slipping inexorably through his fingers and the disappointment was almost more than he could bear. His will to live, so strong and so tumultuous, rose up in one wild rebellious flare; and in that consuming fire he wrote those cruel letters to his love, which are so painful to read and which have been so much criticized. Yet let those who have passed through their own Gethsemane, and have prayed that the cup might pass from them, reproach him, for they and they only have the right to do so.

If Fanny was hurt by those letters, and hurt she must have been, she understood and forgave him. How well she understood is witnessed by a passage in one of her letters to Medwin, Shelley's biographer, who wrote to her asking her whether the accounts of Keats's violence of nature were true.

"That his sensibility was most acute, is true," she answered, "and his passions were very strong, but not violent, if by that term, violence of temper is implied. His was no doubt susceptible, but his anger seemed rather to turn on himself than on others, and in moments of greatest irritation, it was only by a sort of savage despondency," (how well that phrase describes Keats's neurotic moods!) "that he sometimes grieved and wounded his friends. . . . For more than a twelve month before quitting England, I saw him every day, often witnessed his sufferings, both mental and bodily, and I do not hesitate to say, that he never could have addressed an unkind expression, much less a violent one, to any human being."

And yet he wrote to her what seems to us unkind. His first two little notes are still under the influence of the peace her actual companionship gave him. "I have your ring on my finger," (that ring she had kissed before she gave it him), "and your flowers on the table. I shall not expect to see you yet because it would be such pain to part with you again." And later. "For this week past I have been employed in marking the most beautiful passages in *Spenser*, intending it for you, and comforting myself in being somehow occupied to give you however small a pleasure." Three years later she lent the book to Fanny Keats, writing: "You will find the more pleasure in reading as you will find the best parts marked by one who I have heard called the best judge of poetry living—they were marked for me to read and I need not tell you with what pleasure I did so. Keep them as long as you wish for I never open them now."

But when he had been away for a little while, the torments of imagination and of uncertainty began to take hold of him.

"Yesterday and this morning I have been haunted by a sweet vision—I have seen you the whole time in your shepherdess dress. How my senses have ached at it! How my heart has been devoted to it! How my eyes have been full of Tears at it! Indeed I think a real Love is enough to occupy the widest heart—Your going to town alone was a shock to me—yet I expected it— *promise me you will not for some time, till I get better.* Promise me this and fill the paper full of the most endearing names. If you cannot do so with good will, do my Love tell me—say what you think—confess if your heart is too much fasten'd upon the world. Perhaps then I may see you at a greater distance, I may not be able to appropriate you so closely to myself. Were you to loose a favorite bird from the cage, how would your eyes ache after it as long as it was in sight; when out of sight you would recover a little. Perhaps if you would, if so it is, confess to me how many things are necessary to you besides me, I might be happier, by being less tantaliz'd. Well may you exclaim, how selfish, how cruel, not to let me enjoy my youth! to wish me to be unhappy! You must be so if you love me—upon my Soul I can be contented with nothing else. If you could really what is call'd enjoy yourself at a Party—if you can smile in peoples faces, and wish them to admire you *now*, you never have nor ever will love me. I see *life* in nothing but the certainty of your Love—convince me of it my sweetest. If I am not somehow convinc'd I shall die of agony. If we love we must not live as other men and women do—I cannot brook the wolfsbane of fashion and foppery and tattle. You must be mine to die upon the rack if I want you. I do not pretend to say I have more feeling than my fellows—but I wish you seriously to look over my letters kind and unkind and consider whether the Person who wrote them can be able to endure much longer the agonies and uncertainties which you are so peculiarly made to create—My recovery of bodily health will be of no benefit to me if you are not all mine when I am well. For God's sake save me— or tell me my passion is of too awful a nature for you. Again God bless you.

J.K.

"No—my sweet Fanny—I am wrong. I do not want

you to be unhappy—and yet I do, I must while there is
so sweet a Beauty—my loveliest my darling! Goodbye!
I Kiss you—O the torments!"

The next letter, which was written after the blood-
spitting, when he was staying with Leigh Hunt, is even
more terrible.

"I am tormented day and night," he writes. "They
talk of me going to Italy. 'Tis certain I shall never
recover if I am to be so long separate from you: yet with
all this devotion to you I cannot persuade myself into
any confidence of you. Past experience connected with
the fact of my long separation from you gives me
agonies which are scarcely to be talked of. When your
mother comes I shall be very sudden and expert in asking
her whether you have been to Mrs. Dilke's, for she might
say no to make me easy. I am literally worn to death,
which seems my only recourse. I cannot forget what has
pass'd. What? nothing with a man of the world, but
to me dreadful. I will get rid of this as much as possible.
When you were in the habit of flirting with Brown you
would have left off, would your own heart have felt one
half of one pang mine did. Brown is a good sort of Man
—he did not know he was doing me to death by inches.
I feel the effect of every one of those hours in my side
now; and for that cause, though he has done me many
services, though I know his love and friendship for me,
though at this moment I should be without pence were
it not for his assistance, I will never see or speak to him
until we are both old men, if we are to be. I *will*
resent my heart having been made a football. You will
call this madness. I have heard you say that it was not
unpleasant to wait a few years—you have amusements—
your mind is away—you have not brooded over one idea
as I have, and how should you? You are to me an object

intensely desirable—the air I breathe in a room empty of
you is unhealthy. I am not the same to you—no—you
can wait—you have a thousand activities—you can be
happy without me. Any party, any thing to fill up the
day has been enough. How have you pass'd this month?
Who have you smil'd with? All this may seem savage
in me. You do not feel as I do—you do not know what
it is to love—one day you may—your time is not come.
Ask yourself how many unhappy hours Keats has
caused you in Loneliness. For myself I have been a
Martyr the whole time, and for this reason I speak; the
confession is forc'd from me by the torture. I appeal to
you by the blood of that Christ you believe in: Do not
write to me if you have done anything this month
which it would have pained me to have seen. You may
have altered—if you have not—if you still believe in
dancing rooms and other societies as I have seen you—
I do not want to live—if you have done so I wish this
coming night may be my last. I cannot live without
you, and not only you but *chaste you*; *virtuous you*. The
Sun rises and sets, the day passes, and you follow the
bent of your inclination to a certain extent—you have
no conception of the quantity of miserable feeling that
passes through me in a day.—Be serious! Love is not a
plaything—and again do not write unless you can do it
with a crystal conscience. I would sooner die for want of
you than——

Yours for ever
J. Keats."

It is no wonder that after this wild, miserable letter
Fanny complained that he ill-treated her in word, thought
and deed; and it need scarcely be said that there was
nothing to justify the accusations he threw at her.
Charles Brown and Fanny Brawne were on very good

terms, which is to the credit of both of them, seeing how prone Brown was to be jealous of those who were close to Keats. (He quarrelled violently with George Keats, Reynolds and Dilke, and had taken, on Keats's authority, "one of his funny odd dislikes" to Woodhouse.) But with Fanny Brawne, judging by his letter to her, and her references to him in her correspondence with Fanny Keats, he remained on terms of sincere and admiring friendship. That they ever flirted with each other in Keats's sick-room is unthinkable, but Fanny had a lively manner and Brown was fond of cracking a joke. The Valentine, which he sent her, possibly that very year, and which was handed down by word of mouth to her children, shows very well the joking, affectionate, entirely unsentimental terms they were on.

> "Whene'er we chance to meet
>   You know the reason why
> You pass me in the street
>   And toss your head on high—
>
> "Because my walking stick
>   Is not a dandy twig
> Because my boots are thick
>   Because I wear a wig.
>
> "Because you think my coat
>   Too often has been worn
> And the tie about my throat
>   Is at the corners torn."

("There is something," writes Fanny Brawne's daughter, "about his hat being shabby and about his gloves being in holes and then——")

> "To see me thus equipped
>   What folly to be haughty—

> Pray were you never whipped
>   At school for being naughty?"

It is possible when they met in Keats's sick-room, they may have felt something of the subconscious complicity that two healthy, unnervous people do feel, in the presence of someone who is ill, however much dearer the invalid may be to them both, and it may have been this that caused Keats to write, as he did in February:

"MY DEAR FANNY,—I think you had better not make any long stay with me when Mr. Brown is at home. Whenever he goes out you may bring your work," and which prompted this wild outburst of retrospective jealousy. But actually it is not Brown of whom he is jealous, that is proved by the moving request that Keats made to him only a few weeks later: "I think without my mentioning it for my sake you would be a good friend to Miss Brawne when I am dead. You think she has many faults —but, for my sake, think she has not one—if there is any thing you can do for her by word or deed I know you will do it."

No, it is life itself which he resents with this aching bitter jealousy. Fanny, however much she loves him, however constant she is to him, will go on living, will see the spring and the flowers, will eat and drink and sleep and sometimes be happy and perhaps love again, and he will be divided from her for ever. All his love of life, all his longing for her bring him to bitter gall and to despair. He felt as Abelard did when he forced Heloise to take the veil that she might not have part in a world in which he could no longer share.

"To be happy with you seems such an impossibility!

it requires a luckier Star than mine! it will never be . . .
If my health would bear it, I could write a Poem which
I have in my head, which would be a consolation for
people in such a situation as mine. I could show some
one in Love as I am, with a person living in such Liberty
as you do. Shakespeare always sums up matters in the
most sovereign manner. Hamlet's heart was full of such
Misery as mine is when he said to Ophelia 'Go to a
Nunnery, go go!' Indeed I should like to give up the
matter at once—I should like to die. I am sickened at
the brute world which you are smiling with. I hate men
and women more. I see nothing but thorns for the
future—wherever I may be next winter in Italy or
nowhere Brown will be living near you with his in-
decencies——" (This might refer to Brown's language
and manner of expressing himself or more likely to his
behaviour with Abby.) "I see no prospect of any rest.
Suppose me in Rome—well, I should there see you as in
a magic glass going to and from town at all hours,——I
wish you could infuse a little confidence in human
nature into my heart. I cannot muster any—the world
is too brutal for me—I am glad there is such a thing as
the grave—I am sure I shall never have any rest till I
get there. At any rate I will indulge myself by never
seeing any more Dilke or Brown or any of their Friends.
I wish I was either in your arms full of faith or that a
Thunderbolt would strike me.

God bless you.

J.K.—"

CHAPTER XVIII

The journey to Italy—Joseph Severn—The voyage in the "Maria Crowther"—Arrival and quarantine at Naples—Journey to Rome.

PART of Keats's torment can be attributed to the one little sentence we find in the beginning of his letter to Fanny: "They talk of me going to Italy." A warm climate was supposed to be good for diseased lungs. They had talked of sending Tom to Lisbon, but he had not gone, and he had died in the raw chill of an English December. With the best will in the world, with unwearying kindness, his friends were determined that John Keats should have every chance of life. He was bound to submit, but his instinct rebelled. The thought of the journey to Italy, of the parting from Fanny, was horrible to him. It was a nightmare that with slow, inexorable steps came nearer and nearer, from which there was no escape.

He managed to conceal his mental unhappiness, if not his physical state, pretty well from the outside world. Mrs. Gisborne in her private journal wrote that she met him at the Hunts': "We talked of music, and of Italian and English singing; I mentioned that Farinelli had the art of taking breath imperceptibly, while he continued to hold one single note, alternately swelling out and diminishing the power of his voice. Keats observed this must in some degree be painful to the hearer, as when a diver descends into the hidden part of the sea you feel an apprehension lest he may never rise again." And Mary Novello Clarke, the wife of Cowden Clarke, records that she saw Keats just before he left Mortimer

Terrace, "half-reclining having had two or three chairs arranged as a sofa," and lying there, "quietly while he talked placidly and pleasedly with the friends who had come to see him and take leave of him before his journey."

Leigh Hunt, who was intimate with him and saw him every day, naturally knew far more of the real state of the case. "Seeing him once change colour," Hunt records, "in a manner more alarming than usual, as he stood silently eyeing the country out of the window, I pressed him to let me know how he felt, in order that he might enable me to do what I could for him; upon which he said, that his feelings were almost more than he could bear and that he feared for his senses. I proposed that we should take a coach, and ride about the country together, to vary, if possible, the immediate impression, which was sometimes all that was formidable and would come to nothing. He acquiesced, and was soon restored to himself."

But even Leigh Hunt did not apparently realize in what a weak and shaken state his nerves were. He did not take it very seriously when Keats discovered that a letter written to him by Fanny Brawne had been kept from him for two days and was finally delivered with the seal broken, the act of a spiteful housemaid under notice of dismissal. But for Keats it was too much; he had probably been on the rack for this letter, hour after hour, post after post, and he flung out of the house, determined not to set foot in it again. He went back to Hampstead with some idea of finding his old lodging in Well Walk, but when he called on the Brawnes, Mrs. Brawne, shocked at his appearance, insisted that he should come and stay with them.

We have no knowledge whether he was happy in that last month that he spent with Fanny under her own roof. Dilke writes: "The constant feeding of his passion wore him out; this is his own expression." But Severn, in Rome, writing to Mrs. Brawne, tells her: "He has many, many times talked over 'the few happy days at your house, the only time when his mind was at ease.'"

But he was very ill. "I am excessively nervous," he wrote to his sister, "a person I am not quite used to entering the room half choaks me;" and the thought of parting with Fanny was anguishing. "This journey to Italy," he wrote to Taylor, "wakes me up at daylight every morning and haunts me horribly. I shall endeavour to go through with it with the sensation of marching up against a Battery;" an expression which he used in his letter to Shelley; while Leigh Hunt, whom he had asked to come and see him, "for I feel really attach'd to you for your many sympathies with me, and patience at my lunes," writes that, when he and Keats were sitting together on a bench in Well Walk, Keats "suddenly turned towards me, his eyes swimming with tears, and told me he was dying of a broken heart."

One cannot help sympathizing with Fanny Brawne's outburst, written after she heard of his death, that the "Doctors were ignorant and unfeeling enough to send him to that wretched country to die, for it is now known that his recovery was impossible before he left us, and he might have died here with so many friends to soothe him and *me* with him."

But with the best motives in the world the inexorable preparations for the journey to Italy went on. Taylor raised the funds for it in a very generous manner. He bought the copyright of *Endymion* for £100, gave Keats a draft on an Italian bank for £120 and procured another £100 partly from Lord Fitzwilliam, who gave fifty, and partly from five other friends of Keats, including James Rice, who guaranteed £10 each.

For a companion Keats naturally first thought of Charles Brown, but he was in Scotland and could not be got hold of in time, and it seemed as if he might almost have to sail alone, until William Haslam procured for him the companionship of Joseph Severn. Both these young men were very old friends of Keats. They had known John, George and Tom when they were living together at 76 Cheapside, when John was at Guy's Hospital. Not a great deal is known about Haslam, who was a solicitor, except that he was a good and practical friend to Keats. "I cannot forbear mentioning Haslam as a most kind and obliging and constant friend," Keats wrote to George and Georgiana. "His behaviour to Tom during my absence and since my return has endeared him to me very much." And now it was owing to his suggestion that Severn was persuaded to go to Rome with Keats.

Joseph Severn was two years older than Keats but infinitely less mature in every way. He had early shown an aptitude for drawing and had been apprenticed by his father to an engraver, a trade he loathed, and from which he finally broke away in order to become a painter. He was mainly self-taught, and in 1817 was fortunate enough to win the Royal Academy's Gold Medal with the picture Keats wryly referred to when he wrote: "You had best put me in your Cave of Despair." Severn was a very handsome, rather girlish-looking young man, with a lovable, sunny, confiding nature. He was not very well-educated and he had a wondering, enthusiastic admiration for Keats. He would bring over his work to Well Walk or Wentworth Place in order to have the chance of listening to Keats talk. "There was" he wrote "on my part the reception of such intellectual largesse with a warm feeling of gratitude." Keats, on his side, seems to have looked on Severn with a sincere but rather patronizing affection. "You are the most astonishing innocent I ever knew," he said on one occasion. Indeed Severn rather reminds one of a nice puppy in his timid but persistent following after of Keats.

Though he had always longed for the chance of studying in Rome and hoped to win a travelling studentship from the Royal Academy, it was mainly out of friendship for Keats that Severn made the sudden resolve to accompany him to Italy at two or three days' notice.

The poor young man had a dismal beginning to his journey, for on September 17th he left his home in the early morning, after having been knocked down by his father, a man subject to violent and sudden fits of temper, who disapproved of his son's journey to Rome. He reached the docks where he found Keats with John Taylor and William Haslam and went aboard the *Maria Crowther*. That day they slipped down the estuary and anchored at Gravesend. By a most irritating coincidence Charles Brown was also at Gravesend that night. The smack, on board which he had hurried down from Scotland as soon as he received Keats's letter, was anchored alongside the *Maria Crowther* and neither Keats nor Brown had any suspicion of the other's presence.

The next day Severn went ashore to buy some medicines, adding at Keats's special request a bottle of laudanum, and the fourth passenger came aboard. (They had already been joined by a Mrs. Pidgeon at the docks.) Miss Cotterell was a pretty, gentle girl, also in an advanced stage of consumption. "It has been unfortunate for me," wrote Keats to Mrs. Brawne, "that one of the passengers was a young Lady in a Consumption— her imprudence has vexed me very much—the knowledge of her complaint—the flushings in her face, all her bad symptoms have prayed upon me they would not have done so had I been in good health." "I have a thousand times wished (her) at the bottom of the sea as I know she made it worse for your brother," wrote Fanny Brawne.

They had an unpleasant voyage down the Channel. The *Maria Crowther* was a merchant brigantine neither well-found nor comfortable. The five passengers all slept in one small cabin, which was frequently under water. Nor were things made any easier by the fact that Keats and Miss Cotterell seemed to need entirely different treatment. If the windows were shut, she would faint and remain insensible for five or six hours, according to Severn. If they were open Keats would be taken with a violent cough and with blood-spitting. The thought of that tiny cabin containing five people, frequently sea-sick, two of them consumptive, suffering from hæmorrhages, is very terrible.

On the 19th of September they were off Dover Castle and already beginning to feel the motion of the English Channel. In fact, all four passengers were sick over the rail! "Keats," Severn records, "did it in the most gentlemanly manner." The next day they went through a really bad storm, and in the evening the water began to come into the cabin through an opening in the planks. "This made us rather long-faced," writes Severn, "—for it came by pail-fulls—again I got out and said to Keats, ' here's pretty music for you,' with the greatest calmness he answered me only by: ' Water parted from the sea.' " (This was the first line of a popular song from Arne's opera *Artaxerxes*.)

They were blown twenty miles out of their course by this storm; and calms and contrary winds kept them beating about the Channel for many more days.

They landed at Dungeness and again at Portsmouth, when Keats went to call on Mrs. Snook at Bedhampton, from whose house he and Brown had written that light-hearted letter, full of horrible puns, less than two years ago. He again, most unluckily, missed Brown, who, had he only known it, was staying at Chichester with old Mr. Dilke.

"I was very disappointed," he wrote to Brown, the next day when they lay off Yarmouth in the Isle of Wight, "at not meeting you at Bedhampton, and am very provoked at the thought of you being at Chichester to-day. I should have delighted in setting off for London for the sensation merely—for what should I do there? I could not leave my lungs or stomach or other worse things behind me. I wish to write on subjects that will not agitate me much—there is one I must mention and have done with it. Even if my body would recover of itself, this would prevent it. The very thing which I want to live most for will be a great occasion of my death. I cannot help it. Who can help it? Were I in health it would make me ill, and how can I bear it in my state? I dare say you will be able to guess on what subject I am harping—you know what was my greatest pain during the first part of my illness at your house. I wish for death every day and night to deliver me from those pains, and then I wish death away, for death would destroy even those pains which are better than nothing. Land and Sea, weakness and decline are great separators, but death is the great divorcer for ever. When the pang of this thought has passed through my mind, I may say the bitterness of death is passed. . . . I am in a state at present in which woman merely as woman can have no more power over me than stocks and stones, and yet the difference of my sensations with respect to Miss Brawne and my Sister is amazing. The one seems to absorb the other to a degree incredible. I seldom think of my Brother and Sister in America. The thought of leaving Miss Brawne is beyond every

R

thing horrible—the sense of darkness coming over me—
I eternally see her figure eternally vanishing. Some of
the phrases she was in the habit of using during my
last nursing at Wentworth Place ring in my ears. Is
there another Life? Shall I awake and find all this a
dream? There must be we cannot be created for this
sort of suffering."

They landed once more on the Dorset coast and
visited Lulworth Cove, where Keats, "for a moment,"
says Severn, "became like his former self." It was the
last time that he trod on English ground.

After this the voyage was comparatively quick, and
after such minor excitements as seeing a whale, and
being fired on by a Portuguese man-of-war who took
them for a privateer, they arrived in Naples on October
21st, thirty-four days out of London.

In Naples the ship was forced to remain in quarantine
for ten days. The Bay must have looked very lovely as
they sailed into it in the golden October morning. "The
white houses," wrote Severn, "were lit up by the rising
sun, which had just begun to touch them, and being tier
above tier upon the hill-slopes, they had a lovely appearance, with so much green verdure and the many vine-
yards and olive grounds about them. Vesuvius had an
immense line of smoke-clouds built up, which every
now and then opened and changed with the sun's golden
light, edging and composing all kinds of groups and
shapes in lengths and masses for miles. Then the mountains of Sorrento to the right seemed like lapis lazuli and
gold; the sea between being of a very deep blue such
as we had not seen elsewhere, and so rich and beautiful
that it gave great splendour to all the objects on shore."
But Keats, who had so loved beauty and the old classical
Mediterranean civilizations, would not really enjoy all
this. Although at first he was, Severn states, "simply

entranced" with the beauty of the Bay and the City, and was able to talk of "the classic scenes he seemed to know so well," making it "all live again, that old antique world when the Greek galleys and Tyrrhenian sloops brought northward strange tales of what was happening in Hellus and the mysterious East," he could not enjoy it with anything like his full capacity. "O what an account I could give you of the Bay of Naples if I could once more feel myself a Citizen of this world," he wrote to Mrs. Brawne. "I feel a spirit in my Brain would lay it forth pleasantly—O what a misery it is to have an intellect in splints!" He could not write to Fanny herself. "I dare not fix my Mind upon Fanny," he wrote in this same letter. "I have not dared to think of her. The only comfort I have had that way has been in thinking for hours together of having the knife she gave me put in a silver-case—the hair in a Locket—and the Pocket Book in a gold net—Show her this—I dare say no more."

It is all over with the extravagant endearments, reproaches and sweet words of earlier days. "Good-bye my love, my dear love, my beauty—love me for ever," was how he had been used to write to her. But now he has only strength for six small words, written as a postscript in his letter to her mother, heartbreaking in their bare simplicity. "Good-bye Fanny! God bless you." It was the last word that she ever had from him.

The ten days of quarantine passed in a sort of feverish, desperate gaiety. A Lieutenant Sullivan and six men, sent by the Admiral to inquire the name and status of the ship, thoughtlessly came on board and were therefore, according to the strict regulations, imprisoned with the crew and passengers. Miss Cotterell's brother also came to join them, providing them with extra delicacies of fruit, fish and fowl, which, however, could hardly have counterbalanced the bad air and the stifling cabin. There

was continuous chaff and merriment, "for," writes
Severn, "after our advent and our boarding by Lieutenant
Sullivan and his crew, we were encircled by joyous
Neapolitans; for it seemed that the uncommon accident
of having an English naval officer and six man-of-war's
men entrapped into quarantine on board a small merchant schooner, brought hundreds, I am tempted to say
thousands, to laugh and be merry at the expense of the
blunderers. Mr. Cotterell translated the jokes and jibes,
and caused us and our visitors continual roars of
laughter. All kinds of chaff went on, and Keats was not
behind either Mr Cotterell or Lieutenant Sullivan in
witty puns and remarks." It must have been an unhappy
feverish merriment. Keats wrote later to Brown that:
"I . . . at my worst, even in quarantine, summoned up
more puns, in a sort of desparation, in one week than
in any year of my life."

Perhaps there was some real pleasure in the sight
of the gay little boats, flitting across the vivid blue
waters, in the sounds of the guitars and the harsh,
stirring Neapolitan voices, and in the taste of the
warm Southern fruits. But it was not England. His
treasure and, in consequence, his heart were elsewhere.
"Keats," writes Severn, "was never tired of admiring,
(not to speak of eating) the beautiful clusters of grapes
and other fruits, and was scarce less enthusiastic over
the autumn flowers, though I remember his saying
once that he would gladly give them all for a wayside
dog-rose bush covered with pink blooms." The flowers
that grew in the fields of Edmonton, in the lanes round
Hampstead possessed his thoughts. Ten months earlier,
after his first attack of blood-spitting, he had written
to Rice: "How astonishingly does the chance of leaving
the world impress a sense of its natural beauties on us.
Like poor Falstaff, though I do not babble, I think of

green fields. I muse with the greatest affection on every
flower I have known from my infancy—their shapes
and colours are as new to me as if I had just created
them with a superhuman fancy. It is because they are
connected with the most thoughtless and happiest
moments of our lives. I have seen foreign flowers in
hothouses of the most beautiful nature, but I do not
care a straw for them. The simple flowers of our spring
are what I want to see again."

At last the quarantine was over and they landed in
Naples, but there was a horrible reaction in their spirits.
Naples they found extremely noisy and smelly. They
were probably both overtired and dispirited, for Severn,
who wrote in one mood, "The fun, the laughter, the
singing, all helped to increase the brilliant holiday scene,
so much that at the expiry of our 'isolation' I could
not help feeling regret—for, altogether, it was to me a
scene of such splendour and gaiety as I had never
imagined and did not expect to realize again," now wrote
to Haslam: "We are just released from the loathsome
miseries of quarantine—foul weather and foul air for
the whole ten days kept us to the small cabin—surrounded by about 2,000 ships in a wretched hole not
sufficient for half the number, yet Keats is still living—
may I not have hopes of him?" While Keats wrote to
Charles Brown the saddest and most desperate letter
that he ever wrote:

"*Naples.* 1 *November.*

"My Dear Brown,—Yesterday we were let out of
Quarantine, during which my health suffered more
from bad air and the stifled cabin than it had done the
whole voyage. The fresh air revived me a little, and
I hope I am well enough this morning to write to you
a short calm letter;—if that can be called one, in which

I am afraid to speak of what I would fainest dwell upon. As I have gone thus far into it, I must go on a little;—perhaps it may relieve the load of WRETCHED-NESS which presses upon me. The persuasion that I shall see her no more will kill me. I cannot q . . ." (Brown makes the following note on this passage: "He could not go on with this sentence nor even write the word 'quit,'—as I suppose. The word WRETCHEDNESS above he himself wrote in large characters.") "My dear Brown, I should have had her when I was in health, and I should have remained well. I can bear to die—I cannot bear to leave her. O, God! God! God! Everything I have in my trunks that reminds me of her goes through me like a spear. The silk lining she put in my travelling cap scalds my head. My imagination is horribly vivid about her—I see her—I hear her. There is nothing in the world of sufficient interest to divert me from her a moment. This was the case when I was in England; I cannot recollect, without shuddering, the time that I was a prisoner at Hunt's, and used to keep my eyes fixed on Hampstead all day. Then there was a good hope of seeing her again—Now!—O that I could be buried near where she lives! I am afraid to write to her—to receive a letter from her—to see her hand-writing would break my heart—even to hear of her anyhow, to see her name written, would be more than I can bear. My dear Brown, what am I to do? Where can I look for consolation or ease? If I had any chance of recovery, this passion would kill me. Indeed, through the whole of my illness, both at your house and at Kentish Town, this fever has never ceased wearing me out. When you write to me, which you will do im-mediately, write to Rome (*poste restante*)—if she is well and happy, put a mark thus X; if——

"Remember me to all. I will endeavour to bear my

miseries patiently. A person in my state of health
should not have such miseries to bear. Write a short
note to my sister, saying you have heard from me.
Severn is very well. If I were in better health I should
urge your coming to Rome. I fear there is no one can
give me any comfort. Is there any news of George?
O, that something fortunate had ever happened to me
or my brothers!—then I might hope,—but despair is
forced upon me as a habit. My dear Brown, for my sake,
be her advocate for ever. I cannot say a word about
Naples; I do not feel at all concerned in the thousand
novelties around me. I am afraid to write to her—I
should like her to know that I do not forget her. Oh,
Brown, I have coals of fire in my breast. It surprises
me that the human heart is capable of containing and
bearing so much misery. Was I born for this end? God
bless her, and her mother, and my sister, and George,
and his wife, and you, and all!

Your ever affectionate friend,
JOHN KEATS."

Without in the least doubting Fanny Brawne's love
for Keats, nor the grief which, hidden as it was, she felt
over his death, one cannot help feeling that by this time
they had moved on to different planes. Her letter to
Fanny Keats which follows was, it must be remembered,
written to a girl younger than herself, whom she wished
to spare, and whom she hardly knew. One can only
admire her for her reasonableness and her self-control,
yet it does seem that a great gulf now separates her from
her suffering lover. An inevitable gulf; he was passing
through the dark gateway towards death, and she
remained in life. Hers was the right, the reasonable and
the courageous attitude—only if she had seen Brown's
letter, and it appears she had (she had certainly seen the

letter to her mother), it seems strange that she *could* control herself to write so unemotionally:

"My dearest Girl,—I am really affraid you will think me a troublesome correspondent but this time I do not write on my own account but by your brothers wish. Mr. Brown has received a letter from him dated November the 2nd from which I find he has not yet written to you, as he wished someone to do it for him. In the letter we received the 24th of October" (the one to Mrs. Brawne with the postscript to Fanny) "he said they had to stay on board ten days longer to perform Quarantine. So far they had had a tolerable voyage from the time they left Portsmouth. He did not think himself better or worse but his spirits were not very good. When he wrote to Mr Brown they were just arrived on shore, their sufferings during the quarantine were beyond anything we can imagine. From your brother I never expect a very good account, but you may imagine how lowering to the spirits it must have been when Mr Severn who I never imagined it was possible for any thing to make unhappy, who I never saw for ten minutes serious, says he was so overcome that he was obliged to relieve himself by shedding tears." (A later passage in Severn's letter to Haslam.) "He, however, says your brother was a little recovered, at least quite as much so as he could expect, the day after his arrival. He says, if he can but get his spirits good, he will answer for his being well in a moderate time; which shows he does not consider he has any complaint of conse-quence. . . . The Physician to whom our friends were recommended was at Rome when they reached Naples and they had made up their minds to go to Rome. I have written to him to-day and directed the letter there. If you would like to write to him mention it, and I will get the direction, for I cannot give it you now as it is a foreign one and I should make some mistake so I will ask Mr Brown again when I see him. I should like to have given you a better account but I must say that considering all things it is as well as we could have expected." (This sentence, even given the circumstances, seems curiously hard and un-understanding, so that I think it is only right to quote the words that she wrote after Keats's death: "I know my Keats is happy, happier a thousand times than he could have been here, for Fanny, you do not, you never can know how much he has suffered.")

As will be seen from the above letter, Severn and Keats soon left Naples and went on to Rome, partly in order to be near Doctor Clark, and partly because of the disturbed political situation of Naples. King Ferdinand, "Bomba," had lately stolen away, abandoning the new constitutional government and leaving his people to the Austrians. Keats, who as far as he had any political opinions, was a follower of Leigh Hunt's and Hazlitt's Liberalism, was disgusted by this, and by the sight of a couple of armed sentries posted on the stage when they went to the opera. It was only the custom of the age and country, but he broke out in a frenzy: "Severn, we'll go at once to Rome, for, as I know I shall not last long, it would make me die in anguish if I thought I was to be buried amid a people with such miserable political debasement."

Keats had recovered a little since he wrote to Brown. He had unbosomed himself to Severn, which must have been a great relief, even if Severn were not the ideal confidante. He had been able to drive a little around the city with Charles Cotterell, who was very grateful to them both for their kindness to his sister, and he

managed during the five days they spent at Naples to
get through Clarissa Harlowe in nine volumes.

On the 4th or 5th of November they set out for
Rome, in a small carriage so slow that Severn was able
to walk beside it nearly all the way. The roads were bad,
and the accommodation poor, and though Severn, with
his usual sunny temper, enjoyed it, he records that
"Keats, on the other hand, had become very listless, and
seldom seemed even relatively happy, except when an
unusually fine prospect opened before us, or the breeze
bore to us exquisite hill fragrances or breaths from the
distant blue seas, and particularly when I literally filled
the little carriage with flowers. He never tired of these,
and they gave him a singular and almost fantastic
pleasure that was at times almost akin to a strange
joy."

They crossed the vast dun-coloured Campagna, which
Keats said was like an inland ocean, only more mono-
tonous than the one they had just left, and paused a
moment to observe a cardinal shooting small birds. ("He
had an owl tied loosely by a stick, and a small looking
glass was annexed to move about with the owl, the light
of which attracted numerous birds. The whole merit
seemed to be in not shooting the owl. Two footmen in
livery kept loading the fowling pieces for the cardinal,
and it was astonishing the number of birds he killed.")

Finally, about November 17th, by the Lateran Gate,
they entered Rome.

CHAPTER XIX

The last chapter—The house on the Spanish Steps—Keats's physical sufferings—Death.

IF Keats, at nineteen, immured in the dirty, squalid confines of the Borough, could have known that he was a few years later to spend three months in Rome, he would have been overjoyed. But it came too late. The eternal city was to him like a cardboard simulacrum invested with a complete unreality. "I have an habitual feeling of my real life having passed and that I am leading a posthumous existence," he wrote to Brown.

The first month was not too bad. It was a warm, sunny winter, and Keats was able to leave the little house on the Spanish Steps which Doctor Clark had found for him and Severn, and stroll about the upper terrace, and among the ilex and olive groves of the Pincio. He was forbidden to go sight-seeing, but he had a little horse on which he could ride about. In these excursions he was sometimes joined by a Lieutenant Elton, a tall, handsome young officer, also suffering from tuberculosis.

As they strolled on the Pincio the eyes of Paulina Borghese, Napoleon's lovely amoral sister, lit on this young man and her long, languishing, desirous glances followed him every time they passed and repassed on the fashionable promenade. "This so jarred on Keats's nerves," records Severn, "though he thankfully acknowledged that he was not the attraction, that we were obliged to go and take our walk in another place." This little incident shows how tormented he was. He could not bear the thoughts of life, of love and of desire.

"There is one thought enough to kill me," he wrote

to Brown; "I have been well, healthy, alert &c., walking
with her, and now——" And Fanny, so far away, was
she smiling with her long, almond-shaped eyes, at some
man as Paulina Borghese smiled at Elton?

> "To-night, if I may guess, thy beauty wears
>   A smile of such delight,
>   As brilliant and as bright,
> As when with ravished, aching, vassal eyes,
>   Lost in soft amaze,
>   I gaze, I gaze!"

So he had written in the *Ode to Fanny*.

He was, however, a little stronger than he had been.
He was able to read and to study Italian, and he even
began to toy with the faint, shadowy hope of being
able to write once more, planning in his head a poem on
the story of *Sabrina*. Severn procured a pianoforte and
was able to play to him, which he enjoyed much,
exclaiming with delight over a volume of Haydn's
Symphonies: "This Haydn is like a child, for there is
no knowing what he will do next!" It was not such a
very long time, measured in the span of years, since
he had lain listening in the darkness to Charles Cowden
Clark playing in the schoolhouse at Enfield.

He was strong enough, moreover, to take a very
decided line of action over the catering; an anecdote
very characteristic of the earlier, young, impulsive,
mischievous Keats. Severn's account of the incident is
entertaining:

"In our first Roman days," he writes, "we got very
odd and very bad dinners sent in, as the Roman custom
is, from a Trattoria or restaurant. This was the more
intolerable as we paid a crown for each meal, and as
each, for all their cunning disguises in sauces and spices,
was more unpalatable than the other. We put up with

this annoyance for more than a week, although we made daily complaints to the padrona di casa, but one day we both pronounced the dinner to be unfit to eat. Keats hit on an expedient by which we always got good dinners afterwards. He would not tell me what it was to be. When the porter came as usual with the basket, and was beginning to set out the dinner, Keats stepped forward, and smiling roguishly at me, with a ' Now, Severn, you'll see it,' he opened the window, which was over the front steps, and taking up each dish one after the other, he quietly emptied the contents out of the window and returned the plate to the basket—and thus disappeared a fowl, a rice pudding, cauliflower, a dish of macaroni, &c. This was all done to the amusement of the porter and the padrona. He then quietly but very decidedly pointed to the basket for the porter to take away, which he did without demur. ' Now,' said Keats, ' you'll see, Severn, that we'll have a decent dinner; ' and sure enough in less than half an hour an excellent one came, and we continued to be similarly well treated every day. In the account, moreover, the padrona was discreet enough not to charge for the dinners thrown out of the window."

Severn, meanwhile, was enjoying himself in Rome. Doctor Clark was extremely good to the two young men, and it must have been a relief for Severn to place Keats under medical care. Moreover, Clark began to introduce Severn to Roman society, beginning with the sculptor Gibson, at whose studio Severn was enchanted to find himself in company with Lord Colchester. He attempted to retire, but Gibson caught him by the arm and made him enter.

"Indeed," writes Severn rapturously, "the act, slight as it may seem, was like sunshine to me."

Severn was anxious to win the Academy's travelling

scholarship, and Keats was all interest and generous enthusiasm for his friend's plans—although in his general despondency and his knowledge of the world's lack of enthusiasm for young talent, he thought Severn's chances of prevailing against the "host of tradesmen in Art" very slight. He had been at a dinner of artists, he now told Severn, where they were discussing the award of the gold medal which Severn had received from the Academy. "Someone"—the quotation is from Severn's memoirs—"scornfully explained that the picture was very inferior, but that as the artist was an old fellow, and had made frequent attempts for the prize, the Council had given the medal out of pity and not for any merit. Keats, after a few moments, expressed his disgust at such a mean lie, having first awaited a flat contradiction from one of the three artists present beside Hilton, who knew it to be a lie; and he declared that he would not any longer sit at the same table with such traducers and snobs; that he knew me intimately, had seen my picture and recognized its merits; that, as they well knew, I was a young man, and that the picture was my first attempt for a prize of any kind. He then rose from the table and abruptly left the party. . . . He became much excited when he recounted this villainy," Severn goes on, "for with his ready sympathy he placed himself in my position. Although small of stature, yet on these occasions of acts of meanness, he seemed to rise to a larger stature, and the effect was a marvellous contrast to his charming manner when he was tranquil."

It must be recorded for the credit of human nature that two of the artists present, Hilton and De Wint, whom Keats upbraided as snobs and traducers, were two of those who contributed £10 towards the journey to Italy. It is to their credit, and it also shows that there must have been something very fine in the generous integrity of the young man's anger, that could evoke generosity rather than resentment in response.

Severn soon set to work on the "Death of Alciabides," which was the subject he chose for his scholarship picture. "Keats continued to be anguished on my account," he wrote, "for he knew as well as I that my prospects in great measure depended on my producing another picture in competition for the student's pension; but with my agitation for the poor fellow it seemed impossible that I could execute such a work for such a purpose, in what were then my circumstances." It was natural that Severn, on the threshold of what seemed a promising career, should have occasionally repined a little at being kept from it. Would it have seemed strange to both young men had they known that Severn's fame, not only posthumously, but during his life-time, would be to be known as the "friend of Keats," that the only pictures of his ever to please posterity are the numberless portraits he drew all his life long of his dead friend?

But this moderately peaceful existence soon came to an end. Out of a blue sky on December 10th Keats was suddenly attacked by a most violent hæmorrhage. Doctor Clark was sent for, and instantly bled him, according to the barbarous medical practice of the day, taking away about eight ounces of black, thick blood. It was a disastrous day. Keats had never had much hope of his own recovery; one of the tortures of his condition was his medical knowledge, which enabled him to follow and to predict the course of his disease, and now he was quite in despair. He attempted to rush from his bed, exclaiming: "This day shall be my last," and was only restrained with difficulty by Severn. Next morning the bleeding broke out again.

The next three weeks were very terrible. For a while

the body conquered. The medical treatment of the day did nothing to alleviate the horrible suffering. Doctor Clark was as kind as he could be. He came round as often as he could, frequently during the night. His wife prepared food for the two young men with her own hands. But medical science prescribed bleeding and starvation. Keats was, at one time, only allowed one anchovy and one slice of bread per day. He was ravenously hungry, and kept calling for food, crying out that he was being starved to death, which indeed was not far from the truth. He knew far too much about his own condition, and would insist on describing to Severn the progress the disease would take and the horrible stages it would go through. It was·at this time that he wanted to take the laudanum he had made Severn buy at Gravesend, not so much to spare himself but to save Severn the strain of nursing him—as he had once nursed poor Tom. When Severn refused to give it to him, he fell into a violent rage. The thought was an agony to him and added to his tortured despair. He kept recapitulating all he had lost, all he had had hoped to have in life. His temper and his nerves were fretted to breaking point. "His imagination and memory," wrote Severn, "present every thought to him in horror."

But the agony calmed at last. The tearing struggle was over. The will to live, so fierce and potent, the mainspring of his love and of his poetry, was finally conquered. Severn, exhausted by the struggle, which indeed he seems to have borne with wonderful patience and kindness, saw in this some occasion for hope. "I said that 'the first good news I had should be for the kind Mrs. Brawne,'" he wrote to that lady on January 11th, 1821. And he goes on to tell of the reasons he has for hoping for Keats's recovery: "Now," Severn writes, "he has changed to calmness and quietude, as singular as productive of good, for his mind was most certainly killing him. He has now given up all thoughts, hopes, or even wish for recovery. His mind is in a state of peace from the final leave he has taken of this world and all its future hopes; this has been an immense weight for him to rise from. He remains quiet and submissive under his heavy fate. Now, if anything will recover him, it is this absence of himself." Severn was ever optimistic, but there was someone else who saw far more clearly what it meant that the resentment, the bitterness against death, the panting, feverish desire for life, were at last vanquished. "Mr. Severn says that for the first time he feels a hope," wrote Fanny Brawne, "he thinks he shall bring him back to us. Surely, that is saying a great deal—and yet the reason he gives for the hope destroys it, for the last three days, the letter was dated the 11th of January, your brother has been calm, he had resigned himself to die. Oh can you bear to think of it, he has given up even wishing to live—Good God! Is it to be borne that he, formed for every thing good, and, I think I dare say it, for everything great, is to give up his hopes of happiness, so young too, and to be murdered, for that is the case, by the mere malignity of the world. . . . I am sure nothing during his long illness has hurt me so much as to hear he was resigned to die."

He had not been able to write to her for a long time. He could not now bear even to read her letters. A glance at one of them "tore him to pieces." "He kept continually in his hand," wrote Severn, "a polished, oval, white cornelian, the gift of his widowing love, and at times it seemed his only consolation, the only thing left him in this world clearly tangible." He was slowly but surely slipping away from everything. He would not have most of his letters read to him, for, he said, "he had already journeyed far beyond them." "The hope of death," wrote Severn, "seems his only comfort. He talks of the quiet grave as the first rest he can ever have."

At one moment he craved for books, but it was only for a little while, then they too passed from him. Severn would read aloud to him from Jeremy Taylor's *Holy Living and Dying*, "from which," Severn states, "he received great comfort." One wonders what that free, unconfined spirit found in the dogmatically pious Jeremy Taylor. Perhaps he liked it since it was concerned with death, the only subject that now held reality for him. Perhaps there was something in him that responded to the stern Ecclesiastes-like sentences: "Man is like a thing of nought: his time passeth away like a shadow . . . So is every man; he is born in vanity and sin; he comes into the world like morning mushrooms, soon thrusting their heads into the air, and conversing with their kind of the same production, and as soon they turn into dust and forgetfulness. . . . A man is so vain, so unfixed, so perishing a creature, that he cannot long last in the scene of fancy; a man goes off and is forgotten, like the dream of a distracted person." It must have been in this spirit that he asked Severn to have carved upon his gravestone:

"Here lies one whose name was writ in water."

The world was fast slipping away from him. He would fix his large, lustrous, hazel eyes, burning ever larger in his wasted face, on Doctor Clark as he came in every morning, mournfully and sternly inquiring: "Doctor, how long is this posthumous life of mine to last?" Fame, ambition, even love, seemed dreams within dreams. There remained only the little incidents of the present time, the tiny spark climbing along a thread fixed by Severn from the base of a burning candle to the wick of an unlighted one, so that Keats cried out: "Severn, Severn! Here's a little fairy lamplighter actually lit up the other candle"; the description Severn gave him of the cemetery where he was to lie—the grass, the many flowers, the flocks of goats and sheep tended by a young shepherd. "Violets were his favourite flowers," wrote Severn, "and he joyed to hear how they overspread the graves." ("I hope you have good store of double violets," he had written two springs ago, to his little sister. "I think they are the very Princesses of flowers, and in a shower of rain, almost as fine as barley sugar drops are to a schoolboy's tongue.")

He had dreaded a slow death, and feared he might linger on all through the spring and might suffer at last a slow, delirious death-stage, but Fate, so little kind, was kind to him in this.

About half-past four on the 23rd of February he suddenly called out: "Severn, I—lift me up, for I am dying. I shall die easy. Don't be frightened. Thank God it has come." The phlegm was boiling and tearing in his throat and chest, but about eleven at night he slipped into death, so quietly that Severn thought he slept.

APPENDIXES

I

THERE has been some confusion over the date of Keats's first coming to London and over the order of his various lodgings. I have, throughout this chapter, gone by Professor Garrod, whose interpretation seems to me by far the most probable.

II

"THE cause of the sore throat is interesting. Those who harbour tubercle germs, that is to say, tubercle bacilli, in their lungs cough them up embedded in the expectoration; in a small proportion of such cases some of the bacilli lodge in the larynx, and these set up inflammation usually followed by destruction. If this is what happened to Keats, he must have been coughing up tubercle bacilli from his lungs before the sore throat began when he was on the west coast of Scotland, but there is no evidence of this: indeed, it is hardly likely that he could have performed the severe feat of the long walk with Brown had he been coughing up tubercle bacilli. Tubercular disease of the larynx begins slowly: the origin of his sore throat was quick. In those days there was no knowledge of the proper treatment of tubercular disease of the larynx; it almost always got worse and worse till death; but . . . Keats's throat did not trouble him for months together, and it became better as time went on. Hoarseness, loss of voice, cough, and pain in swallowing are all common symptoms of tubercular disease of the larynx. Keats, as far as we know, never complained of any of these. There is no allusion to his throat during the last year of his life, but if a patient has tuberculosis of the larynx this becomes rapidly worse as he slowly declines to death, and it is hardly conceivable that he, the doctors who attended him from his first bleeding onwards, and Severn, who was with him for months before he died, should all omit to mention any symptoms due to tuberculosis of the larynx if it had been present. A post-mortem examination was made, but there is no mention of any disease of the larynx."

From *Keats as Doctor and Patient* by Sir William Hale-White.

III

FOR many years it has been uncertain where Brown met this young Irish girl and whether or no he married her, but the matter has just been much elucidated by a most interesting letter written by Mrs. Mona Osborne, Charles Brown's grand-daughter, to Mr. Edgcumbe, the Curator of the Keats Museum. With Mrs. Osborne's and Mr. Edgcumbe's permission the letter is here printed in full:

> "27 *Great South Road*
> *Auckland, S.E.2.*
> *New Zealand.*

June 30th 1939.

"There is something about which I have meant to write to you. I have had some correspondence with Mr. Fildes in connection with his biography of my grandfather, and he made some reference to his not being married, that was the first time I had ever heard that there had been any suggestion that there was no marriage. For almost as long as I can remember I have known that they were married in the Roman Catholic

Church, which did not in those days of Catholic disability constitute a legal marriage. The history of it was as follows,—as I remember it. Abigail O'Donaghue's people in Killarney were much mixed up in Fenian activities, she was something of a firebrand and they sent her to England to keep her out of it. I don't know what she was doing in London, but she became a friend of someone who was keeping house for my grandfather. This person went away, either temporarily or permanently, and she came in as a substitute. She was a good-looking woman; I know that because when my father was a boy he was sent home to pay a visit to his grandmother; something was going on in the house on one occasion between him and his cousins, and they did some dressing up. The cousins then chaffed my father because they said he looked like a girl. His grandmother said, ' You need not mind that Carlino, for you are like your mother, and she was a very pretty woman.' She also had a great gift of repartee and sometimes when Keats was being monopolised by Fanny Brawne my grandfather went to Abigail's domain downstairs to provoke this gift, and the give and take that it involved. When he decided to marry her, some of his friends tried to persuade him not to, but I remember only Leigh Hunt's name in connection with this, and I don't think he used his influence either way. She was extremely bigoted and consequently would be married nowhere but in her own church.

"When my father was dead and we were leaving New Plymouth, we went through all his old papers, etc., before we destroyed them. We found his birth certificates in which he was described as son of Charles Brown and Abigail Brown (born Donaghue); that is as far as I can remember. I am not certain about the ' born ', it may have been ' maiden name ', I merely remember it was not ' nee ' as is used now. I was rather surprised at the spelling ' Donaghue ' instead of ' O'Donaghue,' because my father had always referred to it as ' O'Donaghue ', and it was so spelt in letters from my grandfather's lawyer Mr Skynner, that we happened to go through at the same time. It was through Mr Skynner that my grandfather and later my father always made her an allowance. When my father went back to England in 1848 or thereabouts his O'Donaghue uncles had wanted him to go to Killarney. I am not certain if he wanted to do so, but Mr Skynner strongly advised against it, he considered that they merely wanted to see if they could get any money out of him to assist them in their political activities. This matter was twice referred to in the letters from Mr Skynner that we went through. There was also a letter to my Father from his Mother, written somewhere in the 1870's. It was occupied chiefly with a tirade against the English for dispossessing the O'Donaghues in Tudor times. It was signed ' A. Brown.'

" When my grandfather intended to emigrate to N.Z. with my father, he thought it advisable for my father to marry first and bring his wife with him, and as the lady would be his companion especially, rather than my father's, he proposed to pick her himself, and to pick someone whose tastes, etc., coincided with his own. My father's preferences were simply not to come into it. My father said in fun, ' Hadn't you better marry her yourself ? ' and my grandfather replied very shortly, ' You forget, my boy, I am married.'

" My grandfather was businesslike, and left a will in my father's favour. But two of his cousins had already put in a claim to what there was of an estate, as my grandfather's marriage was not legal. However their claim came to nothing.

"After hearing from Mr. Fildes that there was supposed to have been no marriage, I mentioned the matter to my brother, to my half-sister, and to the children of my two eldest half-sisters (now dead) and such a supposition was quite new to them and they were all frankly amused. They could not take the suggestion seriously.

(*Signed*) MONA OSBORNE."

IV

DILKE wrote to Brown on the 31st of July, 1824, putting George Keats's case as follows (Haslam & Brown had accused George of borrowing £700 from John):

John's property at first was £1,500. More than £1000 was expended before he came of age; after that his living expenses must have amounted to £200 a year, and he had lent £170. Therefore, when George went to America he had not one shilling and was already indebted to John, who, however, left him £300. George had more money than John, because John's premium, hospital and living expenses after leaving Mr. Hammond cost him money, whereas George was taken into Mr. Abbey's without expense, lived with him, and was given £100 when he left. The funds having risen, George, when he came of age, inherited £1,600, but owing to advances to John he only took £1000 with him to America. The money John had after George left came from Tom's estate which altogether amounted to £1,100, on which Fanny had a claim for £100. John took out £100 and sent £100 to George, and after Fanny's share was deducted, £540 was left to be divided between the two brothers. They each took £100, leaving £340, and George took the remainder, borrowing John's share of £170.

Thus it will be seen, according to George's story, he only borrowed £170 from John, and that was hardly borrowing, since he had lent him £300 on his first voyage to America. In fact, far from his owing John £700, John owed him £130.

Brown answered this letter on the 6th September, 1824, but he says nothing particularly conclusive, since all his statements were repeated from John or from Mr. Abbey, both of whom were very vague about money. On January 20th, 1836, however, nearly six years later, he retorts with a broadside.

George, he says, stated that John had not one shilling when he, George, left for America in June, 1818. On June 4th, 1818, Abbey, Cook & Co., who were, of course, the boys' trustees, held £500 of John's money, minus £31 9s. 2d., which he owes them for tea, coffee and cocoa. John paid his tradesmen's bills and possibly Tom's for £140. Brown calculates that with interest he had clear of all debts £336 16s. 11d.

George further states that he lent John £300 before he left for America. Brown says that on their first day's walk towards the lakes John told him that George had repaid him £70 or £80 lent to him while under age. John did not think it enough, and regretted that George had not kept a regular account.

Thirdly, and most important, George states that he arrived in America the second time with £700. If John had only lent him £170, he would, in that case, on his own showing only have had £440.

This is quite true, and I do not at the moment see how it can be got over. George might have borrowed the money from other sources, but it is difficult to see from where. Abbey, who strongly disapproved of John having lent his brother anything, almost certainly did not supply it.

V

Did Keats have a Cockney accent?

This is an interesting point which has lately been raised, and some critics and reviewers have boldly asserted that he did, basing their argument on a paragraph in Professor Garrod's last edition of Keats's poems, a wonderful monument of scholarship and research.

Professor Garrod himself is much more cautious in his statements. No action for libel would stand! But he does seem to give some grounds for such a theory. He is discussing the variants in Keats's text, and he writes:

"Even 'folorn' is interesting; and when Keats iterates it—' Folorn! the very word is like a bell '—it might be thought to assume importance—indeed an almost dangerous importance. Did Keats so sound the word? And if he did, is not the verse thinner in tone?[1] It is hateful to think that he sounded the words ' exhaltation ' and ' exhalt,'[2] as he spells them, that he pronounced 'aerial' as 'ærial,' and ' horizon ' as though it rhymed with ' Morrison; ' that he alters ' open ' to ' hopen,' and writes ' ear ' for ' hear,' ' hear ' for ' ear; ' interesting to speculate whether he habitually said ' forster ' for ' foster,' ' vauted ' for ' vaulted; ' pleasant to find him preferring ' steril ' to ' sterile.' That he said 'P'raps ' for ' Perhaps ' consistently right down to March, 1818, is certain. Similarly, once at least, he writes—and scans—' partic'lar.' Nor did he shrink from ' sea-spry.'" [3]

[1] Folorn appears in Keats's autograph fourteen times; forlorn once only ("End." III, 227).

[2] At "End." II, 882. Buxton Forman may be right in supposing that "arbour" stands for "harbour"; but I have given Keats the benefit of the doubt.

[3] Compare the confusion of "say" and "sigh" in line 9 of "O blush not so . . ."

Let us take some of these points separately, and let us remember that Keats was an excessively careless writer. He made a large number of slips of the pen, frequently left out letters, transposed words, and omitted to erase, especially when he was working on a rough draft in hot blood.

The question of forlorn is at least a moot one. Professor M. R. Ridley (*Keats's Craftsmanship*, Oxford University Press, 1933) has the following note: "The reading 'folorn' has exercised critics who wonder sadly whether Keats so pronounced the word. It is true that he more often than not wrote it so. But it is also true that 'r' is the letter he is most careless about, and it is perpetually dropping out in his writing. So that we may suppose that Keats's pronunciation was better than his writing."

Keats's spelling was extremely shaky, and I do not see why we should think he pronounced the "h" with which he chose to spell exaltation, than we should imagine that Professor Garrod would pronounce the "h" when he writes exhumation or exhalation.

We now come to "aerial" and "horizon." The two lines are:

"So happy was he, not the aerial blowing,"
and
"Far round the horizon's crystal air to skim."

But Keats in his early work frequently puts in two weak syllables instead of one between the beats; especially when he has a "the" which he often scans as "th'." In the first ten lines of "Endymion" alone, we have two examples.

In *Otho*, 11.11.23, where he writes "hopen" for "open," it seems more probable that he intended to change it to "honest," then realized that he wanted to use "honest" in the succeeding line, wrote open again and forgot to erase the "h." The "ear" and "hear" variants also seem more like carelessness than confusion.

The real root of the matter seems to be whether he saw no difference between "spray" and "spry," "say" and "sigh." It hardly seems possible, nor is the evidence very convincing.

In "Eve's Apple," when Keats first wrote out the poem in a letter to George, the line stands as:

"O sigh not so! O sigh not so!"

It is transcribed by Woodhouse as:

"O say not so! O say not so!"

To me "sigh" appears the more probable reading, since the last stanza runs:

"There's a sigh for aye, and a sigh for nay,
And a sigh for I can't bear it."

Professor Garrod's edition, however, uses "say."

Now, how Woodhouse came to have a different reading we do not know, but if the fault was in his copying it proves nothing, and though it is possible that a man with a strong Cockney accent might dictate "say" so that it sounded like "sigh," it would be a very strange accent indeed that would cause "sigh" to sound like "say."

In fact, the question when raised seems to crumble on exact evidence and we have no proof either way, though it does seem hardly likely that a man who had a precise theory of vowel sounds, and the beauty of whose poetry largely depends on them, should have spoken with an accent that materially deforms them.

INDEX